THE MINING LAW OF 1872

THE MINING LAW
OF 1872

Past, Politics, and Prospects

GORDON MORRIS BAKKEN

UNIVERSITY OF NEW MEXICO PRESS

ALBUQUERQUE

12 11 10 09 08   1 2 3 4 5

Library of Congress Cataloging-in-Publication Data

Bakken, Gordon Morris.
The mining law of 1872 : past, politics, and prospects / Gordon Morris Bakken.
     p. cm.
Includes bibliographical references and index.
ISBN 978-0-8263-4356-7 (cloth : alk. paper)
1. Mining law—United States—History. 2. Mining law—United States.
3. Mineral industries—Environmental aspects—United States. I. Title.
     KF1819.B316 2008
     343.73'077—dc22
          2008014524

Designed and typeset by Mina Yamashita.
Composed in Minion Pro, an Adobe Original typeface
designed by Robert Slimbach.
Printed by Thomson-Shore, Inc. on 55# Natures Natural.

To Elwood Bakken
Karma Wen Kiang Bakken
Ocean Chi Kiang Bakken
of
Bozeman, Montana

Contents

Disclosure Statement and Acknowledgments

> The *Saline,* and Sulphurious Vapours, I take to be the
> True *Demogorgon* of the *Philosophers,* or *Grandfather* of
> all the *Heathen Gods,* i.e. *Mettals.* . . .
>
> —Conyers Purshall,
> *An Essay at the Mechanism of the Macrocosm: or the*
> *Dependance of the Effects upon their Causes* (1705)

I started work on this book in 1967, and in the course of time I have many personal and professional debts to acknowledge. Martin Ridge encouraged me to write an author disclosure statement because he was so taken by William Cronon's in *Nature's Metropolis.* Starting on the statement was no easy task, but like Bill Cronon, I must start the narrative in Madison, Wisconsin.

I was born in Madison, Wisconsin, on January 10, 1943, to Elwood Severt and Evelyn A. H. (Anderson) Bakken, both children of Norwegian parents, Severt and Mabel (Grinde) Bakken and Nordahl and Mildred (Jacobson) Anderson. My father was a high school graduate with business school training. My mother was a high school graduate with business school training who worked in factories, retail food, and government. Dad worked for Wisconsin Life Insurance until his untimely death on March 13, 1969. My mother's parents were farmers in southeastern Dane County, and Severt Bakken worked for The Kipp, a defense industry employer on Madison's east side. Mom and Dad lived two doors down from the Bakkens, and I spent my first five years a few yards from the Bakken front porch on Talmadge Street.

My earliest memories are of my grandparents, who had a substantial influence on my life. The Bakkens worked though the Great Depression at reduced wages and increased gardening. They introduced me to the joy of fishing, and I hounded my grandfather, aka "Whitey" at The Kipp, to take me fishing. I learned much about the sport on Park Lake in Pardeeville. The Bakkens attended Trinity Lutheran Church, which had one service in Norwegian until the 1960s. The Andersons introduced me to the joy of farming, and I spent much of my first sixteen years working on the farm. There was plenty for grandchildren to do on the farm. Cows needed milking, eggs required gathering, weeds demanded pulling, and tobacco worms clamored for extermination. Gramps paid a nickel a bucket for worms. Gramps also needed mice and rats terminated and gave me my first gun when I was five years old. After instruction in the finer points of shooting, I was unleashed on the vermin. Later in life I would outfit long-range .22 rifles with ten-power scopes to increase my efficiency. I saved my money so that I could buy a .410 shotgun at age twelve to start rabbit hunting, but I knew I needed an adult with me to hunt. I recruited my father, who had to buy a shotgun to go into the field and even commandeered my mother on one occasion to walk with me on rabbit safari across the road from the main farmhouse. One thing all taught me was law-mindedness, even on a farm without a game warden in one hundred miles.

The experiences on the farm were formative, and I reflected on them to my grandparents in a letter of January 15, 1964:

God has given me very many great gifts and experiences for which I am thankful. I have in my very short life seen many of the aspects of life many men have never experienced. From my grandma and grandpa Bakken I learned fishing, boating, and other childhood experiences. Some people have never seen lakes. From You I learned of the earth and growth, things which in themselves [are] very precious and I also got a great American heritage. My early experiences with my BB gun to the present are part of the American heritage of the early frontier that I am glad to be a small part [of] now. Down on the farm—and I am so glad there was a farm to visit—I learned of agriculture although a very small portion, but I consider myself very fortunate because I have seen so many of my schoolmates who know nothing of the country and growth in nature. From the country I also saw Christianity at the grassroots—the religion which is different in feeling from the city. The congregations have a greater feeling of continuity and strength in knowing your neighbors are beside you. It is a very different feeling.

The aspects of right and wrong from my parents and the free social movements and ideas from my Aunt and Uncle [Morris and Marjorie Bakken of Milwaukee] have also played a part in my knowledge. The right and wrong I learned early and now I can see an aspect of a restrained temperament and detachment which lets me see a little more clearly what is God's purpose and ways for man.

From my many friends I have known good and evil and for this I am thankful for from the knowledge of evil is the striving for good attained. When you know what it is you are fighting, it is much easier to combat the evil.

Now in Erika I have found someone to share my life. I pray to God it will be a good life and I am sure it will be for without this faith what is there left. The faith is always there when all else fails and God never fails.

It's been a long thank you, but as you see I have a lot to be thankful for. The car [they gave me a 1964 Pontiac Tempest for my twenty-first birthday] has given me a head start in life I otherwise would have been without, but I feel that the other things I have learned from you are more valuable. I have never said much about it, but I thought I had better. I have learned so much you can't find in books "down on the farm." There would be no way to start repaying you. This is just a small attempt. I got to admit to you as I have to Mother that I envy you very much. You have lived such a full and fruitful life so much closer to God that I shudder at my feeble attempts. I only hope I can experience the fellowship you so apparently have and live as full and fruitful a life.

Thank you, again for the car. I never shall forget it—that's mainly what the bankbook is for. I hope I can tell my grandchildren about my grandparents and tell them of the things I learned by just being there at the time. I won't be so long as time goes.

My folks left Talmadge Street soon after my brother, Richard Elwood, was born and our bedroom became too small for both of us. We moved to a larger three-bedroom home on Maywood Street about eight blocks away and closer to Oscar Mayer and Company, a cattle- and hog-kill operation and major employer on the east side. You could smell the money growing when the wind was right, but we did not have a railroad track at the end of the block. Instead, we had the flight path into Truax Field to contend with at almost every hour of the day. I also left Lowell School and started attending Emerson School through sixth grade.

At Emerson School I came to love science, mathematics, literature, and history in that order. I also learned how the rule of law operates. If you fought on school grounds, you ended up in the principal's office. On my second visit for fighting on school grounds, I learned this important distinction. Thereafter, I conducted my fistfights off school property. Actually, the fighting became somewhat of an art form. I asked my parents for a soft bag and started to improve my left jab and right cross. Dad had a great time setting the bag up in the basement, and I had a great time trying to smash the bag off of its mounting. All of this preparation paid off because on more than one occasion I had to confront multiple assailants of my brother at my mother's insistence. Dick was a punching bag of preference for two of the neighborhood's larger inhabitants, and on one occasion I had to confront three. I learned an important lesson on this occasion: take out the largest one first with the first punch, and the rest will run or fall as the case may be.

Emerson School also had a baseball program that was full of lessons. The teachers supervised the program, but the kids really ran it. At the conclusion of the fifth grade year, I approached Bob Juell and asked if a merger of teams might be in order. After all, our two teams were beating all of the rest and splitting the difference when we met on the field of honor. Not barred by antitrust law, the merger took place, and the 1955 Yankees emerged to go on to an undefeated season. The teachers heard complaints throughout the season and changed the play-off rules for our "world series." The reasoning went something like this: since the Yankees are undefeated and there is no reason to believe that would change in the "series," an all-star team must be formed to test the Yankees. So it was, and the all-star team soundly defeated the Yankees. I learned that you have to know who can make the rules when you start to play the game.

Emerson School also had an excellent library. I must have been their number one customer. Every week I consumed *Scientific American* and other science magazines. I went through their collection of Jack London in a month. Seeking further adventure, I started on books on English big game hunters in Africa. I developed an interest in nonfiction and maintained it. In sixth grade I spent the year trying to understand Einstein's Theory of Relativity, but my reasoning and math skills were not up to it. The experience taught me limits and the need to expand knowledge.

In this period, I started spending more time on the farm. At age seven, I could reach the clutch of the Allis, and driving instruction began. Once I could drive the tractor, I could plow. Once I could lift a sack of oats, I could participate in the grain harvest. The whole of the summer became a feast for me of work in the fields and developing a social life with my farming peers, particularly Lloyd Peterson, the youngest son of the hired man, Pete Peterson. Lloyd and I would regularly make trips to the cornfields to cut corn for the cows, to the hay fields to bale and put bovine nourishment into storage in the barn, and to explore the finer points of sniper fire on gophers and sparrows.

Nordahl and Mildred also introduced me to the finer points of simple living and simple social pleasures. Grandma cooked one kind of main meal: meat and potatoes. She fried hamburger until it was hard and then boiled it to get gravy for the potatoes. She boiled chicken until it fell off the bone and then made gravy from the stock for the potatoes. They grew their own protein and potatoes. They kept an apple orchard and garden plot. Our food, including our bread, was produced and consumed on-site. It was the same for company and festive occasions, just the plates were different. On the social side of things, the

Andersons were part of a large farming network that gathered anytime there was a birthday or anniversary to celebrate with food and a card game. Gramps taught me how to play euchre and five hundred before I was five. I remember my shock at one of these card parties of being handed an eight-club hand and told to play it with Ben Wolfe against players with about a hundred years of experience on their side. Gramps had confidence, but I lacked one trick that night. At five I had survived playing with the big boys.

That was Saturday night, and the next morning we went to church at First Koshkonong Lutheran Church, just down the road. Actually, the first Lutheran church in Dane County had been built by the Andersons, and a monument to that 1844 church still stands on Anderson land. The Albion Prairie was definitely Lutheran country. In addition to church attendance, I was active in Luther League at Trinity in Madison, attending a national meeting to take communion with Martin Luther King Jr. I also went beyond confirmation to take additional adult instruction in religion, receiving my diploma in High School Bible Studies from the Lutheran Sunday Church School at Trinity on June 4, 1961.

Going to seventh grade meant going to Madison East High School, just a few blocks farther to walk. Although only a few blocks farther, it was a transition of miles, with students from several other grade schools entering your class and with those big seniors testing the mettle of the twelve year olds. The first day of class with Ray S. Stasieluk was most informative. In the middle of his introduction of the course, Mr. Stasieluk stopped and told Jim Laurie to step forward to his desk. Jim did so, and Mr. Stasieluk told him that he had caught him talking when he was speaking and told him to bend over the desk. Mr. Stasieluk pulled a paddle out of his desk and waved it in Jim's face, telling him that he was going to hit him with it. In fact, he was going to hit him with it until he could not hear a sound from him. After asking Jim whether he understood what was going to happen, he invited the whole class to come forward and stand in a semicircle to watch. Jim bent over and gripped the desk firmly. Mr. Stasieluk took a full swing and broke the paddle over Jim's butt. Jim's knuckles turned white, but he did not utter a sound and went back to his seat. It was silent in the classroom for the rest of the year.

East was more than a blue-collar school with absolute discipline. It was filled with inspiring teachers pushing the envelope. Betty Lehnherr continued the fine work started by Emerson's English faculty. Jeannette Jordan made Latin interesting, while Mary Benson and Ruth (Aunt Ruthie) Conlin taught mathematics without fear or favor. Robert Woollen's band and orchestra classes were inspirational. I had converted from piano and choir in grade school to flute, necessitated mostly by four years of dental braces. Robert Brill's American history class was exacting, and Pete Ross gave the U.S. Marine insight on world history. Mr. Ross clearly missed the Marine Corps, but it was peacetime again, and there seemed a greater potential in teaching. I was one of his greatest fans. In 1959 we formed a Marine rifle club on campus, and Pete instructed us in the finer points of using the M1 rifle and Marine Corps philosophy. Doug Mullen taught eighth grade American history and offered extra credit of one course grade point per three-page biography of any person found in the textbook. I wrote 147 biographies, and Doug told me in 1991 that that record was never beaten. I suspected that my math skills were atrophying at this point because 90 was an A in the course.

East High School also was a place to meet new people. I made friends with James R. Beckman, Herschel Weber, Gary Sanders, and Dennis Felton. We would be fast hunting companions and drinking buddies for years. Dennis and Gary died young, both from cancer. Jim was one of the very few to get a Ph.D. from that working-class class of 1961. At sixteen I struck up a relationship with Jolynn Gildin, a striking redhead almost three years my junior. That relationship melted away in my senior year when I fell for Diane Lang, a brilliant and beautiful woman in my class. That was a one-way deal; Diane loved another. We remain close friends.

East was a great football power in those days and even won a state basketball championship during my tenure beneath its towers. I was a spectator except for a letter in curling on the (Gary) Sanders rink. My brother, Richard, was a far better athlete than I and went on to be a champion curler, winning not only the city title as we had in 1961 but many state bonspiels. Cousin Jim was at West High School setting plenty of records for the family before he went on to a distinguished career in the NFL. In fall 1961, Beckman and I were attending the East–Central High School football game, criticizing the opposition in our newly found tongue, German (we were big freshmen at the university). One of the Central fans turned and told us in no uncertain terms that she did not appreciate our language and that she could understand every word. She was Erika Reinhardt, a displaced persons refugee from Germany; we would marry in 1964.

Going to the University of Wisconsin from East High was no certain thing. I told my father that I wanted to go to college in 1960. He reached into his pocket and pulled out a dime, telling me that there was one at the end of the bus line. That was how I determined where I would go to college. Getting the money to pay tuition was a matter of negotiating with Grandpa and Grandma Anderson. They agreed to fund the experiment. No one had ever gone to college in six generations, and they certainly did not see why I just didn't take the farm and do honest work. Looking back, I made a mistake in not taking over the farm.

The problem was money, but I set my sights on scholarships. After all, I had graduated twenty-third in a class of 468 and scored in the ninety-eighth percentile on the National Merit Scholarship Qualifying Test. The money day was in November 1960 at the University of Wisconsin field house. We were taking the final test, and I would get a composite ninety-fifth percentile but finish out of the money because of a seventy-eighth percentile score in English and an eightieth percentile in social studies. The ninety-eighth percentile in math and ninety-fifth in science could not overcome my deficiencies. I had maintained part-time work in grocery stores as a box boy and at the Harry S. Manchester department store on the east side. College demanded more, so I found a job with City Wide Insulation. That lasted until I fell two stories off the scaffolding, but Oscar Mayer had a job for me on the slice pack line the next week. College was affordable with the generous contributions of my parents and grandparents.

I entered the University of Wisconsin in September 1961 as a chemistry major. Three coaches thought I was Jim Bakken's brother because we look alike and at the time I was 197 pounds of power lifter. Jim left for the Los Angeles Rams that year, but I could not kick. In fact, I could not exempt myself from taking one year of sports via the mandatory physical test all freshmen endured. I managed to find my way to the library on occasion but could be found every night in one of the State Street bars. It would take me three semesters to flunk out, be reinstated on strict probation, become an English major, and get serious about higher education. In retrospect, what I should have done was join the Marine Corps directly out of high school, taken advantage of military education opportunities, put in my twenty, and started a graduate program in 1981. But I got serious about education rather than the alternative some of my peers took getting their heads straight via Camp Pendleton. Three years later I would graduate on the dean's high honor roll with more than forty units of history bulging my transcript. In my junior year I read one of my English professor's monographs to determine whether I wanted to get a Ph.D. in English literature or in history. I chose history despite taking Spencer and numerous poetry courses.

Part of the reason for my enthusiasm for history came from my professors. They were the best the nation had to offer in the 1960s, and they were at Wisconsin, the best graduate school for history in the 1960s. I was fortunate enough to have Avery Craven, Richard Current, Charlotte Erickson, Paul Wallace Gates, and James Norris pass through as visiting professors. Stanley I. Kutler and Allan G. Bogue were most stimulating and compelling. Norman Risjord, William R. Taylor, Lawrence Vesey, Richard Sewell, James Morton Smith, Edward "Mac" Coffman, John DeNovo, Paul Glad, William A. Williams, William L. O'Neil, David Shannon, Morton Rothstein, David Lovejoy, and Stanley N. Katz contributed mightily to my interest in American history. Great professors and a wealth of diverse graduate students in the 1960s combined to make history at Wisconsin the best. The Wisconsin Law School was little different. Great professors like James Willard Hurst, Gordon Brewster Baldwin, and Richard Bilder encouraged careful analytic thought. But time was of the essence, and I wanted to get out as soon as possible.

I expedited my education by taking summer session classes every summer except 1962. I graduated in four and one-half years (forgot to take freshman geography) with about thirty-four more units than I needed;

sprinted through the M.S. (I took a B.S. with a major in English) in a year and one-half, writing the thesis during the summer; and completed the Ph.D. in two and one-half years by overloading units every semester and researching the dissertation every summer. In fall 1968, after the Summer of Love, I was looking for a job and on the road. In summer 1968 Erika and I made a second sweep of Rocky Mountain state historical societies. I owe a great debt to the professionals at the Arizona Pioneer Historical Society in Tucson, the Nevada Historical Society, the Colorado Historical Society, the Montana Historical Society, the Idaho Historical Society, the New Mexico Historical Society, the Wyoming Historical Society, and the Utah Historical Society. Particularly memorable were hours spent with Merle Wells discussing my dissertation project.

Jobs were posted at the American Historical Association convention in New York City. Erika accompanied me on the journey, but there were no jobs. My interview with Humboldt State University did not materialize, and I do not know what happened even to today. Upon my return to Madison, Kutler asked whether I would be going to the Organization of American Historians (OAH) convention to look for a job. I answered in the negative and told him that I was going to finish law school (I finished over thirty units while working on the dissertation). Then the telephone rang. It was Warren Beck for California State University, Fullerton (CSUF). Would I be at the OAH? No! Would I be willing to pick him up at the Madison bus station and take him to the airport in return for an interview? Yes! Erika encouraged me to do all of this and not to give up the dream I had worked so hard to achieve. I remembered Warren's textbook on New Mexico, so I brushed up on all of my New Mexico notes and picked him up at the bus station. We had a two and one-half hour talk, and away he went. I continued to write the dissertation and take law classes. My father died that spring semester, and I had a great deal to do to put my mother in good fiscal shape. Dad had left $25,000 and a house. Fortunately, my mother had a job. I took the cash and invested it in the stock market until it ran into six figures and mother bought an apartment building to generate monthly income. The offer from Fullerton did arrive, and I accepted. We sold most of the furniture that we had paid for before the wedding, put some things on a moving van, and jumped in the car to go West.

My cousin had rented an apartment in Brea for us, and we moved in the day before classes started. I found myself with constitutional history and methodology courses filled with eager students who were well dressed and not too concerned about the course of the war. I noted that California professors did not dress formally for class, and I quickly abandoned my coat and tie. The first week of class, Tom Flickema told me to report to football practice on Wednesday night and to be prepared to play on Saturday. It turned out that the department had a (touch) football team that played the fraternities. I would play wide receiver and free safety for seven years. After football season, I was told to report for basketball practice, and that Saturday I met Judy Flickema. Practice was at a school behind their home. In the course of the "game," I was propelled though the air with such force that I lost all of the skin and a good deal of the flesh on one hand as I met the asphalt. I walked back to the Flickema residence to pick pieces of asphalt out of the wound with tweezers while cold water flushed the blood down the drain. I was back at "practice" the next week. Spring brought softball season, and I found myself in center field. At the end of the academic year I asked Flickema why they hired me. Was it for the department teams or constitutional history? Tom told me that I won out because I already had an article in print and they needed a wide receiver. After all, Jim Bakken was a wide receiver and kicker, and perhaps the genes would tell. Decades later Tom confessed that he was the one that decked me in that first basketball game. He resented a rather physical rebound play and wanted to show the "kid" something. Not knowing who put me down, I was a far more gentlemanly player for the rest of my career in the paint.

Ray Billington gave me a far more important shove. On a visit to the Huntington I asked him about Frederick Jackson Turner and the law. Ray told me that there was little in the Turner collection of interest and that I should start writing the legal history of the American West. It was territory few had explored, and Ray told me that there was great potential in the enterprise. This started a thirty-five-year pattern of research at the Huntington supported and encouraged by Martin Ridge, John Phillip Reid, and Peter Blodgett. Interestingly, Harwood Hinton, editor of *Arizona and the West*, had taken a chance on western legal history by publishing my article in 1969. Not much later, Doyce Nunis Jr., editor of the *Southern California Quarterly*, would be equally supportive and published several of my articles on California legal history.

In addition to teaching American constitutional history, western history, and methodology, I was going to "publish my way out." The 1960s had demonstrated that Wisconsin graduates were entitled to first-rate jobs, but with that entitlement came the burden of publishing more and better history than our competition at Harvard and Berkeley. I had not landed at Stanford or Ohio State as others had for their first jobs. My entitlement would require a demonstration of worth. I published six articles in the first two years, won a research grant from the Penrose Fund of the American Philosophical Society in 1971, and left Fullerton for the Wisconsin Law School for the third year as a Russell Sage Fellow of Law. I was almost out! Working with Willard Hurst at the Wisconsin Law School was another mountaintop experience. Being paid more on a fellowship than I was earning as an assistant professor was an economic boon. Angela would turn two and Jeffrey Elwood was on his way that spring, but would the year get me out? No. The market stayed cold.

I returned to the heat of California resolved to publish more and more. I did, but nothing happened other than tenure and promotion. I was teaching two sections of Historical Methodology every semester and two sections of American Constitutional History every semester. I also "won" an introductory course in graduate methodology, a social science methodology graduate seminar, and American legal history. Undergraduate teaching consumed more time than I ever imagined. I finished the law degree in August 1973 with another visit to Madison for summer session and received another Penrose Fund grant. When I returned to Fullerton, I found a new administrative job had opened for a person to represent the university in faculty grievance proceedings. I inquired of the job with Vice President Miles McCarthy, and he encouraged my application. I got the job and stayed in it for twelve and one-half years. During that period, I taught one to two courses for the History Department including American constitutional, American legal, and American military history. In addition, I taught environmental law for the new environmental studies graduate program in spring 1977 and, in summer 1978, administrative law for the Political Science Department. In fall 1977 I taught American History Survey for the first time. During the summer 1978 I attended a National Endowment for the Humanities Summer Seminar at the Huntington Library conducted by Eugene Hollon. There I met lifelong colleagues Ricardo Griswold del Castillo, Robert T. Smith, and Robert Carriker. Dozens of articles and two books later, I returned to the faculty full-time in 1986. Those books were substantially supported by an American Bar Foundation grant and an American Council of Learned Societies grant-in-aid in 1979.

Other books followed, as did a second American Bar Foundation grant and a Project '87 Summer Seminar at Princeton. I would make the short list for four good research professorships but never get that final interview. My family would ask why I kept publishing and sacrificing so much with absolutely no return on my effort. After all, full professors who had published as few as two articles were making exactly as much as I was with five books. I started answering the questions with intellectual curiosity phrases and applied for more grants. The John Randolph and Dora Haynes Foundation provided summer grants for mining history research in 1988 and 1991. The California State University Summer Stipend in 1990 and the James H. Bradley Senior Fellowship at the Montana Historical Society furthered my mining history research. In 1990 I signed a contract with the University of Oklahoma Press to write a book on the Mining Law of 1872.

At the turn of the century, I would have fourteen books and thirty-eight articles dressing up my resume, but I would still be teaching eight courses a year, sometimes with six to eight preparations per year. In terms of faculty compensation, high school teachers with the same number of years in service were now making up to $10,000 per year more than the average full professor. The level of doubt and disillusionment had numbers to go with it.

I busied myself with other things, as the kids demanded more and more time. I coached soccer teams for ten years despite the fact that I had never seen a game or played before. I read soccer, took a college soccer class, and spied on successful coaches. Ten years later the two teams had seven club silver medals (second place in cup play) and one Orange County gold medal. I coached Little League for six years and the eighth grade football team at Tuffree Junior High School for one season. In Little League I umpired for six seasons. I refereed soccer for twenty-seven seasons. At Redeemer Lutheran Church in Placentia I served on the council for thirteen years and as congregation president for two years. I also taught Sunday School, Vacation Bible School, and confirmation classes for a decade.

My work in the administration led to other diversions. Labor relations became the fine art of public sector collective bargaining. In addition to representing management at the university, I served as chief negotiator for C.S.E.A. Local 167 in its first contract negotiation. It was the only local that used a hired gun, and we came out third best on language and first on money in the state. I also started teaching labor relations and collective bargaining at the University of LaVerne and dabbling in consulting work. Labor consulting work led to natural resources law consulting work. I found that I could make a quarter-million dollars with my expertise on the outside, but it took too much time away from scholarship. In fact, this book has been delayed twice by very lucrative consulting contracts and two writing projects with substantial stipends. Scholarship for its own sake was giving way to dollars for security in investment. However, when I realized that I was a career state college professor for life with five to eight preparations per academic year, it was very easy to take a leave and receive $350 per hour for my time. Academic life has a way of blending scholarship with real-world values, reminding the scholar of just how little monographs are worth on campus. Off campus research and analytic expertise had clear and substantial value. On campus, the people who set salaries care little and pay less. Worse yet, having a faculty union that opposed merit pay and produced contracts that consistently diminished the working conditions of full-time faculty gave little solace.

Yet all of the presidents of CSUF have supported my research and professional activity. All of them were published professors who understood the value of publication. I am in debt to L. Donald Shields, Jewell

Cobb, and Milton Gordon for their support. I cannot say as much for others in the chain of command. Perhaps one example would suffice. Presenting a research grant to my history colleagues for recommendation seemed harmless enough, but when the recommendations went to the dean, I was last in order. The dean followed the advice of my colleagues, and the project was not funded. I turned to extramural sources and received two research grants for the project. The book soon followed. Later I learned that my colleagues believed that the weakest proposal should receive the highest recommendation to promote egalitarian collegiality. In the 1990s we would have a collective bargaining agreement and merit salary increases in various forms. Things improved on the salary side as a result. Publishing really mattered to the university, at least to some administrators and a minority of the faculty, albeit a growing minority of faculty.

I also am in debt to some very important colleagues who consistently read my manuscripts or gave me direction. James Willard Hurst always read my works and responded within weeks with those characteristically terse missives typed on that famous manual machine. Jackson K. Putnam and Warren Beck read and criticized with abandon. Jackson was a great editor. John Phillip Reid and Martin Ridge always supported my efforts and provided good advice.

But scholarship has consequences. All of those weeks away on research trips, all of those weekends lost at conventions, conferences, and presentation, and all of those nights locked up in the study working on the next book eroded my marriage to Erika, and it ended in 1999, if not earlier. I turned inward and worked to complete more scholarship. A book with the University of Oklahoma Press with thirty-eight authors, a six-volume reprint series on the American West coedited with Brenda Farrington, an American West anthology coauthored/coedited with Brenda Farrington, and a special issue of *Journal of the West* with the focus "Western Legal History Undercover" were the fruits of single life. The year 2000 brought more hints of a research professorship or a visitor's position in a law school, but as usual the hints and inquiries were designed to promote the interests of faculty factions seeking to hire their favorite rather than promote my candidacy. It also brought more work at the university as chair of the History Department personnel and recruitment committees as well as the Faculty Merit Increase Appeals Committee. All of this certainly kept the emotional distress of breaking up off center stage, but it lingered in the paperwork of setting up a new household in the ambiguity of the economic consequences of divorce as well as the emotional crisis atmosphere that attends the dissolution.

Summer 2000 brought the dissolution paperwork to a close at the courthouse, but there would be lingering documents to sign. Yet a trip to Montana proved most worthwhile. I ventured into the fire-ravaged reaches of Bozeman, Helena, and Big Timber to see family and friends. I stopped in Helena to have dinner with Chuck Rankin, the editor of *Montana: The Magazine of Western History*. Chuck has been a long-time friend, honest editor, and supporter. The dinner conversation turned to his move to editor-in-chief at the University of Oklahoma Press, the demise of my western legal history book series there, and this book manuscript that I owed the press. Chuck's most supportive advice about the manuscript and his hope that it had the potential to liberate me from the eight-course load were inspiring, but my reality by then was confirmed. Gordon, you just cannot get out except by retirement or death. The bibliography just did not matter on that front, but the advances you made in scholarship and the careers that you promoted would bring solace beyond the two bottles of wine we finished that night. Almost a week with my son, Elwood, and his wife, Karma Kiang, was equally motivating. They found the value of place in Bozeman and put the search for material security far down the list for life goals. Elwood worked as a carpenter, found more time to read than ever before, and turned to substitute teaching and volunteer work at the Pioneer Historical Museum. They had no compulsive drive to get out to greener pastures. They found them in the people of Bozeman and its environment. Perhaps I could too, just perhaps. The week ended, and I had to return to the world.

As noted above, the turn-of-the-century bibliography was lengthy but of little consequence in moving to a research university or improving my teaching load. In fact, the spring 2001 semester put me into two new preparations with a total of four preparations for the semester. During intersession I managed to finish a book chapter for *California History* and another for a U.S. State Department publication, but with two new courses in sight, my time was spent on teaching. It was during this time that I warned two of my former students, both A.B.D., about the pit of preparations and how it tends to suck time down a black hole with little reward. Be that as it may, it was during this intersession that I bought thirteen new bookcases and started moving my library out of boxes in my office and to a configuration for research and writing. With babysitting every Thursday with my granddaughter, Erika Lyn Henderson, and four preparations, I sought sanity in order. In order, perhaps, I would have the efficiency to finish one book and start writing on world history.

April 29, 2001, was the birth date of my second granddaughter, Emily Grace Henderson, and another life check. The book chapter was finished, and the State Department chapter was still languishing on my desk awaiting revisions despite seven weeks of dust collecting. I spent five hours in my office on May 5 and another eight hours at the keyboard on Sunday, just to catch up on correspondence and administrative paperwork. I wanted to catch up, encouraged by a kind word from the University of Oklahoma Press regarding this book manuscript. I also saw the errors of my ways in a word from a professor at the University of Oklahoma who would be teaching one course in the fall and had the rest of the year off to work on a book. Next year I would have only six preparations for the eight courses I had to teach in addition to the two summer session courses starting in four weeks. I saw a window of two weeks to do serious scholarship. I had to seize the moment.

The two weeks quickly diminished to one week because of babysitting duties and a horde of paperwork stampeding across my desk. Albeit short, the week was productive. The State Department chapter won approval, and I finished the week with a very fruitful discussion with Clark Whitehorn at *Montana: The Magazine of Western History* regarding the article Elwood and I had written on the pollution of the Missouri River.

California History and the American Military Heritage summer session courses filled with thirty-five eager students each. The student writing was just as bimodal as ever. My spring semester historical writing course had produced a profound understanding of a generation of students who could not write. Fully 35 percent of the students in that course would be taking the course over or changing majors. The summer session students were not different, but I held them to the four papers in five weeks in California History. The American Military Heritage students had thirteen books to master in five weeks and one twenty-page paper to complete. At least, I know that I did my best to maintain some semblance of standards.

I returned to this biographical exercise, started after I read William Cronon's *Nature's Metropolis*, and assumed that such a disclosure was now a necessity. In June 2002, with another seven preparations under my belt during the academic year and three summer session courses almost in the grade book, I had time to write. The reason for this return to writing was a reading of the "Self and Subject" roundtable in the June 2002 *Journal of American History*. Richard White's words were particularly telling for me, but I just could not get the Norwegian heritage so faint in memory to resonate with Phil Deloria's passionate words. Regardless, one thing stood out when I finished reading the entries: teaching load. I just had a hunch that the panel did not teach seven or eight preparations per year, and I just needed to "get over it."

"This book will simply take longer" was the recognition of the fall semester. At least, my edited work *California History: A Topical Approach* would be out in September 2002, and I only had six preparations among the eight courses the next year. I pledged to do more. The meaningful event of the fall semester was conducting the 8:00 a.m. and 11:00 a.m. services at First Lutheran Church of Fullerton on November 10. Several of the parishioners noted that I conducted the service with ease, and I told them that I had preached for almost a decade when needed at Redeemer Lutheran Church in Placentia in the 1970s.

December 2003 rolled around, and Sage asked Brenda and me to have the *Encyclopedia of Women in the American West* in a month early. That request resulted in a flurry of editing activity, and the first 708 pages went to Thousand Oaks on time, but the next month of calling authors, e-mailing authors, and editing entries pulled down more time.

My frustration with students who could not write, seldom attended class, and complained when they did poorly on examinations grew to the point that I eliminated review sessions, instituted an attendance policy, and lowered grades for grammar errors on examinations. For the first time I graded without downside limit. A graduate student earned an N+ on a final paper because of grammar errors; one-fourth of the fall 2002 graduate seminar students failed because of the inability to write.

The good news was that Erika Lyn turned four on January 3, discovered that grandpa had a birthday one week later, and started reading. Emily Grace Henderson expanded her vocabulary and turned two on April 29. I started believing that there was hope for the future of America in its children. I started looking forward to my year off to complete work on this book despite the fact that the world history textbook was due on March 10. It would only take another two months away from research and writing. It don't mean nothing.

Page proofs for the encyclopedia arrived on May 2 just as an article zipped out on e-mail and a book review went by snail mail. Two of the authors for the encyclopedia were dead, one at age thirty-six, the other at eighty-two. The semester was just about over. California still did not have a budget, and our student enrollment set another record just when the number of classes declined dramatically. Sage Publications offered another encyclopedia project. This time Alexandra Kindell, a gifted student and professional editor at Iowa State University, joined me on immigration and migration in the American West. It was a very good time to be on leave.

The leave started in September, after a trip to Montana to see my son and his wife and to take my daughter, her husband, and their two children to Yellowstone Park. Grandchildren do not travel well for more than an hour, so the trip to the park was memorable. The need to see Elwood and Karma in Bozeman was manifest because Elwood had broken his collarbone that spring and Karma has just lost their first fetus. The trip yielded some research material for the book and a good deal of family healing. That healing time was made even more important when Elwood called on September 4, 2003, to report that he had lost sight in his right eye and was going to Billings for a brain scan. It was a good time to be away from classes.

Waiting for the results of the brain scan turned my attention to writing on ancient and medieval India for the world history text. The work reminded me of how far civilization had come from the time of Islamic invasions, Buddhism's slaughter in India, and the power of fundamentalism. Amid my writing and reading, Jason Forgash called to get his M.A. thesis on Islamic warfare back on track after an almost two-year tour of Afghanistan and Iraq with his Arabic-speaking U.S. Marine Corps unit. He was glad to be home, and I was glad to have him back working on the thesis, now even more marketable. He had been a guest lecturer in my American Military Heritage course on two occasions. He also was a graduate teaching intern in the course in summer 2005. Jason returned to Iraq in 2006, and on July 23 a sniper dropped him with a single round in the stomach. I talked with him two weeks later at the U.S. Naval Hospital in Bethesda, Maryland. Surgeons reconnected his stomach to his intestines on October 14, and he was home in time for Thanksgiving.

In November 2003 Elwood's eyesight recovered enough for us to go hunting in the Absaroka-Beartooth Wilderness Area. It was a great time for sharing, as we had never hunted together and we were working on an article on the economics of big game hunting in Montana. We shared the pain of ascending the mountain and riding to camp, enduring four hours of cold. We experienced a whiteout snowstorm and seven hours of descending the mountain in two to four feet of snow. Elwood exclaimed at the base of the mountain that he knew that if the men on the Battan Death March could make it, he could. I suggested that the more apt historical analogy was the Marine Corps attack in a different direction at the Chosin Reservoir in the Korean War. It was a bonding experience like no other in our lives. Our hunt also made an economic impact on Montana, and we put two bucks into Elwood's freezer.

On May 30, 2004, Ocean Chi Kiang Bakken joined the Montana branch of the Bakken family. She is doing well at this writing. I had the joy of seeing the newborn and the parents in July 2004 and returned again on November 17 to visit and return to the Absaroka-Beartooth Wilderness Area looking for the elk that eluded us in 2003. I managed to fall off Buttercup on the first day of the hunt, break ribs, walk down the mountain in four hours, and arrive at Urgent Care in Bozeman twenty-two hours after the fall. The attending physician pronounced me in pain, issued a prescription for painkillers, and wished me well. I was back in the bunkhouse on the third day of the hunt and shot the only elk for our party of eight. Elwood took a nice buck the next day, and we had another freezer full for the year. I also looked forward to escaping the rigors of another year of eight preparations and students in need of writing repair.

The 2004–5 academic year yielded relief in the form of the editorship of *California Legal History*, the journal of the California Supreme Court Historical Society. Harry Scheiber at the University of California–Berkeley Law School was stepping aside, and I had the blessing of the society board as editor. Thomas Klammer, the dean of the College of Humanities and Social Sciences and always a supporter of scholarship, quickly gave me a one-course load reduction and a graduate assistant.

I started the 2005–6 academic year on a three-course load for the first time in thirty-six years. I also had a better 2005 hunt, with both Elwood and me bagging four-by-four whitetail deer and Elwood taking his first shot at an elk. We both returned saddle sore and thankful to Bob Bouvee's Big Timber Guides and Mike Lovely's Rollin' Bounder Outfitters for a third great hunt. In 2006 Elwood and I filled both deer and elk tags. Elwood had his first elk and another fine whitetail. With the end of the hunt came the final revisions responding to the second round of outside reader comments. Those final revisions turned out to be merely another stage stop in this book's trek. Spring and summer 2006, after the publication of *The Encyclopedia of Immigration and Migration in the American West*, edited with Alexandra Kindell, focused on the next round of revisions, with particular attention given to the actual language of the Mining Law of 1872.

The year 2007 was filled with promise. *World History: A Concise Thematic Analysis* came out after six years of crafting by twelve hands and Andrew Davidson's expert editing. The *Mining Law of 1872* book was in press at the University of New Mexico Press. Brenda Farrington and I returned our *Women Who Kill Men: The Feminine on Trial* to the University of Nebraska Press and two outside readers. My *Icons of the American West* was in press at Greenwood Press. I continued to work on *The Death Penalty in America*'s four volumes for Praeger Press. Newly under contract were *Activist Minority Women in the American West* with Texas Tech University Press, coedited with Clifford Trafzer and Sandra Schackel, and *The World of the American West* with Routledge of New York. In November I flew to Montana for our annual elk hunt. Elwood harvested a symmetrical three-by-three mule deer and a very large elk cow. I took a three-by-four mule deer and a five-point bull elk. This was the second year in a row that we filled all tags thanks to Mike Lovely and Bob Bovee's expertise as guides and gentlemen.

The year 2008 started with the Phi Alpha Theta Biennial Convention in Albuquerque. I chaired two sessions and commented on four military history papers. In panel sessions, I spoke on how to get published and how to publish a student journal. On January 19, I watched my granddaughter, Erika Lyn Henderson, score two goals from her fullback position to win the Orange County Commissioner's Cup for her soccer team, the Pirate Girls (U-9). The next week I received the copyedited version of *The Mining Law of 1872*. I thank Elisabeth A. Graves of Leesburg, Virginia, for her expert work on the manuscript.

This book owes much to many and particularly to the staff of the University of New Mexico Press. Two anonymous readers did an outstanding job hacking out hundreds of pages of legal detail, mining chemistry, and peripheral subject matter. I deeply appreciate their insights and owe them a great deal for this book's focus. In particular, I must thank Bob Spude for his insightful comments and making me aware of Amigos Bravos. Bob also passed on valuable newspaper sources that make this book far more informative. All errors contained herein are my responsibility.

—Gordon Morris Bakken
Fullerton, California

INTRODUCTION

To equate time with hope

is to ignore the opportunity for things

to become worse. A future is young, briefly

and once—the past

you can hold in your hands, loosely, and carve.

> —Christopher Cessac, "Letter of Introduction to Gostan
> Zarian from Troia" in *Republic Sublime* (2003)

On October 6, 2004, the Santa Fe *New Mexican* reported that members of Amigos Bravos, an environmental group, staked a twenty-acre mining claim on prime environmentally significant public land abutting the Pecos River. Janice Varela of Pecos, New Mexico, and campaign manger for Amigos Bravos's mining reform campaign stated that the claim was "a mock claim" to highlight the absurdity of the Mining Law of 1872. The Mining Law allowed people to go onto the public domain and stake claims to minerals with little effort or cost. Amigos Bravos symbolically staked this claim to make clear to an uninformed public that "special places" were "threatened by mining." "Right now, mining trumps all other uses [of public land]—including recreation, agriculture, wildlife habitat," the Santa Fe *New Mexican* recorded. According to Amigos Bravos, the Mining Law of 1872 was the basis of the problems with the management of our public lands and public policy.

From a world history perspective, Pulitzer Prize–winning author Jared Diamond writes in *Collapse: How Societies Choose to Fail or Succeed*, "The General Mining Act passed in 1872 . . . provides massive subsidies to mining companies, such as a billion dollars per year of royalty-free minerals from publicly owned lands, unlimited use of public lands for dumping mine wastes in some cases, and other subsidies costing taxpayers a quarter of a billion dollars per year."[1] Diamond places this federal statute and the mining industry's use of it among the greatest failures of judgment in world history rivaling the Easter Island and Mayan collapses.

To put the environmentalist and scholarly perspectives in context, this book involves three topics: western American mining, the law, and the environment. These three histories have different trajectories. This book retains some of mining history, focuses on legal choices and the reach of the law in addressing the degradation of private and public property, and puts the operational level of law in the environment into historical perspective. Along the way, we will observe people making decisions about specific situations. Individuals made these choices within a mining culture. As Jared Diamond observes, "The mining industry evolved in the U.S. with an inflated sense of entitlement, a belief that it is above the rules, and a view of itself as the West's salvation—thereby illustrating the problem of values that have outlived their usefulness."[2] In individual decisions about specific cases we will see this evolution and its consequences for the mining industry in the late twentieth century.

The problem with western mining historiography until Duane Smith's *Mining America* (1987) was our lack of awareness of mining's role in environmental degradation.[3] The classic image of the California gold rush miner was the bearded forty-niner with pan in hand squatting next to a stream agitating the gravel to reveal gold. What the classic picture and conventional history did not see was all of that gravel washing downstream. Historians saw exactly what William Z. Walker described on September 10, 1849, in Bear River, California:

> The method of operation was very simple: one man dug the earth and put it into a seive attached to a cradle which a second man washed rocked and pured water upon after Sufficiently washing the earth it passed thro' the seive in the bottom of the cradle which is open at one end where it passes out leaving only particles of gold and black sand in the bottom. In the seive

SUTTER'S MILL, 1851.

FIRST DISCOVERY OF COLD IN CALIFORNIA, January 19th, 1848.

Photographed by HOUSEWORTH & CO from Reid's famous Painting.

Figure 1: Sutter's Mill, the site of the discovery of gold in California in 1848. Courtesy of the California History Section, California State Library.

remains particles of rocks roote &c which are thrown away. After wasing a sufficeint quantitty of earty (generally from 20 to 50 pansful) the contents of the cradle are put into a pan washed: Which opperation is performed by dipping the pan in the ater and shaking and stirring it to keep the contents loose and puring the water off, which repeated untill the sand is all floated off with the water; the gold being much heavier sonn deposits itself in the bottom of the pan.[4]

What we did not envision was thousands of miners doing the same. What we did not watch was the turbidity of the stream increase, the clear water growing dark with debris, and the trout choking to death down the creek and washing ashore. What we did see was the ingenuity of the miners to fashion rockers and Long Toms to more efficiently wash gravel and reveal gold. What we saw was the industry of miners and entrepreneurs building huge flumes to convey even more water to even larger machines to wash the gravel and yield gold. We marveled at the engineering that conveyed whole rivers into nozzled washing systems blasting gravel out of hills and funneling even more pay dirt through even larger machines. Historians told those stories of American enterprise, ingenuity, and fortune. It was a gold rush without environmental consequences that produced great wealth. What we did not see was the ever-growing volume of debris produced by pans, rockers, Long Toms, and hydraulic mining systems.

Property owners as well as the residents of Butte, Montana, only had common-law remedies available to them when air or water pollution descended on them. Until the dawning of America's environmental age in the 1960s, we did not care to see the refuse disgorged upon the earth and sky by the processing of pay dirt. Once free, placer gold was dredged, panned, and scooped up for washing, miners turned to hard-rock tunneling into the mountains. This mining technique was not new, and historians looked at the same issues cast in a different light. Prospectors with the same beard, Alkali Ike of Arizona mining lore, and wearing Levi's wandered into the mountains, staked claims, and sold them to capitalists who brought money to the mountains. Now histories of silver, gold, and copper joined the miner's parade in books and articles. Now the gold mountain was the silver of the Comstock Lode or the copper mountain of Butte. Historians loved the tales of the war of the copper kings, the fortunes and failures of silver strikes, and the high jinks of instant bonanza kings. Yet the heaps of waste piled outside the mines, the slag, tailings, and slimes dumped into streams, or the acid rain or poisons poured into the air by smelters seldom aroused historical attention until the 1980s.

The history of mining case law was even more uninteresting. Mining law evolved from the private property culture of America, with antecedents in English common law. The law of property was adapted to the conditions of the mining camp, ushered into federal mining law, and applied by judges who understood American property law. What miners and legislators did was to define how a person could acquire an interest in real property, how that interest could move to an absolute private interest in real property, and how those interests could be used. If this sounds like a first-year property course in law school, it is because of the twists and turns in the law as it matured. Further, the law of property contained the law of nuisance. English experience with conflicting uses of property created what became known as the law of nuisance. Simply put, the law tried to redress cases where one property owner dumped something into water or air that interfered with the use of property by another. However, as Jared Diamond has argued, "Early miners behaved as they did because the government required almost nothing of them, and because they were businessmen."[5] Nineteenth-century miners only had to deal with lawsuits filed by other property owners claiming damage at common law. Early-twentieth-century mining corporations confronted the complaining ranchers and farmers who thought their livestock and crops damaged by toxic mine waste and smelter smoke. Plaintiffs witnessed "how mechanisms of proof and habits of inference can be hijacked to serve the interests of the powerful."[6] Late-twentieth-century miners had to deal with statutes, administrative law agencies, state and federal compliance agencies, and the like to continue to mine. The legal complexity of the twenty-first century makes mining a very different enterprise than it was in 1872 when Congress passed the General Mining Law. The critical difference is environmental regulation at the state and federal level. Mining now goes through a permitting process that often takes years, long after the discovery of a valuable mineral deposit.

The central focus of this book is the Mining Law of 1872 and the legal and environmental issues that have evolved from its application. The 1872 law built on the Mining Law of 1866. The 1866 law opened public lands to all U.S. citizens and aliens who had declared their intent to become citizens to lode-mining claims. The statute recognized the legal force of state, territorial, and mining district laws and regulations. Local mining district regulations dotted the law of western mining since 1849. Significant among these and specifically written into federal law was the "apex rule" allowing extralateral pursuit of veins outside the sidelines of a claim. Miners holding the apex could excavate outside their claim boundaries following a vein. This particular provision came to mining law via Nevada's Comstock Lode. Claims were to be no more than three hundred feet along a vein. A mining claim owner could receive a full patent from the federal government and thereby full title to the land for $5.00 per acre. The statute distinguished agricultural and mineral lands and provided that rights of way for roads, ditches, and canals could be granted over any mining claim. In 1870 Congress extended federal law to placer claims. Claims could be up to twenty acres per person, and eight people could associate to claim 160 acres. Miners could obtain a patent for $2.50 per acre.

In 1872 Congress refined its work on mining. It declared that the public lands were free and open to mining. Miners had to file a claim or location on the vein or placer. The claim had to be recorded, thus giving notice to the world about the location of the claim and its claimants. Miners had a right to live on the claim and develop it. The claim could be up to fifteen hundred feet long along the vein and six hundred feet wide. The width limitation was new. The 1866 law did not provide such a limit, but local mining district regulations and state and territorial laws applied to claim size. The end lines of the lode claim had to be parallel, and the apex rule still applied. Claimants had to have a monument on the ground with legal notices posted. Where lode claims intersected, the senior locator prevailed. Claims had to locate valuable minerals. Miners could locate up to five acres for a mill regardless of whether a valuable mineral was discovered on the site. The 1872 law gave people a right to take pick and shovel or bulldozer blade to the public domain in search of valuable minerals. After they filed the claim, they had to expend $100 working each claim every year to maintain their rights in that location. The statute was another way for Congress to spend land for development and put decisions on use into private hands by leaving any environmental consequences to the common law of the state or territory.

The Mining Law of 1872 was written to deal primarily with local issues such as claims, but the statute had wide-ranging implications for the nation. Its authors saw lone prospectors much like yeoman farmers moving westward to scratch out a living and individually create the wealth of the nation. Congress knew of local mining districts that made needful rules for the exploitation of the wealth they found in the rock matrix. The Mining Law of 1872 regularized those rules and created some uniform mining regulations for the future exploitation of the earth. As time passed and corporations replaced prospectors, the General Mining Law in the hands of Congress became frozen in legislative inertia, and corporate interests kept it unamended in any meaningful way. By the twentieth century, entrepreneurs found the General Mining Law to be a tool to extort land developers, erect hunting shacks, or develop ski resorts. Environmentalists soon noted the impact of mining, and the Mining Law of 1872 became a symbol of corporate greed and congressional inertia. The Mining Law of 1872 had environmental and land-use implications that Congress had not anticipated in 1872. More importantly, when mining was recognized in light of environmental pollution, Congress failed to revise the General Mining Law in the midst of the environmental legislation that poured out of Washington in the 1970s. In the 1990s Congress again failed to act, but the Mining Law of 1872 was steadily restrained by state and federal environmental regulation as well as litigation and tribal assertions of the desecration of their sacred places.

CHAPTER 1

An Act to Promote the Development of the Mining Resources of the United States

And there was I, another specimen of

nature's bumbling excell, trying to make

a case that I could rest, fumbling

through the last century's language:

the mind loves its old home; then trying

something newer; *the pattern which connects*;

and settling on some half-remembered lines,

spores of a thought I couldn't grow without

consulting again the spirit reader who wrote them;

It's as if we were told at the outset—every grain

Of dust, each waterdrop, to be suffused

With mind, with our minds. This will be paradise.

—Alison Hawthorne Deming, #15 in
The Monarchs: A Poem Sequence (1997)

The Mining Law of 1872 entitled "An Act to promote the Development of the Mining Resources of the United States" was the codification of the American experience in mining in the American West.[1] This much-discussed statute is seldom narrated for its contents. We need to start by knowing exactly what Congress put on the books.

Congress declared that all valuable mineral deposits on the public domain were "free and open to exploration and purchase." Citizens
and persons who had declared their intention to become a citizen of the
United States could occupy and purchase these lands. Such exploration,
occupancy, and use of these lands were subject to the "regulations pre-
scribed by law, and according to the local customs or rules of miners, in
the several mining-districts." These mining district rules prevailed "so
far as the same are applicable and not inconsistent with the laws of the
United States."

This first section made the public domain open to all for the exploitation of our national mineral wealth. Congress did not lease mineral
lands as it had for lead mining. It spent land as it had in the several statutes, including the Homestead Act, to put Americans in possession and
eventually ownership of valuable property. In 1872 that made sense in
terms of public policy, but by the 1950s American public policy started
focusing on environmental degradation. Exploration and mining had
caused massive environmental problems. Miners violated American
Indian sacred places. Occupancy for purposes other than mining and
the patenting of those claims putting the property into private hands
for golf courses, hotels, housing, and casinos indicated that the original
purpose of the statute had been thwarted. Several chapters to follow will
discuss this process and the reaction of policy makers.

The second section of the act dealt with hard-rock or lode claims.
Congress provided that such claims were "governed as to length along
the vein or lode by the customs, regulations, and laws in force at the
date of their location." This covered the California gold rush claims
and subsequent mining strikes up to May 10, 1872. Thereafter, Congress
provided that lode claims were to be no more than fifteen hundred
feet in length along the vein or lode. Further, no location of a claim
could be made "until the discovery of the vein or lode within the limits of the claim located." Regarding the other dimension of the claim,
Congress limited it to "three hundred feet on each side of the middle of
the vein at the surface, except where adverse rights exist at the passage
of this act shall render such limitations necessary." Finally, lawmakers
declared, "the end-lines of each claim shall be parallel to each other."

This section cleared up some confusion on the mining frontier, and chapter 5 addresses the process.

Section 3 provided locators with exclusive use and enjoyment of their claim plus extralateral rights. Locators without adverse claims had "exclusive right of possession and enjoyment of all the surface" within the location. That included all "veins, lodes, and ledges throughout their entire depth, the top or apex of which lies inside of such surface-line extended downward." Rights to veins extending outside the claim boundaries depended on their position "between vertical planes drawn downward . . . through the end-lines . . . so continued in their own direction that such planes will intersect such exterior parts of said veins or ledges." Congress specifically provided that such extralateral rights did not allow a locator "to enter upon the surface of a claim owned or possessed by another." This provision was part of Nevada's Comstock Lode heritage and the Mining Law of 1866. The issue of extralateral pursuit was a hot litigation matter well into the 1920s. Chapter 8 focuses on the cases, the process and resolution of the disputes, and the ultimate business solution of the problems.

Congress addressed the problems of subterranean exploration for valuable minerals in section 4. Tunnels excavated for the development of a vein or lode or for discovery gave the tunnel owners "the right of possession of all veins or lodes within three thousand feet from the face of such tunnel, to the same extent as if discovered from the surface." Other prospectors on the surface who located a claim "after the commencement of the tunnel, and while the same is being prosecuted with reasonable diligence," did not hold valid locations. There was an exception. If the tunnel owners did not "prosecute the work on the tunnel for six months," then they had abandoned "the right to all undiscovered veins on the line of said tunnel." Chapter 6 tells some of the tale of abandonment in broad brush and in specificity regarding section 5 of the statute.

Section 5 set national standards for some aspects of mining. Mining district regulations had to conform to federal, state, or territorial law regarding "location, manner of recording, amount of work necessary to hold possession of a mining claim." That said, Congress set minimum federal standards. A location must be "distinctly marked on the ground so that its boundaries can be readily traced." How that was done remained for local mining districts or state or territorial law. Records of mining claims after the passage of the Mining Law of 1872 had to contain "the name or names of the locators, the date of the location, and such a description of the claim or claims located by reference to some natural object or permanent monument as will identify the claim." Congress wanted greater certainty for mining just as it had provided for land claims on the public domain under all of the public land statutes. Congress set the minimum work requirement to maintain a claim at $100 per year. For claims filed before the act's passage, "ten dollars' worth of labor shall be preformed or improvements made each year for each one hundred feet in length along the vein until a patent shall have been issued." Failure to perform annual work or improvements worked an abandonment of the claim. Congress did provide a preference for original locators and their heirs, assigns, or legal representatives, allowing them to resume work after abandonment but before a valid location by a third party. Abandonment and location were continuing legal questions frequently resolved by lawyers and in court. Chapter 6 deals with these questions and the work requirement. Chapter 14 continues the discussion in the context of congressional reform of the statute.

Congress also protected co-owners from slothful, deadbeat former locators. Where a co-owner had not performed his proportion of work or contributed to improvements, his co-owners still had to pony up the work or dollars for improvements. In such a case, after one year of nonperformance, co-owners had the right to give notice to the delinquent. After ninety days, failure to contribute his proportion worked a forfeiture of "his interest in the claim." Congress gave miners a single mechanism to solve a business problem.

In section 7 Congress established a procedure for the processing of adverse claims. The adverse claim had to be filed during the sixty-day publication window. The claimant(s) had to do so under oath, stating the nature, boundaries, and extent of the adverse claim. The filing of the adverse claim stopped the patenting process but required the adverse claimant within thirty days to "commence proceedings in a court of competent jurisdiction, to determine the question of the right of possession." The claimant had to "prosecute the same with reasonable diligence to final judgment." Failure to do so resulted in a waiver of the adverse claim. After judicial judgment, the rightful possessor was to "file a certified copy of the judgment-roll with the register of the land-office, together with the certificate of the surveyor-general that the requisite amount of labor has been expended, or improvements made thereon." The rightful possessor had to pay five dollars per acre for the adjudicated claim to the land office. Once all the documents were filed and fees paid, the commissioner of the general land office issued a patent for the property. In the case where multiple parties were adjudicated possessors, the section provided that "each party may pay for his portion of the claim" and the appropriate certificate of patent issue. Congress also provided for proofs of citizenship filings and the simple statement that nothing in the statute "shall be construed to present the alienation of the title conveyed by a patent for a mining-claim to any person whatever." Like any other real property in America, a patented mining claim was alienable in the free market economy.

Section 8 of the Mining Law of 1872 told the surveyor-general that on unsurveyed land, he must adjust survey lines "to the boundaries of such patented claims, according to the plat or description thereof, but so as in no case to interfere with or change the location of any such patented claim." If the claim was on surveyed land, the description of the location must "reference to the lines of the public surveys, but need not conform therewith." These directions to claimants and surveyors hoped for greater certainty of property descriptions.

Congress in section 9 repealed sections 1, 2, 3, 4, and 6 of "An act granting the right of way to ditch and canal owners over the public lands, and for other purposes" of 1866, commonly called the Mining Law of 1866. The repeal did not affect existing rights. Patents for mining claims under the 1866 act were to proceed, but if no adverse claim was pending, then patents were to issue under the 1872 statute. Further, mining patents in force under the 1866 act where no adverse claim existed had "all the rights and privileges conferred by this act."

Section 10 tinkered with the Mining Law of 1870 entitled "An Act to amend an act granting the right of way to ditch and canal owners over the public lands, and for other purposes." Congress declared that it stayed in force except for the patenting process that was not governed by sections 6 and 7. Further, regarding placer claims on surveyed land that conformed to legal subdivision, "no further survey or plat shall be required." Henceforth, all placer mining claims locations "shall conform as near as practicable with the United States system of public land surveys and the rectangular subdivisions of such surveys." Claim size was limited to twenty acres per individual claimant. If a placer location "cannot be conformed to legal subdivisions, survey and plat shall be made as on unsurveyed lands." Congress also provided that "proceedings now pending may be prosecuted to their final determination under existing laws," but if there was no conflict with existing laws, the 1872 act's provisions prevailed. Finally, where agricultural land existed on the public domain segregated by mining claims and was less than forty acres, any qualified person could enter that property for homestead or preemption purposes.

Section 11 added another wrinkle to the Mining Law of 1870 that brought placer claims under federal law by addressing the patenting of placer claims. Placer mine claimants were required to stipulate that a vein or lode was contained within the boundaries of the placer claim if the vein or lode was known to exist. Then the patent included the vein or lode with the payment of five dollars per acre for the vein or lode claim and $2.50 per acre for the remainder of the placer claim acreage. The wrinkle was that if the claimant knew of the mineral deposit and did not make the declaration, then "a conclusive declaration that the claimant of the placer-claim has not right of possession of the vein or lode claim" arose as a matter of law. In the alternative, where the vein or lode was not known and a placer patent was issued, the placer patent would include both the placer and the vein or lode deposit. The problems for practical miners and possibilities for speculators abounded in the provisions.

Section 12 provided for the survey of claims, filings, and notices. Congress authorized the surveyor-general of the United States to appoint "as many competent surveyors as shall apply for appointment to survey mining-claims." Applicants paid surveying fees and publication costs. The surveyor-general could designate newspapers in a land district for the publication of mining notices and fix the rates charged. Applicants for patents had to file sworn statements regarding these charges. Land office registrars and receivers had their fees fixed for services. Finally, Congress provided that nothing in this section changed anyone's rights under the Mining Law of 1866 or the grant to Adolph Sutro of a right of way to drain the Comstock Lode granted in 1866.

In section 13 Congress provided that affidavits required by the statute could be verified by "any officer authorized to administer oaths with the land-district where the claims may be situated." So, too, testimony and proofs could be similarly taken. Such documents had the same force as if "taken before the register and receiver of the land office." In controversies over the classification of lands as mineral or agricultural, the same procedure prevailed. Congress provided notice procedures for the parties to such contests and held the register responsible for requiring proof that the notices had been given.

Congress provided for cases where two or more veins intersected in section 14. The lawmakers declared that "priority of title shall govern, and such prior location shall be entitled to all ore or mineral contained with the space of intersection." That said, Congress gave the junior locator "right of way through said space of intersection for the purposes of the convenient working of the said mine." The priority provision also prevailed when "two of more veins unite." In this case, the prior locator "shall take the vein below the point of union, including all the space of intersection."

Section 15 dealt with milling and other adjunct mining usages of the public lands. Locators of a vein or lode could claim lands for mining or milling purposes, and "such non-adjacent surface ground may be embraced" in a patent application. Survey and notice provisions applied to this ground. Congress limited future claims to five acres. Finally, a mill or reduction works owner "not owning a mine in connection therewith" could apply for and receive a patent for the mill site. The sixteenth and last section of the act simply repealed "all acts and parts of acts inconsistent" with the new act and provided that "nothing contained in this act shall be construed to impair, in any way, rights or interests in mining property acquired under existing laws."

Pulitzer Prize–winning author Jared Diamond has declared that "the General Mining Act passed in 1872 . . . provides massive subsidies to mining companies, such as a billion dollars per year of royalty-free minerals from publicly owned lands, unlimited use of public lands for dumping mine wastes in some cases, and other subsidies costing taxpayers a quarter of a billion dollars per year."[2] This is an observation from the perspective of a world historian schooled in Montana's mining experience. From the long view of a Western historian, the Mining Law of 1872 did just about the same things that federal land disposal acts did. It put public lands into private hands in the hopes that farmers and ranchers would produce a bounty of food and fiber. These farmers and ranchers would in turn pay property taxes and build up the export capacity of the United States. These farmers and ranchers paid no royalty to the government, albeit they paid purchase price or fees to gain title to the property they occupied.

In passing the Mining Law of 1872, lawmakers put mineral lands into the hands of private businessmen in the same hope. Although this public policy of spending public lands for national economic and social goals resonated with the Mining Law of 1872, there were distinctions. The unintended consequences of the Mining Law of 1872 soon became manifest. Further, the environmental degradation caused by mining practices soon ravaged the West, and Congress failed to meaningfully act.

CHAPTER 2

LOCAL MINING DISTRICT REGULATIONS

History repeats itself

with a stutter.

—Lawrence Ferlinghetti, "First, the News"
in *How to Paint Sunlight* (2001)

The Mining Law of 1872 has its origins in the California gold rush. Local mining district regulations formed the basis for congressional legislation and judicial inquiry. The national hysteria that drove thousands westward got down to earth when gold seekers assembled in a placer mining locality to write property rules governing their local district. In their worldview, the 1849 miners needed rules to define what constituted a claim and what the size of the claim should be, to require that the claim be recorded, and to define the limits of use of property. Miners were little concerned with the underlying title to the land they claimed. American Indian title was not extinguished, Spanish and Mexican title under grant was unclear, and whether California was public land by virtue of the Mexican War was not a concern. What concerned miners was their assertion of a property right in placer grounds against other miners during a mining rush. What they wanted was some sense of certainty in the ground they were working.

This assertion of a claim of right in real property was nothing new in American history. English colonists rarely respected American Indian title, and the Spanish also took Indian lands and enslaved the survivors of conquest. The Treaty of Guadalupe Hidalgo had ended the Mexican War, but the impact of Spanish or Mexican grant titles was unclear in 1849. Argonauts, whether American emigrant or immigrant entrepreneur, claimed mineral lands unoccupied by another miner. Information flowing back to Congress told of wealth, massive emigration, and a need

California placer miners at the head of the Auburn Ravine. Courtesy of the California History Section, California State Library.

for a mining law. Following American legal tradition for public lands, Congress wrote statutes granting preemption rights for those pioneers in the West. Even more fundamentally, Americans knew that property was liberty and liberty equaled private property. The American Revolution was based on this protection of the ancient constitution of Britain and the assertion of the sanctity of private property.[1]

When Congress set out to write mining law for the California gold rush and the Comstock Lode in Nevada, it had precedent. Congress legislated for mining in a variety of ways before the gold rush to California. In the General Land Act of 1785 Congress reserved one-third of all gold, silver, lead, and copper in mines sold or otherwise disposed of under the act. In 1807 Congress inaugurated a leasing system for the lead mines of Indiana Territory. In the 1840s leases extended to the Lake Superior copper-mining lands. Under an act of March 3, 1829, the United States sold lead-mining tracts to the public. Land sales extended to copper lands in 1847 including the Chippewa District in Wisconsin.[2] Leases and sales guaranteed interests in land or the certainty of private property.

Miners took a gamble, but they did not want to gamble on their rights to a particular piece of ground. This gambling context explains, in part, why Congress in 1872 did not impose a royalty fee on mining the public domain. Milton B. Stevens wrote to his mother from Salmon Falls, California, on December 9, 1849, that "we are making from 8 to 25 Dolars per day. This is but Small pickings."[3] Gordon C. Cone confided to his diary on February 12, 1850, that "gold digging in California is attended with great uncertainty. In the first place there is but few places that gold is found in anything like an aboundance, and there places have all been dug out."[4] Stanford Johnson in New Diggings, California, wrote to Daniel Johnson on December 28, 1850, observing that "it is true one gits a fortune very quick but wher there is one that gits a fortune there is thousands that dont git anything at all."[5] The days of placer bonanzas in California passed quickly, and by the time Congress legislated in 1872, the nature of mining had changed. For the miners, the risk of the venture remained.

The gambling nature of mining was not confined to California's placers. Enoch Root wrote to his sister from Laurette, Colorado, on April 15, 1862, and reported that "times are very dull here at present."[6] Two weeks later he wrote to his aunt that "if these mines continue to prosper my money is laid out at a good advantage, otherwise the claims are of little value. This winter hay has brought fabulous prices selling for sixty and eighty dollars per ton."[7] Root, like other miners, turned to enterprises like farming if the mines did not prosper and the claims had no buyers. Henry Harmon Clark in Virginia City, Montana, told his brother on December 30, 1864, "One man can hold 200 feet on a leed, the law here makes leed claims real estate so that a man is not obliged to work them. We are going to get hold of some claims if we can without paying much." His hope for fortune was clear: "There will be a great many fortunes made at it here in a few years capitalists from cities east have sent agents out here after specimens of quartz. It will be known next season whether they are good or not."[8] The local mining district regulations

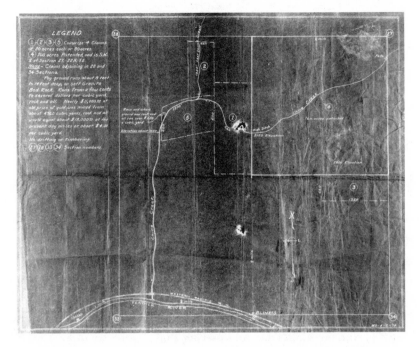

Placer locations, Butte County, California, 1934. Courtesy of the California History Section, California State Library.

had converted a claim into real property. It enabled speculation without the investment of time, labor, and capital. Fortune depended on buyers, however, with capital.

Clark had moved from the placer mining phase of gold seeking to hard-rock prospecting. Clark explained the important difference to his brother in August 1865: "We bought a claim paid 2.50 dollars down we dug a drain ditch and become satisfied that it would not pay very well, after putting on 3 weeks work found a chance to sell for the same we paid and sold but had to wait 3 weks for part of the pay."[9] Clearly, placer mining required money and a great deal of labor. Clark worked with two men from Iowa and got nothing for their toil. He went on, writing, "The surface mines dont pay very much. The big money I think is the quartz ledges and in time they will be worked." As for him, "I am getting a few quartz claims. They may be worth something sometime."[10] Cornelius Hedges of Helena adopted the same strategy, combining the practice of law with speculating in mining claims. He wrote his parents in 1865, "I don't know as the claims will be worth anything but hope and think so. I have about 10,000 feet of Lode claims that may prove rich but nothing is known yet. In fact noting is sure here but what one has in his hands."[11] Charles Francis Clark of Austin, Nevada, declared in 1868 that "I am going to quit working for nothing." He turned to selling apples, citrus, and blackberries to miners who had money.[12] The contrast is simple. Practicing law enabled speculation in claims, and farming provided a living after mining failures.

Despite the gamble, some miners chased their dream of a paying mine all over the West. Hutch Stevens was poking around Lead, South Dakota, in 1893 when he wrote to his sister Matilda that "notwithstanding the financial troubles that seem hovering over us, Lead seems to keep up her spirits."[13] In 1894 he observed from Grangeville, Idaho, that "nearly all successful people owe there prosperity to industry, economy, and accumulation and not to speculation or bonanzas."[14] In 1895 Hutch was in Altman, Colorado, complaining that water had to be hauled uphill at a cost of forty cents.[15] The next year from Florissant, Colorado, he told his sister of prospecting Wyoming from the Bald Mountain to North Park and then "east to the Laramie River and from there to the east side of the Medicine Bow Range." He "found nothing in there that I thought good and came back."[16] A decade later Hutch was in Steamboat Springs, Colorado, and in 1907 he wrote from Lovelock, Nevada, telling his sister that "in the Humboldt Mountains . . . wages are high but expenses are frightful." Still an optimist, Hutch pursued "my mine," and he rejoiced, "What a glorious thing hope is. Well it buoys us up and keeps us from sinking."[17] In December Hutch was reported missing from his gold claims near Fitting, Nevada. Peter C. Stevens left Salt Lake City in search of Hutch, thinking he had "met his death by foul play."[18] As late as March, Peter reported from Fitting that it was "impossible to find a trace of Hutch."[19] But spring cleared away the mountain snow, and Peter returned to Salt Lake City with Hutch's remains. Apparently he had "accidentally shot himself" hunting sage hens as Peter had only found "the bones and nothing but the skeleton remained. The chicken was laying near him and was not eaten."[20] Hutch's fowling piece had done him

Cornelius Hedges.
Courtesy of the
Montana Historical
Society, Helena.

in still searching for his mine. The gamble was one with mining and another with the frontier environment.

The depression years certainly did not make mining any more secure. A mining stock crash could follow a national economic problem. O. H. McKee of San Francisco wrote to Robert Keating in Nevada on December 10, 1879, that "very many here have lost their cash dollar and very many more have lost about everything they possess."[21] W. H. Cscanyan, the vice president of the Boreel Mining Company, wrote to R. Chester Turner in 1910 that it was "too bad that some of those properties are vieritable ghost stories and virtually of no value at all, and we have no redress for our labor and money spent in the examinations."[22] Will Pomeroy of Candelaria, Nevada, wrote Dr. Carl Lee Smith of El Paso, Texas, in 1929 explaining that "mining is a cold blooded proposition, and especially when one is spending his own money."[23] Philip R. Barbour of Montana agreed. He told Philip H. Collins of Cleveland, Ohio, that "mining is a very hard game to bet. The odds seem to be about 250,000 to 1. That is someone has figured out that of every 250,000 claims located 1 pays dividends. This should be tough enough for anyone with any gambling instincts."[24]

To minimize the gamble and put mining claims in private property law terms, miners gathered to write rules for their enterprise. William Downie's diary recorded that the Upper Yuba Forks Mining District laws provided for claims to be ten yards in length from the middle of the river, staked with tools left on the claim. Claimants had five days to prepare and occupy the claim. Only persons born in the United States or naturalized were eligible to hold claims. If a company of miners dammed up the river to exploit their claims, they had a right to the bed of the river. Referees had jurisdiction to settle disputes over mining claims. Juries of miners tried crimes, and fair trial was guaranteed.[25] So said these miners, and they put their values into the law of the district. Otis E. Young Jr. has summarized the local mining district regulations of the West in similar terms. The placer claim could be fifty to one hundred feet extending out from the center of the watercourse channel. To be located, it had to be staked and recorded with the district recorder. Miners could only hold one claim in the district, but partnerships could hold contiguous claims. Miners had to work their claims. If they did not do so for a specified length of time, another miner could assert possession by locating it by staking and recording. Typically, this act was called jumping a claim. Miners were to take only the amount of water they needed and were not to interfere with other miners. Disputes found their way to referees, recorders, or miners' meetings. Miners' meetings called all available members of the district together to hear and decide disputes.[26] Although the terms varied, these general provisions dominated the local mining district regulations.

Local mining district regulations were subject to change as personnel in the district shifted with news of the next rush. Regardless of those changes, miners respected the property rights acquired under prior mining district regulations by continuous possessors of claims. James Henry Morley confided to his diary on August 9, 1862: "Found our Beaver Head prospectors returned with good specimens of gold and . . . flattering reports of mines. They had secured each a claim and have today organized a district and made rules governing the same."[27] A month later he wrote of "some three hundred men [in] the mines, who have organized and made rule[s] to regulate mining operations. Our claims are all jumped and Ault is waiting a miners' meeting set for Sunday next to get his back."[28] Ault won. In December, Morley expressed delight when "a miners' meeting called to pass the odious code of civil laws gotten up for the benefit of a few pettifoggers, but they were rejected by a two thirds majority."[29] A similar attempt lost in February, but on April 26, 1863, Morley recorded that "laws passed making quartz leads real estate and setting claim disputes by jury chosen by President [of district]."[30] In 1865, the "Laws of Lincoln Gulch" in Montana provided that "all claim holders have the right to dig drain ditches through the claims below them," but "no persons have the right to empty their tailings or waist dirt upon those below them." The miners' meeting of March 2, 1870, decided in the negative on a motion "whether claim owners of No. 28 had a right to go about 100 feet below their line and take up grade in the drain ditch for the purpose of draining the lower part of their ground." The vote was seven for and twelve against.[31] The folkmoot of the West had decided a case under their local mining district regulations.[32]

John Ryan found things different in Bodie, California. He wrote to R. P. Keating of Virginia City, Nevada, in 1879 that

> laws hear is diferant to any Camp I ever been in yo must first get the ledge before you can locate you myst show the ledge good and gring the recorder on the ground then you are only alowed 100 feet Wide 50 each side of the Ledge you can take up a big lot for a tunnell right ledge or no ledge on acount there some apearently good Claimes left that the ledge was not found or looked for much there is no croppingts hear only slate it takes labor to find a ledge except by chance.[33]

Every miner knew that knowledge of the local district rules was imperative for the successful location of a claim.

When the miner had a claim and staked it, he still had to record it with the local district recorder, later replaced by the county recorder. It was not unusual to find the ancient metes and bounds descriptions recorded. William T. Armstrong's April 19, 1853, claim description was as follows:

> Claim commences at a large Pine Tree marked with the letter A; thence running a North East direction about six hundred yards more or less to a lone cedar tree marked B; thence running Southeast about 5 hundred yards to an Oak Tree marked C; thence running to a large Pine Tree in a Soouth West direction about six hundred yars distant from said oak. This tree is west of a ravine and marked D; thence running Northwest to said Tree inscribed with the letter A.[34]

In the American history of real estate, trees served as a point of beginning, with boundaries defined in terms of trees. However, doubt and uncertainty increased with every windstorm and forest fire.

The parameters of the local mining district regulations formed the foundation for the Mining Laws of 1866 and 1872. Miners had defined the nature of mining property. It had a certain claim size and distinguished placer from quartz claims. Staking the claim to define its boundaries and assert ownership was stated clearly. Miners required that the claim be worked by its owner or be subject to relocation by another miner. Simply stated, if a miner did not work a claim, then that claim was abandoned, and another miner could "jump" that claim and file a location notice. Rights and interests in water brought to the claim and conveyed away from the claim found clear expression in district regulations. Miners required that claims be recorded, making public the location of the claim and its owner. These were culturally rooted rules of American property law transported west and applied to mineralized ground. Congress would have to sort out which of these rules needed to be included in the *Statutes at Large*. In 1866 and again in 1872, our nation's lawmakers visited western American mining and wrestled with the needs of a national economy, the traditions of American property law, and the claims of western uniqueness.

CHAPTER 3

CONGRESS SPEAKS

The General Mining Laws

I am waiting

for the discovery of a new symbolic western frontier

and I am waiting for the American Eagle

to really spread its wings and straighten up and fly right

and I am waiting for the Age of Anxiety

to drop dead

—Lawrence Ferlinghetti, "I Am Waiting"
in *These Are My Rivers* (1993)

Congress knew that something was happening in California in 1849, but matters of slavery, slavery in the territories, the Mexican Cession, and economic dislocation occupied much of its time. A civil war would further distance congressional minds from the need to regulate mining on the public domain. Yet in 1864 legislation would start down the halls, ultimately finding its way into the *Statutes at Large* as the Mining Laws of 1866, 1870, and 1872. These statutes were products of their times, the dominant Republican Party, and the limited knowledge of lawmakers listening to their western brethren.

Colorado Territorial Delegate Hiram P. Bennet, Senator William Morris Stewart of Nevada, Senator John Conness of California, and Representative William "Bloody Bill" Higby of California were instrumental in forming this legislation.[1] Bennet won unanimous consent to introduce a bill "in relation to mines and minerals on the public domain" in March 1864.[2] A month later New York Representative Fernando Wood introduced a bill, limited in geographic scope, designed "to protect all the property which the Government actually possesses" in order to "pay the public debt."[3] The concept was simply to use the mineral lands as a source of revenue. Bennet replied that the silver and gold produced in the West was sufficient to support U.S. currency and that was enough.[4]

Bennet put the miners in that same basket as yeoman farmers:

> The only thing that should be done is to pass some liberal statute to aid the occupant, or else to let him entirely alone to work out his own salvation. A reasonable tax would not be objected to in these war times by miners, but it should be accompanied with statutory protection to the miners in his possessions. With the same propriety the gentleman might propose to drive the settlers off the agricultural public lands because they are producing corn and what as to drive off those who are producing gold.[5]

In Bennet's eyes, the miner and the farmer were performing the same duty as productive Americans. They were working the public domain and producing national wealth. Bennet was not alone in likening miners to farmers merely preempting public land to feed a family and produce a surplus for the market economy.[6] Yet government needed money, and Justin Morrill, noted authority on the public lands and taxation, wanted an ad valorem tax on mineral output.[7] California congressional efforts to kill the tax failed, but the bill drifted off with the course of the Civil War.

In 1866 John Sherman of Ohio introduced Senate 257, a lode claim act with a 3 percent tax on mineral proceeds. William Morris Stewart was now a U.S. senator, and he had orders from his mining corporate clients.[8] By convincing Congress that the bill did no more than validate democratically derived local law, Stewart satisfied his clients. Politically, Stewart assured his colleagues that the miners were all "good Republican voters."[9] The mining law was continuity, democracy, entrepreneurial opportunity, and wealth producing without burdensome taxation imposed on the poor miner.

The Mining Law of 1866 was simple, deceptively so. The mineral lands of the public domain were open to all U.S. citizens and aliens who had declared their intent to naturalize. All state, territorial, and local mining district regulations and laws were recognized under federal law. The apex rule holding that the claimant possessing the apex of a vein had the right to pursue the vein outside the sidelines of the claim was federally recognized in explicit terms. Claim size under the statute was limited to three hundred feet along a vein. Miners could buy their claim for $5.00 per acre if they had made statutorily sufficient improvements. Rights of way for roads, ditches, and canals won federal recognition.

As any observer of statute could infer, the 1866 law was limited in scope, yet it fixed the apex rule on federal paper. The Comstock Lode was not a placer, and mining was not solely quartz mining. In 1870 the House Committee on Mines took up the limitation and included placer mining in a bill that passed the House on a voice vote.[10] In the Senate William Morris Stewart and California's Senator Cornelius Cole sluiced the bill though to a voice vote. It provided for placer claims of twenty acres and associations of eight individuals to claim 160 acres.[11] It was a hydraulic miner's dream.

Congress kept tinkering with mining law in committee in 1871, and in 1872 the mining bill was on the floor. There were numerous inconsistencies and omissions in the 1866 and 1870 legislation. One California senator characterized the 1866 law as "a bill to promote litigation, create controversy, and occasion difficulties."[12] The 1870 statute had included the placer claims, and in 1872 lawmakers provided for a uniform system of location, recording, and working claims.[13] Representative Aaron Sargent of Massachusetts told the lawmakers that the bill did "not change in the slightest degree the policy of Government in the disposition of the mineral lands." Rather, "it simply oils the machinery a little."[14] So it was with the 1872 statute, replacing 1866 language but retaining the authority of state, territorial, and local mining district regulations and laws. Claim size was increased to fifteen hundred feet, and an annual work requirement of $100 was imposed to retain a right in a claim. Patents were $5.00 per acre for lode claims and half that for placers. One legal question received a federal answer when the statute provided that lode claims situated on placer claims could be patented as part of the placer claim. Intersecting lode locations went to senior locators, that is, the first in time was the first in right. Claims were limited to "valuable" minerals, and the law made a distinction between mineral and agricultural lands. Tunnel claims won recognition, and five-acre mill sites could be located on lands not containing "valuable" minerals. As we will see, some of these provisions and the failure of the Congress to define specific mining terms would leave a great deal of work for the courts. Importantly, the statute specifically provided that local law applied to claims filed prior to the effective date of the statute and that all thereafter had to follow the federal law.

The congressional voice most frequently heard in courts was that of William Morris Stewart. In 1866 he declared that "a series of wise judicial decisions molded these regulations and customs into a comprehensive system of common law, embracing not only mining law, (properly speaking,) but also regulating the use of water for mining purposes."[15] In *Sparrow v. Strong* (1865) Chief Justice Salmon P. Chase took an 1865 speech of Stewart's as legal gospel, declaring that "a special kind of law—a sort of Common Law of miners . . . had sprung up on our Pacific coast."[16] To make clear to bench, bar, and Congress what he was citing, Chase had Stewart's entire July 19, 1865, speech included as appendix 1 to that volume of the *U.S. Supreme Court Reports*.

The 1872 law did put a new requirement in the apex rule requiring miners to locate the apex within the claim to have extralateral rights. What that meant would be for the courts to sort out, but that was not the only variegation in mining law and practice. The law made no distinction between horizontal deposits and fissure veins. Silver replacement deposits were horizontal and irregular without a certain dip, strike, or necessary connection. The Moose Silver ledge, vein, or deposit in Colorado's Mosquito Range would be such an exceptional challenge to legal certainty under the law.[17]

Further, those local mining district, territorial, and state laws for mining under which miners held claims were still part of the common law of miners. With all the genius of the California local mining district regulations, subsequent miners were certainly perfecting the mining law. Montana's experience should have given Congress pause, but it did not. Harrison Burns remembered that laws written in Virginia City in summer 1864 were "the only guide that courts and lawyers had to enable them to administer justice." Further, "there was not an acre of land in the territory owned by a private individual. None of the land had ever been surveyed. If a person who occupied a lot abandoned it[s] possession, he lost his claim and anyone else could locate upon it." Regarding mineral lands, "there were some miners' laws as to location mining claims, but these conferred possessor rights only."[18] When the first territorial legislature met in Bannack, Burns noted that "in the chaotic conditions of the laws the members of the legal profession of Virginia City deemed it adviseable to organize and draft some bills to be presented to the legislature for adoption." The legislature received the civil and criminal codes, and "both codes were rush through without change."[19] Included were "An Act concerning the location of Tunnels" and "An Act relating to the Discovery of Gold and Silver Quartz lead, lodes or ledges, and the manner of location."[20] Tunnel claims had to be recorded after location and could be three hundred feet on each side of the center of the tunnel. The legislature specifically provided that this provision was not in conflict with the discovery statute. The tunnel had to be one hundred feet in depth within one year of filing the claim. The discovery law provided for two hundred-foot claims on a lead, lode, or ledge "together with all dips, spurs, and angles emanating or diverging from said lead, lode, or ledge, as also 50 feet on each side."[21] The claim could extend "ten hundred feet along said lead, lode, or ledge in each direction."[22] The territorial legislature revisited mining law in its 1871–72 session and limited claims to two hundred feet by fifty feet and provided for one claim by discovery and one by preemption. The solons also guaranteed property rights in prior claims and made transactions real estate transactions.[23]

Montana's territorial mining law was dysfunctional in the real world of miners. The two hundred-foot claim limit necessitated either cooperative effort or fraud to obtain enough working ground to make a mine pay.[24] Miners filed about twelve thousand lode claims but worked few. Speculation rather than development dominated the practice of the early miners. Further, milling and smelting offered similarly dismal prospects: "The mediocre state of mining intelligence, high transportation costs, the restrictions of Montana's quartz law, and the chronic shortage of ore almost guaranteed failure."[25] Litigation offered another impediment to profit. William H. Hunt, a justice of the Montana Supreme Court and later a federal district judge, observed that "mining properties were often very valuable and that as precedents were few and books seldom readily at hand, controversies over rights to claims demanded resourcefulness of minds which called for superior intellectual power."[26] The Montana legislature was the source of additional confusion. Decius S. Wade characterized the statutes of Montana as fragmentary, confused, mixed in subject matter, inadequate in scope, and a breeding ground for litigation and delayed justice.[27] The 1871–72 legislature amended and changed the law; and "here is the source and beginning of the confusion and contradictions," Wade declared to the Helena Bar Association in 1894.[28] Federal law put this territorial law under the national legal umbrella, leaving it for the courts to sort out meaning, but in 1872 the General Mining Law gave miners and claims more signification.

As we will see, Congress tinkered with mining law and in the 1990s seriously confronted the General Mining Law of 1872 without success. In the interim the mining interests had organized. In 1897 the American Mining Congress emerged as a national lobbying organization. State organizations had nineteenth- and early-twentieth-century origins. In 1914 Robert Chester Turner told of "a movement on foot to organize a California Mine Operators' Association for the purpose of insuring concerted action on the part of the principal mining companies in dealing with employees, influencing legislation affecting mining interests, etc." Turner was "heartily in sympathy with this movement, as it can be developed into a powerful organization and made to be productive of much good to the mining business." Turner had been secretary of the Tonopah Mine Operators' Association, which had evolved into the Nevada Mine Operators' Association, with "nearly every important mining company in Nevada" a member.[29] In addition to organizations, mining interests watched state legislative activities. In 1955 Louis D. Gordon of Reno, Nevada, told Harry Corvin, a San Francisco attorney, that "in addition to my usual duties, the Nevada Legislature has been in session since January 17th and one of my duties is to attend such sessions in order to watch any legislation inimical to the mining industry of Nevada."[30] The miners had organized to protect mining interests. Their ordeal was just ahead.

Decius S. Wade, 1880.
Courtesy of the Montana
Historical Society, Helena.

Contemporaneously, the Anaconda Copper Mining Company decided that underground mining in Butte, Montana, was not profitable and started open-pit operations. Jared Diamond has noted that "until 1955 most mining at Butte involved underground tunnels, but in 1955 Anaconda began excavating an open-pit mine called the Berkeley Pit, now an enormous hole over a mile in diameter and 1,800 feet deep."[31] That decision was rational in the sense that open-pit mining was less costly than tunnel mining. Yet the company knew of the hydrology of Butte since the nineteenth century. Subterranean water had long plagued tunnel mining in Butte, and the Berkeley Pit also filled with acidic mine waters.[32] Today it constitutes America's most costly Superfund site. Jared Diamond notes, "While denial or minimization of responsibility may be in the short-term financial interests of the mining company, it is bad for society as a whole, and it may also be bad for the long-term interests of the company itself, or the entire mining industry."[33] Under the General Mining Law of 1872 Anaconda clearly had the authority to decide how to mine. It did not have to calculate the future costs in 1955. As we will see later, the mining industry's legacy has had negative consequences for many mining companies.

CHAPTER 4

COURTS SPEAK

Mucking Out Waste and Processing Words

Do you need maps of the mountains and the

underworld?

We have maps of the mountains but we lack maps

of the underworld.

Of course you lack maps of the underworld,

there are no maps of the underworld.

—James Tate, "The Workforce"
in *Memoir of the Hawk* (2001)

Remembering the words of Judge Hunt regarding the need for judicial intellect, judges in the period before federal mining law had local mining district regulations, territorial or state statutes, and the common-law tradition to deal with in deciding mining cases. The desire to put the judicial hand on a treatise or a precedent case was often thwarted by the newness of the law.[1] Regardless, judges had the duty to decide cases. Now the meaning of the local mining district regulations and the Mining Laws of 1866, 1870, and 1872 were in judicial hands. As we will see, prior to federal statutes judges had little to contemplate and the common-law tradition was central to judicial interpretation.

In *The Bear River and Auburn Water and Mining Co. v. New York Mining Co.* (1857), the California Supreme Court complained loudly of the lack of legal guidance to decide the case. Justice Peter H. Burnett, speaking for the court, noted that "the judiciary of the State, has had thrown upon it, responsibilities not incurred by the Courts of any other State in the Union," in that it had a new constitution, a new code of law, and new subject matter to deal with in its institutional infancy.[2] The subject matter was mining, and it created "a large class of cases unknown in the jurisprudence of our sister States."[3] The court noted that without direct precedent or statutory guidance, its recourse was to the common-law tradition. Further, regardless of how the court decided the case, one party would sustain great injury. Burnett rhetorically wrung his hands because "no class of cases can arise more difficult of a just solution, or more distressing in practical result. And the present is one of the most difficult of that most perplexing class of cases." The nature of the mining enterprise compounded his difficulty. Burnett reckoned that "there are intrinsic difficulties in the subject itself, that it is almost impossible to settle satisfactorily, even by the application to them of the abstract principles of justice."[4] The problem was that "in our mineral region we have a novel use of water" that "deteriorates the quality of the element itself, when wanted a second time for the same purposes."[5] Basically water was the vehicle for mining profits, and pay dirt must be washed. Lower riparians also wanted to wash their gravel, and the upstream miners sent sludge downstream, destroying their enterprise.

Burnett looked at federal public policy for guidance and found it in the management of the public domain. That policy was "to distribute the bounty of the government among the greatest number of persons, so as most rapidly to develop the hidden resources of this region; while at the same time, the prior substantial rights of individuals should be preserved."[6] Taking the cue from public policy, Burnett concluded that making the diversion of water for mining purposes produced a greater good. The court used the language of property rights and resource exploitation with little regard for environmental consequences.[7] Within a quarter century, the flood of tailings, gravel, and slimes that filled California rivers, flooded its cities, and destroyed its croplands would force a jurisprudential change of heart.

With the Mining Law of 1866, judges had federal language to ponder. Hiram Knowles of Montana opined in 1871 that considering the history of mining for the precious metals in the mineral lands of the United States, and the history of the passage of the act under consideration, it cannot be doubted that Congress intended by it to legalize the mining upon the public domain for precious metals, which up to the passage of the same had been carried on in such a manner as to make those engaged therein trespassers as against the general government.[8]

Knowles construed the statute as giving the miner the equivalent of a patent on the public domain and as against a legislatively granted toll road, the claim was private property requiring just compensation for any taking for a public use.[9] Congress had created a private property interest in land for mining purposes.

The U.S. Supreme Court looked to local mining district regulations for the precedent and wisdom of the work requirement in the General Mining Law of 1872. Justice Miller speaking for the Court wrote that

these mineral lands being thus open to the occupation of all discoverers, one of the first necessities of a mining neighborhood was to make rules by which this right of occupation should be governed as among themselves; and it soon discovered that the same person would mark out many claims of discovery and then leave them for an indefinite length of time without further development, and without actual possession, and seek in this manner to exclude others from availing themselves of the abandoned mine. To remedy this evil a mining regulation was adopted that some work should be done on each claim in every year, or it would be treated as abandoned.[10]

Miller acknowledged the private property aspect of a claim but also the superior public policy requirement that the property be used productively. It was a concept enshrined in American history, public domain policy, and entrepreneurial wisdom.

Congress saw this wisdom when it passed the General Mining Law of 1872. Miller continued that

Judge Hiram Knowles.
Courtesy of the Montana
Historical Society, Helena.

when it came to regulate these matters and provide for granting a title to claimants, adopted the prevalent rule as to claims
asserted prior to the statute, and as to those made afterwards it
required one hundred dollars' worth of labor or improvement
to be made in each year on every claim. Clearly the purpose
was the same as in the matter of similar regulations by the miners, namely, to require every person who asserted an exclusive
right to his discovery or claim to expend something of labor or
value on it as evidence of his good faith, and to show that he
was not acting on the principle of the dog in the manger.[11]

Miller clearly delineated the policy of release of energy in the use of
private property. People who sat on their property contributed nothing
to the national wealth. The Court was consistent with "the current" of
judicial "protection of property in action."[12]

The U.S. Supreme Court also set about the task of defining statutory
language in mining terms. When did a patent applicant have knowledge

of a lode under the 1872 law? There were no maps of the underground until mines had been developed and mining engineers had surveyed the mine. The claimant on the surface looking down a tunnel wanted to see color enough to buy the ground from the federal government and hold title free of that pesky work requirement. Justice Stephen J. Field, once the only justice who had ever seen a mine, wanted actual discovery rather than "mere surmises, notions, and loose gossip of the neighborhood."[13] After multiple cases, differing opinions, and shifting majorities on the issue, the Court settled on discovery and location as a nexus.[14]

The darling of the 1866 law, the apex doctrine, similarly drew judicial heat. Apex litigation made fortunes for prevailing litigants and lawyers on all sides, particularly in Nevada.[15] The U.S. Supreme Court put a damper on apex litigation in 1878 when it held that the location had to be along the lengthwise course of the vein's apex. The end lines of the claim had to be across the strike or course of the vein, and the sidelines, parallel to it. If not so located, the claim only secured as much of the lode as within its boundaries.[16] With that said, the next question was the mining definition of the statutory term *vein*. Moses Hallett of Colorado's Supreme Court and a federal district judge announced in *Iron Silver Mining Company v. Cheesman* (1881) that it was "a body of mineral or mineral bearing rock within defined boundaries in the general mass of the mountain."[17] When the case arrived at the U.S. Supreme Court, Justice Miller acknowledged that a vein was "no easy thing to define."[18] After a review of the cases, Miller adopted Hallett's definition. In 1891 the Court determined that "the apex of a vein or lode [was] the highest point thereof, and may be at the surface of the ground or at any point below the surface." Further, it was "not necessarily a point, but often a line of great length."[19] Apex litigation now had definition from the highest court in the land, and mining engineers needed to be very busy mapping the underworld.[20]

The Mining Law of 1872 gave the federal courts plenty of western mining history and legislative intent to contemplate, but case by case, miners and their lawyers had greater certainty. Yet the conflicts of claimants to mineralized ground continued, and the problem of the unintended consequences of unrestrained environmental pollution soon became evident.

CHAPTER 5

LOCATION, LOCATION, LOCATION

Out here

I can almost understand

how mountains are

words said

at a height—actual sound made manifest as silence,

a summons

—Margaret Gibson, "In the Mountains"
in *Earth Elegy* (1997)

L ocating a mining claim was a matter of finding mineralized ground and posting a location notice of claim to that particular ground. Whether placer ground or hard-rock quartz claim, the concept was the same. Declare your property interest in writing in the center of your ground in a manner giving the people in the vicinity clear notice of your claim. Then you had to stake the claim with posts, blazed trees, or rock piles at the corners of the claim. You had to record the description of the claim with the local district recorder or the county recorder. The Mining Law of 1872 and all of its predecessors clearly required that claim locations be recorded. The description contained the nature of the discovery, and miners gave their claims names, some quite colorful. Now recorded, all you had to do was work on the claim to develop a mine.[1] It all seemed very simple.

However, in the course of events, the reality on the ground was not always what the local mining district regulations, state law, or federal statute provided. Stephen Wilkin of Virginia City, Nevada, wrote to J. M. McDonald in 1879 regarding the problem of finding a location that "in early times, there was much imperfect indexing done."[2] Adam Aulbach of Murray, Idaho, wrote to James H. Hawley in Boise in 1897 that "the Northeast corner stake of the Buckeye cannot be found, but in its place is a stake of the Jim Blaine, said to be 30 or 40 feet to the West. This would jeopardise a part of the best ground in the Buckeye." How to resolve the problem? Aulbach reported that "Mr Heyburn has directed me to reset the stake where I am told it ought to be."[3] Aulbach had written to W. B. Heyburn one week earlier that "unfortunately the Buckeye vein or ledge had its apex in Jim Blaine ground" and "the Blaine was a prior location."[4] A month later attorney W. B. Heyburn wrote Hawley from Spokane, retorting that "I don't take much stock in the apex question. I doubt if it can enter into the consideration of the value of that property at all, but the facts are undeveloped and without an understanding, of course, you never can say just what may arise upon the trial."[5] As we will see, the issue of the apex of a vein was crucial to the right of extralateral pursuit of a vein outside the sidelines of a hard-rock location. The question of the situs of the apex and its position within the location was for expert witnesses and skilled attorneys. Millions frequently turned on the issue in the nineteenth-century West.

Another reason that the exact situs of stakes, end lines, and sidelines of claims was significant was subterranean trespass. L. H. McIrwin of Bellevine, Idaho, wrote to J. W. Brown on October 24, 1897, that "thare is ore in the clame and the partis are working under our end line They moved our Corner Stake last winter so tha Macarter & Redley could mak a sale Tha sold to a French Co. for ten thousan dollars tha claim the notice cont cover the gound as saked but the Sakes has been thare all the time and the work been don in good faith."[6] Howard E. Perry paid out $75,000 in 1930 for trespass onto another quicksilver claim in Texas.[7] The famous war of the copper kings in Butte, Montana, also involved the conversion of ore from a claim outside the location of the mine.[8] A. M. Livermore wrote to Mr. Stevens on June 29, 1868, that "you are hereby notified that I hold you responsible for the value of all the ore that you are hauling away from my claim on the 'Alameda Lode' near Virginia City, Montana."[9] Cornelius B. Nolan reported to Judge Showers in Boulder, Montana, in 1895 that "Ross [Deegan] has a force of men

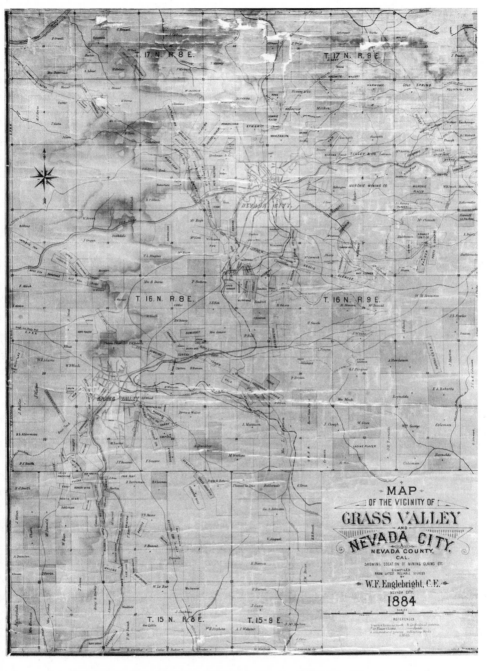

Hard-rock mining claims map, Nevada County, California, 1884. Courtesy of the California History Section, California State Library.

getting out the ore as speedily as possible and doing away with it, and as he is absolutely insolvent every dollar that he takes out is lost to us."[10] Whether a miner was a copper king or an unincorporated entrepreneur, the problem of trespass and ore conversion was an economic and legal concern.[11] Knowing where stakes resided as described in claim filings in the recorder's office often required a surveyor, and staking claims underground further confounded certainty.

You did not need to be a copper king to be at war with other miners. Very early in western mining history, claim jumpers sought advantage in the diggings. J. C. Martin reported from Elk Hill, California, to A. M. and T. E. Bell in 1853 that he had found "the location for 2 first rate claims," but they had been "covered by land warrants by speculatores and not considered worth anything" because the land was unsurveyed and "the location of said warrants contrary to the Act of Congress making the grant to the State and also contrary to the act of the Legislature of Cal. authorizing the issue and locating those warrants." These speculators were "jumping them here without any regard to such claims."[12] Frank F. McKee reported self-help in 1856 in Nevada. Writing from Clinton, Nevada, he reported that Bill "Williams collected together what *loafers* and *pimps* he could find up about the Flat and who were willing to risk their *lives*, their *fortunes* and their sacred honor" in defense of Williams's claim. The crowd of thirty to forty men gave "the poor englishmen a severe pounding," who returned the favor with "a Suit against the Boys for assault and Battery."[13] Charles Camden started prospecting in 1849 but found the greatest returns on abandoned claims, with one twenty-foot-wide claim yielding $4,000 in two months and three days. That "showed what method and double work meant."[14] Camden saw these claims as abandoned and jumpable, albeit only while he made a profit. I. F. Corbiere at Poor Man's Creek, California, thought, "If a person is doing pretty well, he had better remain. Prospecting is very uncertain business and very few make by it."[15] So he said in 1853. Things had not changed much in the diggings by 1866. N. S. Bowen of Jamestown, California, wrote to H. Mills in Martinez, "Some Mexicans and a negro have struck a fine pay chute, [but] sometimes they do not go near their claim for two or three months—some prospectors are watching with a view to jump it."[16]

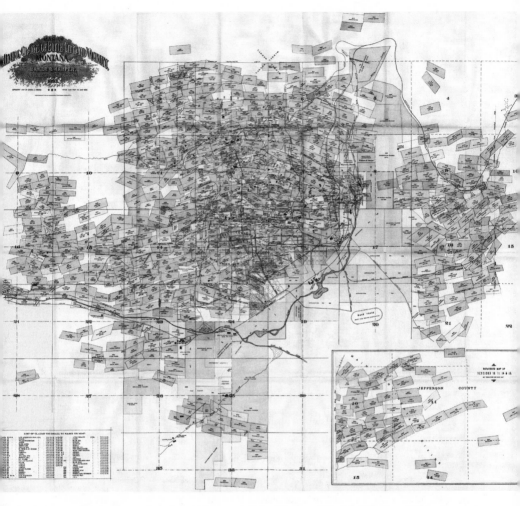

Butte mining claims map. Courtesy of the Montana Historical Society, Helena.

Such claim jumping was not restricted to mining claims. The *Helena Independent Record* reported on May 15, 1887, that the real estate boom in the city had been "suppressed" by the lot jumpers, who had "selfish and grasping propensities of those who are ever ready to take unto themselves what does not properly belong to them."[17] Timothy Donohue of San Francisco reported to William R. Morgan on June 9, 1896, that their lawyer had told him that "the only way [to deal with the Slate Creek jumpers] was to lay injunction on them and law them out of it." Donohue

Forrest H. Anderson,
Attorney-General of Montana.
Courtesy of the Montana
Historical Society, Helena.

demurred due to lack of cash, and he did not "want any lawsuit it might cost more than we bargain for and then get beat."[18] Donohue repeated his themes three years later, telling Morgan that "I am trying to protect our property from jumpers but I dont think I can do it with law suit and that will take money and they might beat us."[19] The need to go to law did not disappear in the twentieth century. Montana Attorney-General Forrest H. Anderson advised Elmer McElroy of Troy in 1962 that "if you have properly located your mining claim and kept up the assessment work as you state then anybody who tries to jump your claim is a trespasser. However, to oust him it is necessary that you hire a lawyer and bring a civil action."[20] Claim jumpers could be legitimate miners relocating the claim open to their interests or persons simply trying to squeeze money out of a miner via an adverse claim and cloud of title.

Part of the location problem was the original claim description methodology and subsequent reformation for hard-rock mining purposes. One Cripple Creek, Colorado, prospector measured "out a mining claim with a clothesline and pocket compass, on the north side of Poverty Gulch." It was a standard Colorado claim of fifteen hundred by three hundred feet, but "what he was doing actually was relocating the old Grand View claim to make it conform more with the trend of the El Paso Lode."[21] The relocated claim was nothing more than an attempt to increase advantage relative to an adjacent paying claim. One 1860 claim in Calavaras County, California, commenced "at the Oak stump on the South side of the dividing ridge between the San Domingo Creek and Murphy's flats about fifty feet north from the wagon road leading from Murphy's camp to said creek," wherever that might be.[22] Stephen Roberts of San Francisco gave W. A. Garvin advice on this matter in 1880: "You should never relocate and use the same name as before and you cannot acquire a title by taking possession."[23] Changing the name of a claim could eliminate confusion in the litigation that surely would follow. Chumasero and Chadwick had similar advice for a Montana miner in 1879: "to avoid any possible questions—that you make some discovery and *immediately* stake the corners." Further, "if you are able to jump and relocate it will be a very pleasant . . . way of finishing up R's fraudulent claims to our Freespeech Lode."[24] A. M. Esler of the Helena and San Francisco Mining Company of Gem, Idaho, told Anton M. Holter in 1889 that "the discoverer of Frisco affirms and will swear that it was located on *Saturday*—while the Gem was located on *Sunday*, but *dated back* to Saturday."[25] Six weeks later he reported that "John Bartlett . . . located the Badger and Black Bear—I took him before [Judge] Clagett, and among other statements under oath, he said that the San Francisco was located on *Saturday*, while the Gem was located the next day after, but *dated back*—making his evidence very material."[26] A month later Ester was employing Pinkerton detectives to investigate "a man who may ingratuiate himself among a class of scoundrels to develope crroked work, which has been done, in the location of mines, and with who we are at law."[27] The value of mineralized land and the willingness of people to put a cloud on title, file adverse claims, and pervert the seemingly simple system created other levels of uncertainty.

Having an abstract to title prepared by an attorney, the usual process in real estate in the nineteenth century, did not make title to mining claims any more secure. Seth Cook in Virginia City, Nevada, told George O. Whitney of San Francisco in 1862 that "I have sometimes thought it would be better to buy up ten or twelve hundred feet of the Sacramento—a controlling interest—than to stand a Law Suit."[28] William Morris Stewart, a mining attorney and later U.S. senator, was in accord: "The Sacramento Co. are mostly miners, who have worked upon the hill from a very early date, and can furnish the most important evidence in the case."[29] Cornelius B. Nolan of Helena, Montana, wrote to Charles Stevens of Boulder in 1890 expressing concern:

> In the abstract of title sent by you the other day for the Crescent Mine, I notice that in the Notice of Location there seems to be what might perhaps be a fatal defect. The location of the claim is not shown by the notice, and nothing would establish from the notice itself whether it was in Jefferson or any other county. Are you sure that you made no mistake in making out the notice?[30]

Those abstracts were based on the paper trail of mining claims, but, as we have seen, descriptions could prove ambiguous. N. B. Ringeling, the superintendent of the Hope Mining Company of St. Louis, wrote from Philipsburg, Montana, to Vice President John T. Field in St. Louis on August 17, 1890, that "the titles to the Comanche Extension are badly mixed and I doubt whether an abstract can be made. I am having title looked up but the Recorder doubts whether title can be traced, as the interests go as low as 4, 5, and 10 feet on the Claims." Further, "there have been transfers since 1867, I think."[31] The jumble of titles made searches like a three-ring circus. Fletcher Maddox of Great Falls, Montana, wrote to Thomas C. Power of Helena in 1900 that there was a further cost-benefit problem in seeking certainty: "We cannot improve on the description in the . . . deed without having a survey of the premises which would cost more than the entire consideration."[32] Power restated real property law to Maddox in reply: "We cannot deed to Mr. Rickard any more than is conveyed to us under the patent."[33]

In 1905 litigation, Cornelius B. Nolan gave his client Daniel D. Sullivan of Mareville, Montana, plenty of latitude: "Guided by the map and references to the different objects noted on the map I succeeded in figuring the quantity of land in the possession of the defendant within the mining claim. You will notice however, that I left two or three of the distances blank and you can fill in those blanks at the time that you sign the complaint."[34] Nolan faced an even more daunting task regarding the Mountain Chief and Chief of the Mountain claims located on October 7, 1902, by Heber and Fleming. On August 21, 1905, he wrote to John Tegen of Stockett, Montana, the proprietor of The Handicap, offering "Fine Wines, Liquors and Cigars," and proposed his opinion that

> there is a very serious question as to whether the locations made are valid. Under the Laws of the United States, in making mining locations they must be described with reference to some natural object or permanent monument. I notice in examining the records that the notices are deficient in that respect although I am not prepared to say that they are so deficient as to invalidate the locations. They are not tied down to any natural object or permanent object; there is the simple statement that they are located in the Rocky Mountains.[35]

Any prudent investor in mining claims could see this red flag.

Lawyers examined public records, ferreted out transactions, and offered opinions on title, just as they had for a century or more on real estate. Corette and Corette of Butte made a living at title opinions. John Earl Corette founded the firm in 1934, but Corette had been practicing law since 1903 in Butte and as general counsel for the Union Pacific Railroad. In 1915 he examined abstracts, legal digests, and case law to tell R. J. MacDonald that "if no other persons were proprietors of any mineral land covered by the land patented to your predecessors in interest at the time of the issuance of the patents to your predecessors, you are the owner of the mineral rights and this includes the right of oil and gas."[36] Similarly, Herbert Van Dam Jr., a Salt Lake City attorney, wrote to Edward H. Snyder, the manager of the Combined Metals Reduction Company of Stockton, Utah, in 1934:

There is nothing in the record to indicate any source of title in the Virginia Louise Company. This is likewise true of a deed Entry #28 from Virginia Louise Mining Co. to Prince Consolidated Mining and Smelting Company describing the California, Prince and Great Western, but I think the correct construction to place upon the deed is that it is intended as a waiver or conveyance of extralateral rights.[37]

In this particular case, the documents were not clear on their face, and only surrounding transactions could lead to the intent of the parties.

In other cases the documents made little sense. On December 23, 1862, Frank J. Huggins gave a warranty deed to A. C. Beritzhoff for an undivided one-seventh interest "in a copper mining claim, known as the *Christian* claim situated one thousand and fifty feet in length, and three hundred feet in width." Edward G. Kenyon of the Gopher Mining District of Calavaras County gave a quit claim deed at the same time.[38] The latter made sense in that title was so uncertain in California, but the warranty deed was virtually absent from real estate practice in the nineteenth century.[39] R. H. Countiss of Chicago expressed the concern of all investors in mineral lands to Robert Chester Turner of Berkeley, California, in 1915: "I do not like the idea of spending any money on the proposition until we know absolutely that titles are perfect."[40] So it was in real estate, whether mineralized or not.

What constituted a valid location became clearer as courts continued to decide cases, but ambiguity remained. James A. Walsh, a Helena attorney, wrote to Charles Benton Power in 1922 with some confidence. Mining law, he offered, required the discovery of a valuable mineral before location, but as sixty days after location were allowed, discovery was not strictly required. Posting a location was required, but putting it in a tin can and nailing the can to a tree was not prudent to him because the posting was not conspicuous. Putting the notice between two rocks with part of the paper protruding was sufficient, he thought. Location work to discover the mineral was clearer, but to be safe, one should be certain to move 150 cubic feet of material. Fractional claims were trickier but not impossible to achieve, even if in conflict with patented claims or prior valid locations. Finally, he told Power, one should be certain to read the law as printed on the back of the location notice, and "there should not be any trouble in locating claims."[41] It was easy for the locator, but as Walsh told T. J. Vaughan Rhys of Hughsville, Montana, in 1925, there was more to it: "As you know, many of these locations are made by men who want to levy tribute on somebody who is trying to develop a mining country. They want to bet hold of a claim and then hold up a man for a high price. You want to block them in that game if you can. Of course when it comes to the mining contest that will be a question of fact for the courts to determine."[42] Rhys agreed, telling Walsh and Nagle on January 15, 1925, that "I believe that the only interest of the locators of the Silver Star in this land is their expectation of 'gouging' us at some future date."[43] What was a mining law giving every entrepreneur the opportunity to make a mine had become a game of position and opportunity for those with no intent ever to develop a mine.

The claim business retarded growth in some mining camps. Gardner H. Smith put it simply regarding Arizona in 1897: "Most of the best properties here are held by men who know practically nothing of the business & some of the mines must change owners & get into the hands of mining men before the camp becomes permanent."[44] Walter Scribner Schuyler noted in his journal on March 15, 1914, that "we posted very inconspicuously a notice of location on a small triangle of ground about which we are doubtful. It probably belons to the company but if not we want to secure it against intrusion." The problem was that "the Wisebone claim is almost entirely on our ground and the Horseshoe may encroach somewhat."[45] On May 19, 1914, he noted that "the Grizzly Claim location . . . now called the Lonesome A. Claim . . . is valuable chiefly to prevent encroachment on the Grizzly but also for the young timber on it."[46] Walter V. Martin of Grand Canyon, Arizona, was more sanguine about the significance of locations. He had just "located four quartz claims just off the group of the original strikes." Whether they were legal or not was not an issue. He observed that he "may get sued for trespassing, but if you fellows wake up it may be beneficial for all of us, as the strike is now rated an eight million dollar proposition. Buy it, steal it, but get possession some way."[47] Mining the miners also was a part of the location business, and the Mining Law of 1872 enabled the practice because locations were virtually low-budget speculations.

Securing defensive space and nonmineral assets was another objective of locations. Andrew C. Smith of Portland, Oregon, argued for defensive space in 1906, writing that

> I fully agree with you that it is necessary to proceed at once in securing patent, and also agree with you that it is well to avoid friction; for this reason, therefore, we will avoid including any ground south or east of us that would provoke a conflict, but we want all that we can get; indeed, I feel like the countryman of may ancestors who said, "Faith, I don't want any land except that that joins me."
>
> You may consider me very foolish in including some of this ground in the patent, but I believe it is necessary to have plenty of elbow room, and in these stock affairs, acreage counts for a good deal.[48]

Fred Gibbs in Arizona used locations like Walter Schuyler did in Pike, California, when he saw trees. Gibbs penned this entry in his diary on October 8, 1932: "In afternoon relined some of survey stakes on detours. Located 'Carbonate' claim for Joe & Myself covering bridge on Santa Fe R.R. back to D.E. ranch with idea of trying to hold that timber."[49] The cutting of trees on mining claims was regulated by the U.S. Forest Service, as Lyle F. Watts, the chief of the U.S. Forest Service, explained to Carl T. Hayden on February 23, 1950. After reviewing the relevant legislation, Watts explained that

> These acts all place reasonable restrictions on the right to use the surface & resources, other than mineral deposits, of a mining claim. Patents issued under these acts convey title to the mineral deposits only with the right to occupy and use so much of the surface as may be reasonably necessary for carrying on prospecting and mining. The use of timber is restricted

to mining purposes and the timber must be cut according to sound principles of forest management. Prior valid claims are of course excepted by these acts.[50]

The law in the books was there, but a reality check often told a different tale. Cut-and-run timbering was not unknown in the American West regardless of the best intentions of the Forest Service. In fact, Charles Baldwin Genug, an Arizona miner along the Gila River in 1863, had found wood more lucrative than mining, farming, ranching, and public service. He had a contract "for supplying the concentration works at Wickenburg with wood . . . about 1,800 cords for a year's run."[51] Trees had dollar signs on them and were easier to cash in than quartz lodes.

Timber was not the only objective of mineral locations. Edward E. Williams, a Phoenix attorney, complained to U.S. Senator Carl Hayden in 1967 that the problem of mineral locations was "becoming acute in Pima and Pinal Counties where very often the ranch headquarters are located on lands with reserved mineral rights and the owners are being harassed by spurious mining claims being located for nuisance purposes."[52] Hayden pursued the issue and heard from the secretary of the interior on December 5, 1967. The Stock-Raising Homestead Act specifically provided for mineral entries on the lands claimed under the act. The law provided that the miner "shall not injure, damage, or destroy the permanent improvements of the entryman or patentee, and shall be liable to and shall compensate the entryman or patentee for all damages to the crops on such lands by reason of such prospecting."[53] The law was on the books. It maintained the Mining Law of 1872 provisions on entries on the public domain and put mineral development as a highest and best use, regardless of the actual uses of the land by "miners."

In the 1930s, when developers saw the depression as an opportunity to put claims together at substantially lower cost, the underlying problem of location deficiencies still plagued enterprise.[54] Howard A. Johnson, a Butte attorney, wrote to I. B. Haviland of Chicago in 1931 with bad news:

The locations were far worse even than the certificates indicated. They were poorly laid out in odd shapes and sizes and some of them even had discovery work done on the old patented claims. Apparently they were not made with proper reference to the map, and there wasn't a thing about them that was done right.

Accordingly we will have to relocate them, preferably on July first, so that location work will eliminate the necessity of representation work for the year ending July 1, 1932. One of the chief objections to the claims as laid out, is that they do not cover the fractions left between patented claims, but lap over on patented claims too much to be of much value. It is hard to imagine how a mining engineer or even a miner of any experience could have made a set of seven locations without at least one of them right in at least one respect.[55]

Johnson had, at least, found a paper trail for these claims, and the patented claims had title passed from the federal government to the claimants.

The law firm of Pope and Smith of Missoula was not as fortunate. On March 6, 1936, they informed Joseph Lancaster of Philipsburg that "we are still unable to find any reference either in county records or from the files at Seattle as to the location of the Buschman or Bonnie Jean claims."[56] Lancaster replied five days later that "I have hunted every file in the office but can find no evidence that these claims have ever been recorded, and I think the best thing to do would be to relocate them, and have them recorded in Helena."[57] This was an important find because the Black Pine Silver Mining Company had acquired "what was known as the Combination Group of mining claims in the Philipsburg district. There are seventy-seven patented claims in this group covering approximately 1300 acres of land."[58] The Combination operated in the 1890s and closed in 1897 because of the low price of silver and litigation. Charles D. McClure gave the mine a second chance from 1916, but it fell into bankruptcy in 1922. It was sold under mortgage foreclosure in 1931, and Black Pine bought it in 1932. Regardless of new money invested, reorganization, and the curing of titles, it was foreclosed again in 1940.

In 1938 the Nevada Porphyry Gold Mining Company sent E. A. Michal out to relocate the Monadnock placer claim with a 4×4 and an "empty tin can" for the location notice. However, he was instructed, "if you find that someone else is on the ground for the purpose of relocating this claim," he was to complete the work on the monument and "jump in your automobile and make the trip to Tonopah as quickly as possible in the hope that you may beat the other people to Tonopah."[59] It was a race to the county recorder's office. The 1930s certainly were times of opportunity, but making a mine was more than timing for some.

Depression also had consequences for the future of mines in general. William A. Clark, one of the Butte copper kings, wrote to Samuel T. Hauser in Helena in 1894 that despite the national depression, "it was necessary to go on hoping to find a body of ore, or to shut down, and let the mine fill up with water, which would mean its closing up entirely, as the ground would cave, and the property in that case be practically worthless."[60] Over a half century later, Montana Congressman Lee Metcalf addressed the House Interior Committee's Mines and Mining Subcommittee regarding the "depressed mining industry in 27 states." Melcalf related that when mine maintenance ceased, "shafts and tunnels shift or fill with water, gas creeps in, supports give way and roofs collapse, machinery deteriorates rapidly."[61] Melcalf received a letter from a Wibaux farmer in 1958 expressing disdain for his support of the mining industry. Metcalf offered that he represented farmers, but not "the silly, the foolish and the vicious ones."[62] Irving Dichter of the International Union of Mine, Mill and Smelter Workers was far more appreciative of Metcalf's efforts to maintain their industry.[63] At the public policy level, politics and mining prosperity grew in proportion to the depths of depression.

Whether in prosperity or in depression, mining locations sometimes ran against competing "entrymen." Chumasero and Chadwick of Helena, Montana, opposed the agricultural entry of Silas S. Harvey on the mining claim of their client in an 1873 letter to Willis Drummond at the U.S. Land Office in Washington, D.C. By their lights, "the land should not be permitted to be entered as agricultural, but only a mineral land." Further, "the Miners who are affected by the entry . . . who live in that neighborhood opposed Harvey's entry."[64] In Arizona Gardner H. Smith reported in 1897 that the speculators were booming "town lots, and its growth is far ahead of the development of the mines." Another reason was conflicting entries, such as the case of the King Soloman mine located "on school section 36 and some one filed on it as grazing land after the miners were located."[65] California's state mineralogist in 1922 reported "numerous inquiries . . . received by the State Mining Bureau regarding" conflicts of mining locations on patented homestead land. He told the miners that they needed "written consent or waiver of the homestead entryman or patentee" and "must pay damages to crops or tangible improvements" if damages were agreed to or must post "a bond or undertaking in an amount set by a court."[66]

Similarly, Indian reservation timberlands were off-limits according to the Interior Department in 1922, and Interior Department classification of lands as timberlands presented additional problems. L. O. Evans wrote from Butte to J. R. Hobbins, a vice president of the Anaconda Copper Mining Company, in 1927 that "the apparent difficulties in securing patents to such claims are at least decidedly formidable" because "there would be imposed upon the mineral claimants a tedious, expensive and uncertain contest at the best, with no substantial assurance of final success."[67] In 1955 Montana Attorney-General Arnold H. Olsen responded to Harold E. Cripe in Racine, Wisconsin, regarding uranium prospecting near Libby, Montana, that "because you are prospecting for uranium does not give you the right to trespass on private land."[68] It was little different in Wyoming. These ranchers "took a dim view of dozens of enthusiastic prospectors gouging out large holes in the sod or wearing automobile trails across their pastures."[69] Conflicts of property rights, land use, and mineral exploration as well as the certainty of mineral locations spanned the American centuries of mining.

Importantly, by 1970 new voices were raised regarding conflicting land uses. Now we will hear two, but later came a chorus with a different tune. In 1970 George I. Erickson, the chairman of the Cascade County Democratic Central Committee, wrote to Montana Attorney-General Robert Woodahl commending the Montana Land Board for delaying the granting of an easement to the Anaconda Copper Mining Company

Attorney-General Robert Woodahl. Courtesy of the Montana Historical Society, Helena.

for mineral development work in the Upper Blackfoot Valley. Erickson declared that it was their "insistence that they [all elected public officials] vigorously safeguard Montana's quality environment for future generations."[70] Woodahl was in accord, writing to Debbie Dorsey in March 1970: "My duty is to insure that the most efficient use of the land is promoted. The most efficient use is not merely the use which will bring the most revenue to the state. Economical, environmental, and aesthetic ramifications should all be considered and balanced to arrive at the most beneficial use to the people of Montana."[71] Times had changed, and priorities had shifted. What was good for mining in Montana was not good for all of the people of Montana. Whether in Montana or Arizona, the Mining Law of 1872 location provisions had numerous unintended consequences that impeded the development of mineral wealth and, for that matter, other land uses in the West.

The action of the Montana Land Board was only part of a larger change in Montana. As Jared Diamond has remarked, "Until 1971, mining Companies in Montana on closing down a mine just left it with its copper, arsenic, and acid leaking out into rivers, because the state of Montana had no law requiring companies to clean up after mine closure."[72] The Montana Land Board was trying to stop an abuse from happening, and the Montana legislature in 1971 required mining companies to clean up their property, "but companies discovered that they could extract the valuable ore and then just declare bankruptcy before going to the expense of cleaning up."[73] But in 1971 America was on the cusp of an environmental age.

CHAPTER 6

IT'S OFF TO WORK WE GO

Perhaps there can be, in this little art,

a seeming to glory—just as loom and thread,

sickle, rip-saw, claw hammer, so too with paper

and quill—*Industry hath its recompence.*

> —Christopher Cessac, "The Tenth Muse
> Lately Sprung Up in America"
> in *Republic Sublime* (2003)

Claim jumping was relocating a dormant claim. Miners who did not work the ground may have abandoned the claim. Public land in the nineteenth century was to be worked to be productive, and it was work that made America great. It was a simple faith and one that miners understood. They did not have to refer to the Apostle Paul to know that if you did not work, you did not eat. So too, our nation's mineral lands called to people willing to work to increase our national wealth. Claims left alone could be jumped, relocated, worked, and made profitable. This was the law of the diggings expressed in local mining district regulations and the Mining Law of 1872. The General Mining Law of 1872 section 5 made the annual work requirement one hundred dollars per claim per year.

In gold rush days, mines were abandoned in favor of the next best rush to another strike on another river or up another creek. Running off a claim for the next bonanza had its risks. So said Americus Vespucius Lancaster about 1857, recalling that "shortly afterwards some parties who had gone to Salmon River in early days and had done some work on the claim, brought a lawsuit against Mr. Lancaster and his partners and won it."[1] Before the uniformity of federal law on the amount of work necessary to maintain an interest in a claim, miners and courts looked at whether the claimant was putting any work into making the claim pay.

The federal requirement of one hundred dollars of work on each claim was evidenced by an affidavit of work done each year filed with the county recorder. The affidavit gave notice to the world that a particular claim was not jumpable. It also forced claimants to make decisions regarding the expenditure. One hundred dollars in the nineteenth century was serious cash, not a twenty-first-century bar bill ($1,589.12 in 2005 dollars based on the Consumer Price Index). Adam Aulbach of Murray, Idaho, told James H. Hawley of Boise in 1897 that "last month I saw that the group was going to be eaten up by assessment work, so I made arrangements to lease the properties." That saved the claimants $400 and saved their interest in the claims when the lease expired.[2]

Time was of the essence in completing the required assessment or representation work on a claim. Richard Saxe Jones, a Seattle, Washington, attorney wrote to attorney William A. Blackburn of Austin, Texas, in 1902 of a timing problem. Jones's client, Colonel Benjamin R. Townsend, wanting to save a few bucks, had died doing the assessment work on his copper claim in the Cascade Range, and Jones urged action. "To stop work would require considerable loss of perishable goods and in addition to that these mines are practically in accessible after Oct. 15th and the law requires the work to be completed before January 1st," he penned. There were other problems. He averred that if not "done during the year a contest would arise which might jeopardize the title to the mines." Jones was justifying his actions of hiring workers for the claims, made even more important by the fact that "there were originally about forty claims, but last year Col Townsend decided to abandon all but twelve, doing the assessment on twelve claims only."[3] The work requirement had to be completed to hold these valuable claims.

Managers on the ground often had to make judgments for absentee owners. Frank D. Brown, the manager of the Henderson Mining Company, gave Charles D. McLure in Rye Beach, New Hampshire, a list of claims "liable for representation or relocation 1903–4" and replied to the demurrer that "I assume the text of the law to be that all ground not represented January 1st of any year *is subject to location*, the question

P. C. Waite working his claim at the Grubstake Cyanide Mill, Red Bluff, Montana, ca. 1906–8. Courtesy of the Pioneer Museum, Bozeman, Montana.

of pryor location not being an entering factor."[4] The question of doing more than the minimum was a management decision. George W. Fowler Jr. of Butte told Anton Holter in Helena in 1903 that he was "anxious not merely to make a perfunctory representation of the claims as required by law, but to open up the mines so that we can sell ore and put the business on a sound financial basis."[5]

There was a difference between doing the minimum and mining the ground, just as there was a difference between filing the affidavit that the work had been completed and actual work being done on a claim. John E. Corette of Butte explained the issue to Gibson T. Knapp of Bisbee in 1915: "Of course, we cannot any of us swear positively that the work was done, but we can swear that the money was paid for the work, and that we have receipts for the same. It is too far away for a personal supervision of the work."[6] The fact of the filing in the county recorder's office gave notice to any potential claim jumpers that the work had been done.

Yet as mining claims changed hands, those notices to potential claim jumpers were not always effective. Edgar W. Smith of Goldfield, Arizona Territory, explained the situation to George U. Young of Phoenix in 1911:

> The letter from the recorder looks bad. Looks to me as if the property had been allowed to lapse before you got a hold of it probably while McFarland was watchman here & that he jumped it. If that is the case, looks to me as tho' he could be beat out of it in court. Since you did the work last year seems as tho' you were doing just that much for McFarland on the quiet. He is doing assessment work on his claims North of here now. Has had nothing to say to me. I will watch him & the Dippe claims (water claims) & if he does not do his work these next 2 1/2 months we can relocate it again in you name on Jan. 1, '12.[7]

The letter from the recorder of Pinal County, G. F. Watson, evidenced the fact that no assessment work had been done since 1908. Smith's letter also evidences another trend in mining claims, the mining claim used to secure a nonmineral asset such as water.

Water and timber were necessities of hard-rock mining. Robert Chester Turner in La Porte, California, told J. H. Wood of San Francisco that the costs of water and timber were under control on a mine because "water power can be obtained from the river by locating it, and fuel & timber are abundant and cheap in the vicinity of the mine so that the cost of working ought not to be very high." Within six months Turner was reporting a wood shortage caused by heavy use for "the pump in the

Grubstake Mill near Red Bluff, Montana, used water to power a waterwheel turning cyanide machinery, ca. 1906–8. Courtesy of the Pioneer Museum, Bozeman, Montana.

Scraping tailings at the Grubstake Cyanide Mill near Red Bluff, Montana, ca. 1906–8. Courtesy of the Pioneer Museum, Bozeman, Montana.

mill well tunnel shaft."[8] Timbering mines and keeping the steam boilers hot required a great deal of wood whether on mining claims or not. Ewald Kipp, an Arizona mining engineer, reported in 1927 that "I am still timber helping to an old timer who has been doing nothing else for the past ten years." It was healthful, as "all of this hard labor with the ax and saw and the pick and shovel are doing me good."[9] H. R. "Dick" Cooke, a Reno attorney, made clear how important the annual assessment work was to Thomas R. White of San Francisco in 1940: "This exclusive right of possession conferred upon the locator by the statute is as much the property of the locator as the vein or lode, subject to the right of the Government to limit the cutting of timbre growing on the mining claim to the necessity for its use in working the mine."[10] Doing the assessment work preserved the rights in timber and kept claim jumpers at bay.

Getting the work out of the way provided a measure of peace. George F. Davis, a Spokane attorney and president of the Sunnyside Mines Company of Virginia City, Montana, told Alonzo Emerson in 1938 that "we will also perform enough exploration work on the Vander Miller vein across the creek to cover current assessment work and then we can file proof of it along with Sunnyside." That filing would "protect our titles to all of the Sunnyside claims to June 1940."[11] For miners, war brought better news than peace. In addition to increased demand for metals, Congress lifted the assessment work burden. John E. Corette told J. J. Carrigan, the manager of mines for the Anaconda Copper Mining Company in 1943, that Public Law 47, 48th Congress, chapter 91, 1st session, H.R. 2370, had "suspended the $100 assessment work requirement." Now only a filing of an annual notice maintained an interest in a claim.[12]

World War II came to an end in 1945, and the demand for metals fell until the Korean War gave demand a nudge, but peace was hard on miners. Mining state representatives went back to Congress trying to give the mining industry a break from the onerous $100 per claim per year assessment work requirement.[13] The mining industry needed cash to pay its bar bills again.

As we will see in a later chapter, a simple regulation requiring that the federal government be paid the $100 in cash would revolutionize the process. Thousands of speculative claims suddenly were open for relocation. Again, as Jared Diamond has observed, "Early miners behaved as they did because the government required almost nothing of them, and because they were businessmen."[14] The work requirement was one of those things that government required miners to do and to attest that they complied with statutory requirements. When government required more than an affidavit in the late twentieth century, miners clearly demonstrated that work and money had a different value on the public lands.

CHAPTER 7

Spurs, Dips, and Angles

In fact, alone, the world itself is gray,

our language indecipherable to us,

my mouth a puddle splashed; and one again

you are the passer-by who looks away

just as it happens, who scarcely could discuss

the strange nuances of an age's burning

securing our extinction, and our yearning.

—Jennifer Anna Gosetti-Ferencei,
"Some Exigencies" in *After the Palace Burns* (2003)

The ability of a hard-rock or lode locator to pursue a vein outside the sidelines of a location into the claim of abutting miners created another problem of certainty in western American mining. This particular "custom" of some miners became general law, confounding claimants, lawyers, judges, and public policy makers. In the nineteenth and twentieth centuries, miners and their lawyers had to deal with the practical aspects of the law, its uncertainty, and its consequences. This was a custom at the Comstock Lode and found its way into federal law courtesy of Senator William Morris Stewart of Nevada. Suffice it to say, Curtis H. Lindley, America's first academic expert on mining law, wrote, "no branch of mining law presents so many intricate and varied questions, and there are none more difficult to treat comprehensively and concisely."[1] How to deal with uncertainty varied over time, but legal and business sense frequently meshed.

With hard-rock miners hacking away spitting distance apart on a ledge, suspicions of creative tunneling and ore theft abounded. Edgar W. Smith of Goldfield, Arizona Territory, told George U. Young of Phoenix of a suspicious neighbor in 1911. "Morris of Mesa, 1/2 owner in the Wasp, south extension of the Mammoth, was out last Sunday," he wrote, "to see what we were doing. Heard we were in under his ground. Fixed him all right & he left satisfied apparently."[2] The problems of extralateral litigation were severe, as O. H. McKee, a San Francisco attorney, explained to Robert Keating, the superintendent of the Savage Mining Company of Virginia City, Nevada, in 1879. First, such a suit would set off "the howl" in the newspapers, and that could adversely affect the value of company stock. Second, delay was costly because an appeal to the U.S. Supreme Court would "thus tie the matter up for a couple of years more during which time new arrangements can be made if desirable."[3] Litigation regardless of the merits increased negotiating leverage because the ore was fixed in the inertia of the law.

As hard-rock mining became big business and capital investment grew, the question of extralateral rights, as the spurs, dips, and angles came to be known, increased in significance. N. B. Ringeling of Montana described part of his problem to Charles A. Cuno in St. Louis in 1891:

> The fact is our vein has dipped out of our north side line and into the Fraction Lode a portion of which claim is claimed by the Garnets.
>
> The vein is being worked as rapidly as possible.
>
> The miners posted outsiders as to we were working and the result is the Garnets thought we were taking their ore.
>
> They no doubt will survey, and try to get out an injunction, restricting us from working within the disputed ground, Fraction Garnet adverse ground or rather the S.S. portion of Garnet claims. I will be in shape soon so that I can get at our ore without entering ground in dispute or within the so called Garnet lines.
>
> If an injunction should be granted the damage would be

very great as it no doubt would prevent us from getting ore enough for the Mill.[4]

Ringeling would get as much ore out before an injunction could halt the work, but that was not always his solution. In 1897, he advised his company's president that he had "two places that are promising for good ore in the tunnel, but both are within the conflict with another claim." He filed "an amended location to close up small gaps east of the Trout Mill," got a deed to another claim, got a quit claim to "improvement &c then made a relocation," and purchased a "timber claim west of the Algonquin Lode."[5] Ringeling had a felt need to acquire claims despite extralateral rights. C. S. Thomas Jr. also took a conservative approach to the Nevada Porphyry Gold Mining Company in 1908, finding "sufficient ore to run the mine at full capacity for 3 or 4 years should be opened up and blocked out ready for stoping. This lessens the chances of a shut down engendered by litigation."[6] Rights were one thing, getting ore out was another.

Another wrinkle in extralateral rights theory was getting the apex of the vein properly fixed within the location. This was a matter of geology as well as law.[7] Again the problem was certainty. The practical problem on the ground could be addressed in several ways. James T. Stanford of Helena, Montana, explained his thinking to Jacob Baur of Chicago in 1907:

> If this vein really does apex on the Davis ground then in pay-
> ing for the balance of the property we will be paying for ore of
> which we have already removed considerably more than half.
> If it does not apex on the Davis ground, then the adjoining
> tract does not apex either and we would not have to pay for the
> privilege of removing that. The advantage of buying the Davis
> interest would apparently resolve itself into a question of policy,
> if the non-apexing theory is correct. That is to say, that if we
> should discover large values on the 500 [foot] level it would be
> advisable to get the Davis interest for the purpose of settling all
> possible rights. For you will recall that the course of the veins

William Scallon.
Courtesy of the Montana
Historical Society,
Helena.

in this immediate section are so mixed up that it is difficult to
determine exactly where any given apex really is.[8]

There was safety in acquiring adjacent ground regardless of the apex
issue.

When it came to extralateral rights litigation, attorneys and mining
engineers had to educate. D. W. Burton, a consulting mining engineer
in Denver, told William Scallon, a Helena attorney, in 1915 that a "Slope
Chart" and colored sketch "would be the most readily understood, especially by a judge or jury."[9] The problem was that neither judge nor jury
was geologically astute. Mining engineer and expert witness Louis Janin
thought that geological ignorance extended further. Writing to James D.
Hague and W. B. Bourn in 1908, Janin offered that

the mining men with whom I am acquainted know very little
about the structure of veins. It is the question of apex and of

equilateral rights that make it of interest to lawyers. It is of decided and satisfactory assistance in understanding your vein systems in this camp. It is the aid it gives in the search of ore that makes it of interest to the miners for it is a rather complete analysis of vein structure and was obtained from my personal inspection of a large area of this district.[10]

Education in the courtroom and on the ground was seemingly a continuing venture for mining engineers.[11]

Alternatives to litigation frequently suggested gave mining engineers more expert work.[12] In 1925 Charles Benton Power of Helena suggested using an "impartial mining engineer" to settle a dispute over the location of the apex to his client, Hattie Atkinson of Denver. He offered that "the expense in this matter would be very small compared with a law suit and it is a matter of fact that it can be determined better by a qualified engineer rather than to have it handled through the courts."[13] Karl Eilers of New York wrote to Power in 1925: "I imagine a lawsuit might be long drawn out and its decision very uncertain." Power concurred and suggested "a neutral surveyor" who could resolve the dispute "without unnecessary and unpleasant litigation."[14] Even the possibility of a divided apex did not change Power's mind on the efficiency of arbitration by an expert engineer.[15] Arbitration might be efficient, but that did not mean that the issues could be just as complex as in law.

The complexity of extralateral pursuit and geologic facts could still confound the process. The law firm of Walsh and Nagle of Helena wrote to Charles Benton Power in 1925 and surveyed some of the issues:

> The agreement to arbitrate is only for the purpose of determining where the lead is, whether it enters the end line or the side line of the Liberty claim. It is conceded that it departs from the side line of the Liberty. If that is the case, then limit of the Liberty rights to follow the dip of the vein would be confined by a line drawn parallel to the in-line, as shown on the maps which you have furnished. If it enters a side line and parts on the other

side line, then the side lines become the end lines and a different question might be presented.

. . . If it should enter at a corner, it might present a nice question as to just where the apex is.

. . . The apex of the vein is the highest point in the vein, so that should be very carefully noted in making the excavations and the exact location of the corner accurately determined.[16]

This message was clear. Experts could make important determinations, but where law and fact intersected between geology and a courtroom were not always so clear.

Staying out of those courtrooms motivated some parties. Robert Chester Turner of Berkeley, California, wrote to R. H. Countiss of Chicago on September 1, 1914, recommending the acquisition of space around their claims. "We would also want the mineral rights to the surrounding territory," he penned, "as we would want to be protected against the possibility of the ore shoot traveling beyond the end lines of the claim."[17] Tying up loose end lines prevented extralateral pursuit litigation. H. A. Guess wrote to W. J. O'Connor, the manager at American Smelting and Refining Company, in 1938 about the North Star, Independence, and Ivanhoe claim groups in Hailey, Idaho, looking for a settlement in an apex dispute. What he wanted was "an amicable settlement of the apex question . . . preferably by conference." He observed that "Mr. Snyder . . . is fearful that if the lawyers, as he says, get into it, the result will be a long, hard fight over the apex question." They needed to get a geologist's opinion and the deliberations of "technical men." Once these were consulted they would have "pretty precise information as to the portion of the orebody that can be rightly claimed by Federal through Federal's apex . . . and . . . by Ivanhoe." This would require "a tri-part agreement upon investigation," but that was better than litigation.[18] Even so, if the parties did agree, they still had to perform, and that was not always the case.[19]

If engineering geology was helpful in settling disputes, the developing law of extralateral pursuit sometimes confounded the bar. An exchange of letters between William Scallon of Helena, Montana, and

Frank T. Donahoe in Washington, D.C., in 1944 evidenced the continuing problems. Scallon was troubled by an opinion of the U.S. Supreme
Court in 1912 involving the Silver King Coalition Mines Company and
the Conkling Mining Company. The opinion discussed the right of a
locator with a location across a vein instead of along it to extralateral
pursuit through the end lines or short lines of the location. The holding
had been interpreted "to mean that the course of the actual end lines—
whether nominally side or end lines—determined the direction in which
the extralateral right could be exercised regardless of whether the course
of the end lines coincided with the direction of the dip."[20] That being
said, Scallon was troubled.

The trouble was the reasoning as well as the language of the Court.
Scallon precisely offered his disquiet:

> Respecting the merits of the opinion, I must say that it is not
> quite satisfactory as a matter of jurisprudence. It is quite plain,
> indeed, to the effect that the nominal end lines may be treated
> as side lines and that the extralateral right may be exercised
> through them, but it is not plain in dealing with the course or
> direction in which the right may be exercised. You will see in
> the sentence quoted above the statement is that if "*the strike of
> the vein crosses the location at right angles, its dip may be fol-
> lowed extralaterally. . . .*" Then follows the words: "whatever the
> direction in which the length of the location may run."
>
> The words last quoted involve a contradiction of the first
> statement, or perhaps a meaningless statement, unless it can be
> given some interpretation that would reconcile the statement
> with the previous ruling.
>
> In explanation of the foregoing, I will say that it is self-evi-
> dent that if the strike of the vein is at right angles to the loca-
> tion, it is at right angels to the side lines of the location, and, as
> a consequence, it is also self-evident that the side lines would
> correspond with the dip.
>
> Whether the judge, in speaking of the vein, meant its apex,
> there is no way of determining from the opinion. To repeat the

matter, and perhaps put it in another way, I may say that when the judge spoke of the vein crossing the location at right angles, he impliedly but necessarily determined—and in effect stated—that the length of the location was at right angles to the strike. So, there was no sense in adding: "whatever the direction in which the length of the location may run." On the supposition of the vein running at right angles to the side lines, there is only one direction in which the length of the location can run, and that is, of course, at right angles to the strike, and this, of course, as already stated, is also the line of the dip.

If the judge was thinking of apex and used the word "vein" as synonymous with apex, the language might then be construed to mean that the extralateral right may be exercised at right angles to the strike of the apex. This would perhaps make sense; but to my notion it would be the introduction of what, in terms, would seem to be an absurdity.[21]

Scallon found other contradictions and offered several criticisms of the opinion. What he needed was the briefs of counsel and any maps offered at trial and brought up on appeal. Perhaps with these in hand, he could ease his analytic mind.

Donahoe's prospecting for litigation clues unearthed a map and some pertinent testimony. The testimony was that the strike of the Crescent Fissure Vein was "substantially at right angles to the length of the claims in which it apexed." This raised other questions for Donahoe:

It is interesting to speculate as to the definition of the extralateral rights of veins crossing a short and a long line of a claim. Are the extralateral rights confined to one plane on the dip of the vein bounded by vertical planes having the bearing of one side of the claim and if so how is such side determined or do extralateral rights [give] any title to ores on their extension downward from the apex in tow planes of the vein bounded by vertical planes parallel to the short line and parallel to the long line respectively.[22]

Donahoe enclosed the map attached to the briefs and promised to write a personal letter.

Scallon's eyes on the map cleared his mind. "The plat makes the whole case plain to me," he declared. The Court decided that "a locator may have the right to pursue his vein on its downward course through its nominal or survey end lines." However, by his lights, the opinion did not "have any direct bearing on the question of what constitutes downward course or whether the extralateral right may be exercised diagonally or longitudinally instead of downwards." That said, Scallon turned to Donahoe's questions. First, "it has been settled that where the location vein of the claim crosses one endline and one side line, the locator has extralateral rights to the extent of the length of the vein within the claim." Further, "where there is extralateral right on the discovery vein there is also extralateral right on any other vein or veins apexing with the claim." Courts had repeatedly held that "there can be but one set of end lines." Second, "the extralateral right is based on the discovery vein and determined by its course." More interesting to Scallon, cases had held "that where an apex of a vein crosses one end line of a claim, the extralateral right attaches—to the extent of the length of the vein or apex within the claim." That holding was a qualification of a prior case. In his mind, "if the doctrine of that case and its predecessor had been logical or strictly adhered to, it would have been held that where the discovery vein crossed one end line and one side line, the side line became the end line and a boundary both on dip and strike." More critically, "it would also have been held that this side-end line, not being parallel to the end line, this lack of parallelism would also have been a reason for denying extralateral right."[23]

Even after decades of precedents, the matrix of geology and law had not fused. Yet decades of litigation did produce some good poetry:

> A dozen lawyers on a side,
> And eminent experts multiplied;
> Maps of the biggest and the best,
> And models till you couldn't rest
> Samples of rock and vein formation,

And assays showing "mineralization,"
And theories of that or this,
And revelation of "genesis,"
And summing-up of sound and fury.
No matter now which party lost—
It took the mine to pay the cost;
And all the famous fight who saw
Beheld, with mingled pride and awe,
What science breeds when crossed with law.[24]

CHAPTER 8

LITIGATION

but oh I wish I knew how it is to be alive

to be able to simply recognize

the horror embedded in memory

waiting patiently

but realizing makes such pain in me

no easy matter—to simply write

what happens now, or then, it is

beyond me on ordinary days

to acknowledge what I know

and what I see. I was carefully

constructed to forget what is

before my eyes. The conqueror teaches that, you know.

so we will never say what is so.

so no one will ever know.

> —Paula Gunn Allen, "Runes #30"
> in *Life Is a Fatal Disease* (1997)

Americans are a law-minded people, bringing the values of the rule of law and the respect for private property with them on the Overland Trail.[1] Miners wrote local mining district regulations to reflect these values. When disputes arose, miners gathered to hear and decide the controversy. With the creation of state and territorial courts, these

miners took their disputes to court. Congress got into the mining legislation business with the Mining Law of 1866 and the General Mining
Law of 1872. Yet federal law did not reduce conflict or thwart litigation.
Conflicting claim boundaries, fraud in sales of mineral property, and the
apex issue in hard-rock mining law dominated legal disputes well into
the 1920s. Litigation kept lawyers busy. Some mine owners used litigation as a tool of business. Others wanted to quiet title to give certainty
to transactions. The impact of litigation in many mining communities
was economic disaster, but the miners did not see this consequence until
well into the late nineteenth century.

Litigation "was the handmaiden of mining," Malcolm J. Rohrbough
has observed of the situation in the nineteenth century.[2] The early trials
etched out property rights in transient camp communities, but as mining matured, the values at stake rose, as did the costs of litigation. For
William Cornell Greene of Arizona, "litigation became a way of life."
Greene "kept more lawyers busy than any other man in the history of
Arizona or perhaps of the whole United States."[3] For Greene, he lived by
the unwritten rule: "All's fair in love, war, and mining."[4] But these mine
owners seldom measured the costs. Howard E. Perry of Texas was stub-
born to a fault in litigation, resulting "in court costs that far exceeded the
money in question."[5] The litigation over the Comstock Lode in Nevada
was staggering. Colonel W. S. Keyes reported "the total costs of litigation in the Washoe District up to January 1st, 1866 . . . at $10 million."
That was 20 percent of the total product of the mines."[6] The cost of litigation in the Aspen apex case of the 1880s was $600,000, but the win-
ner gleaned a net profit of $6 million in the next five years.[7] The New
Almaden Mine litigation lasted twelve years and produced a 3,500-page
transcript in federal court.[8] Louis Janin, an expert witness in mining
cases, confided to his notebook in 1875 that the "Gibson lawyer talk of
compromise." However, "our lawyers . . . appear sanguine of success, but
the case may be lengthy and expensive. They demand retaining fee of
fifteen hundred dollars and more according to length of service which we
now cannot foresee." The lawyers "refuse to name any fixed amount."[9]
The calculus of litigation looked brightest to winners as long as they
could keep paying fees.[10]

The calculus for communities was another matter. Litigation often meant jobs. During the pendency of litigation, mines could be shut down. "Years of litigation had taken a heavy toll" in Julian, California, in the 1870s because of idle mines.[11] A New Mexico mine sat idle for thirteen months during a heated trial.[12] When the Belle of the West mine in Colorado shut down because of litigation in 1883, "the local economy stagnated."[13] Goldfield, Nevada's, Jumbo Mine "produced $1,690,000 worth of ore in 1904, making it the premier mine in the district, by the end of the year, however, the Jumbo was entirely closed down by litigation," and it remained shut "during most of 1905."[14] Robert C. Turner reported in 1912 that "this ground was left because of a dispute between the owners of the Maltman and Sultana or Bovee and Fritz Claims." Sultana had a mill site, and Maltman claimed the minerals: "Both sides were afraid to risk a lawsuit so this ground was tied up."[15] Closed mines cut off jobs.

Mining disputes were not the only business for western lawyers. Most were involved in property and contract work.[16] This also was the case for lawyers who were not house counsel for a mining corporation.[17] Cornelius Hedges reported on his fledgling law practice in Helena, Montana, to his parents in 1865 that "law business is not very good. There are a great many lawyers. I hope to get something better to do."[18] The next month he wrote, "Our business has been pretty good. Our Dist Court adjourned last week. We won every case we were interested in. On one we get $500, for our fee, on the others about $100." That meant that "we are not crowded at all but can live & make something."[19] Two years later he told his father that "all I expect of the law business was a support till I could get started in our Quartz Mill."[20] As 1867 ended, Hedges confided to his mother that "I know I am becoming a better lawyer. I shall keep hold of the law till I am certain that I have something a good deal better."[21] Hedges kept mining as an investment strategy and law as an economic means to a future end.

For other lawyers, mining was part of their litigation compensation. Montana's Cave Gulch placer litigation of 1866 brought the "leading lawyers of those days" to both sides "of the case and every inch of the ground was fought over with all adroitness, legal acumen, and eloquence that could be summoned to the aid of the attorneys engaged."[22] The value of the ground gave all a great interest, but in other cases, attorneys took a share of the ground instead of money to litigate. William Chumasero and Walter F. Chadwick wrote to U.S. Senator Lyman Trumball in 1871 regarding a case they had before the U.S. Supreme Court that "we are now personally interested in the case to the extent of one fourth interest in the ground in dispute and are working it in common with them and we desire your services in the case." Regarding the senator's fee, "the parties connected with ourselves are not without means and we will have to pay your fee."[23] In taking mining claims or patented ground for fees, western lawyers were following a long-term practice of accepting land in lieu of cash for representation.[24]

Time was money with litigation pending. Allen Martin set the parameters for Frederick Oliver in 1879, arguing that "it would be better for him to make some settlement with the banks then to go on with the law as the lawyers would get the money."[25] Money also was leverage, and L. M. Rumsey, the president of the Granite Mountain Mining Company, told Samuel Hauser of Helena, Montana, so in no uncertain terms. In an 1886 letter complaining about Hauser's superintendent and general manager, Rumsey asserted that he had "continuously advised and assisted otherwise peaceable people in said camp, to bring suit against the Granite Mountain Mining Company, to jump their claims, and in every possible way to annoy and make expense for the Granite Company." If Hauser's people "continue in the same unfriendly, troublesome and litigious manner, I will be unable to prevent the Trustees of this Company from ordering our deposits removed from your bank."[26] Following the money was another part of the mining matrix.

In Aspen, Colorado, an apex case "was not a matter of principle; it was over money, millions of dollars."[27] Regardless of precedents and the clear language of federal or state statute, Leadville juries had for years nullified the written law, with local custom giving victory to "the side-line doctrine" and rejecting the monopolistic claims of "apexers."[28] But an 1885 case involving the Durant and Spar claims in Aspen found the apexers in complete control. The defeated at trial appealed to the federal court in Denver of Moses Hallett, one of the West's greatest mining law

Samuel T. Hauser, late
1870s. Courtesy of the
Montana Historical
Society, Helena.

experts. Many felt like Albert Kleinschmidt of Helena, Montana, that a
state court was "not the best tribunal to let our case go to, but the U.S.
Courts are always better for non-residents, as their interests are more
guarded in every particular."[29] Hallett paid special attention to the jury
and sequestered the men during the trial, ran a smooth trial, and charged
the jury with the expertise expected of the West's best. The jury came in
unanimously for the apex locator.[30] The case had split the community
of Aspen, but now the cards and the lode were in the hands of the apex
locator, just as the law required. Regardless of the court decision, the
parties worked to compromise their claims in light of a motion for a
new trial. A new company called the Compromise Mining Company
emerged. Fred Buckley confided to his diary in 1887 that

> Dave Shiller & Geo W. Lloyd preparing descriptions &c for the
> *preposterous robbery* of J.B. Wheeler, known as the Compromise.
> Davis & Boal, who seem to have had entire control of the side-
> line interests know absolutely nothing about mining or the

C. B. Nolan. Courtesy of
the Montana Historical
Society, Helena.

frauds being practiced by Reynolds upon them and Davis has
rejected every attempt to suggest pitfalls for him. Boal is a com-
placent ass.[31]

Despite Buckley's misgivings, compromise was achieved the next year as
the law hung heavy over the mine.

Mining and business in general drew lawyers West. Cornelius B.
Nolan of Helena saw the trend. Writing to B. G. Peck of Camden, New
Jersey, in 1889 he observed that

Helena is a very nice place, and has a climate which is unsur-
passed. In my judgment it is bound to be a big city. Lawyers are
flocking here, as to every part of Montana, in large numbers,
but as to whether they are making money or not is a question
which I cannot satisfactorily solve. I suppose they are making a
living, as there is no account of anyone having starved to death.
I think under a state government the legal business will improve

here. The trouble in the past has been that there were not courts enough, but this trouble will soon be obviated.[32]

However, increasing the size of the bar and the number of courts did not lessen the problems of practice. Nolan also complained in 1889 that "the papers I have received from Morrison authorizing me to act for him are so badly written that I cannot make out what the title of the suit really is." He resolved to give the adverse party "another whirl a little later on."[33] Law practice on the operational level in the West was far from regularized in the nineteenth century.[34]

Litigation brought frustration to more than attorneys. Simeon G. Reid, a Portland industrialist, bought into the Bunker Hill, Idaho, silver strike, but by 1890 "a rash of court litigation over the property discouraged Redd and, though it ended in his favor, he, too, decided he had had enough of the Coeur d'Alenes."[35] Delay in litigation created anxiety. James H. Henley, the superintendent of the Granite-Bimetallic Consolidated Mining Company of Granite, Montana, heard from his attorneys in 1893 that they "were very sorry to have the continuance granted, as we have the time to try it, and have made preparations for trying it, but under the circumstances it was certainly the safest and most economical to continue it."[36] To lawyers, this was not unusual. Cornelius B. Nolan told T. H. Teall of Syracuse, New York, in 1895 that "it is an easy matter with shrewd attorneys to secure delays" and "sometimes delays will occur in the life of a lawsuit, without the consent and against the objections of a party."[37] Delay, motions, evidence, and precedents mattered less to mine owners than certainty. B. F. Graham, the president and general manager of the Lucky Tiger–Combination Gold Mining Company of Douglas, Arizona, expressed his frustration to his attorney, Webster Street, in 1904:

I am very much surprised and disappointed to learn the Costello people have appealed the case which was decided in our favor in August.

It is nothing but a hold-up proposition. They got it down again that they would appeal their case and try to compel us to compromise with them naming a sum of money so we could go ahead and sell the property.[38]

On other occasions, litigation tested the staying power of the parties. The New Almaden Mine in California engaged in litigation costing "more than two hundred thousand dollars" with no end in sight.[39]

Sometimes certainty was secured with compromise, as it emerged in Aspen. In Silver City, Idaho, compromise involved a "purchase in each case" and paying filing fees to record "a judgment roll in each of the six Knott cases."[40] Compromise in the form of settlement out of court, William Scallon told his client in 1897, could be done "without too great a loss" and was advisable because the critical question in the case "may prove to be a delicate matter to handle in court."[41] The transfer of the mining ground in conflict to the adverse party was not an unusual end of litigation. The Lavagnino Conglomerate Mining Company of Utah made a simple notation of such a transfer in 1898.[42] This trend was noticed in the legal and mining communities.

The theme of the speakers at the California Miners' Association convention of 1897 was the evils of litigation. The keynote speaker, Niles Searls, was a forty-niner and a judge. He painted a world where "mining went on for years, agriculture was developed, horticulture, viniculture, and various other resources of this State were developed, and we marched hand in hand, the happiest people upon the face of God's footstool." That all came to an end when mining interests, particularly hydraulic miners, "came in conflict with those of the agriculturalists of the valley. What followed? Litigation—a good thing for lawyers, and a blank, blank, bad thing for citizens." Then, by his lights,

fifteen years of this litigation passed, and we as miners were worse off than when we commenced. Then it was that the intelligent men in the mining population took the sober second thought. They realized that we should do unto others as we would have them do unto us. They realized that a man should "so use his own as not to injure that of his neighbor." This seemed original to some men; it was not original to all.[43]

Searls, the lawyer and jurist, knew he was, in part, restating the law of nuisance as well as the golden rule. Jacob Hart Neff provided a positive note that federal aid had arrived for "restraining dams."[44] But Colonel W. S. Keys closed with the horrors of litigation, trumpeting that "the honest miners are then in the hands of justice, which means injunctions, trials, expert testimony, juries, and the abominable waste of money."[45] Litigation was not the miner's ally in business.

The business of consolidating mining property equally abhorred the uncertainty of litigation. Massena Bullard, a Helena attorney, wrote to William E. Borah of Boise in 1903 regarding a half-million-dollar sale of lode claims and an option to buy the Bingham Consolidated Mining and Smelting Company that "if the sale is consummated the suit will of course be dismissed, but it is probable that the American Mining Company Limited will insist upon fighting the issues tendered by its cross complaints and that can be done before the option expires, so that the pendency of the action may not rest as a cloud upon the title."[46] Five months later Bullard created a stipulation so that the purchase would terminate the litigation.[47] But the time all of this required and its consequences for business caught the public eye, as evidenced by an August 8, 1904, article in the Butte, Montana, *Reveille*:

> The law's delay has been receiving much attention lately from American jurists and business men. There is evidently "too much law." We are told that 14,000 statutes are made annually in the United States. This excessive legislation both to remedy and prevent evil is a poor thing. If more deliberation were used in Making laws and more haste in enforcing them, justice would be served and the lawless spirit more effectively repressed.[48]

Regardless of the recognition of the problem, towns such as Glendale, Montana, suffered when "the mines were finally closed in 1905 as a result of long and costly litigation."[49] Ghost towns and closed mines left an impression.

Buying mining ground with a lawsuit lurking in court cast a chill on acquisition fever. Some tried to assuage doubt with precedent. Robert

Chester Turner wrote Fred Chester in 1897 to make clear that rights were clear. Regarding the "right of holder of mine with regard to dumping tailings and mine cyanide solutions into lake," the tailings dumping right "was given as part consideration for transfer of some land the Flume Co. needed." The cyanide dumping right was "settled in a suit brought against Gov. Waterman, when he used cyanide to clean copper plates in mill. He was using from 1 to 2 lbs. per day & it was decided that this quantity was beneficial rather than deleterious as far as affecting water for drinking purposes was concerned."[50] What could be clearer? C. H. Mallen in Grass Valley, California, explained it to Robert Chester Turner of Berkeley in 1914:

> I explained to him [a mining engineer inspecting the ground] just how Creller was trying to sell the "Union Hill" Property on the strengt of the brunswick pay shoot passing in to their ground, I explained this to Mr. Hunt [prospective buyer] also. I think it is time to throw a "cold chill" on Creller, You are aware of the fact that very few mining companys care to buy amine where there is any chance of litagation.[51]

The certainty of title and quiet possession was significant, but other challenges to the industry would appear in the late twentieth century with environmental awareness.

The Mining Law of 1872 did nothing to stem the tide of lawsuits. Rather, the failure of Congress to provide a comprehensive statute with federal supervision and recording enabled the tool of litigation and its costs to continue into the twenty-first century.

CHAPTER 9

TAILINGS, SLICKENS, AND SLIMES

Yet seeing now the beauty of those fish

down there below the surface

so still and lovely

in their deep dream

dappled in their last deep pool

We fish no longer

turn

and go on

into the deeper pools

of our own lives.

—Lawrence Ferlinghetti, "Hilarious God"
in *These Are My Rivers* (1994)

When the gold rush miners swirled the pay dirt around in their pans and cast the waste away in the running waters, they did not see the trout float belly up downstream. The bodies as well as the tailings of Long Toms, the slimes and slicken of mills, and the tons of tailings from smelters washed away in the waters. They were out of sight and out of mind. What excited miners was the trespass of someone else's tailings on their private property, limiting their access to wealth. The Mining Law of 1872 did not address the problem of tailings disposal or pollution. The common law was the only recourse for early miners.

Today we see the results. As Jared Diamond has noted in his *Collapse: How Societies Choose to Fail or Succeed* (2005), "Until 1955 most mining

Butte, Montana, mines and smelters, September 26, 1922: a landscape featuring tailings and slag dumps as well as smoke from smelter stacks. Courtesy of the Montana Historical Society, Helena.

at Butte involved underground tunnels, but in 1955 Anaconda began excavating an open-pit mine called the Berkeley Pit, now an enormous hole over a mile in diameter and 1,800 feet deep."[1] It is now a Superfund site. We see no fish in the toxic Berkeley Pit, but we do see a changed landscape. Geographer Randall E. Rohe has described it best, noting that "each form of mining left a mark on the landscape."[2] Placer miners left piles of tailings. Hydraulic mining produced land "cut into an intricate pattern of gullies and ravines," making the old terrain "unrecognizable" within a year.[3] Dredge mining piled processed gravel high along the banks of watercourses. Lode or hard-rock mining produced tailings, tailing ponds, stamps, mills, and smelters. All these fixtures and dumps were signatures of mining.

Some early mining districts required miners to tend to their tailings on their property. In the Garnet Mining District of Montana "each miner was required to take care of his own tailings, dumping them on his own ground, that the claim down stream might not be buried under worthless material."[4] But that was clearly not the case for one stream in Colorado: "During the winter of 1859–60 George C. Swadley, and four others placer mined the bar; reportedly they made wages but little more. When the tailings blocked the sluice area and no means were readily available for tailings, the site was abandoned."[5] The experience was mixed for the early placer miners.[6]

The arguments about tailings and their downhill runs did not take long to get into court, and there, public policy arguments took on more substance. In Montana's Wilson Mining District, an upstream miner allowed tailings to flow onto a downstream Argonaut's. The lawyer for the offending miner argued that it was "the custom and usage of miners . . . to locate and take up the same subject to the right of the tailings rock sediment & gravel to flow off & down the natural channel or bed of said gulch."[7] The reply was that there was no such custom for miners, but the jury thought otherwise. A motion for a new trial lost, with a notation by the trial judge that "while I feel confident that there was a preponderance of evidence against any such custom yet there was some evidence to the effect that there was such a custom."[8] The jury decided against the preponderance of the evidence, and an appeal followed. That appeal was successful, with the territorial supreme court siding with property rights in a location. It said:

> To allow the custom of free tailings to govern without restriction, would be in opposition to this principle (that each locator can locate grounds designated for tailing deposits & thereby put junior locators on notice of the boundaries), that parties locating are bound to mark the boundaries of their claims, which shall be notice of the extent of the mining ground and rights

Anaconda Smelter, known as the "Old Works," 1885. The smelter dumped tailings into the Warm Springs Creek, killing cattle in 1885. Courtesy of the Montana Historical Society, Helena.

acquired to subsequent locators, for all the first locators would have to do, would be to pass the mining custom of "free tailings"; then defining boundaries by physical marks would be useless, because if any one located below, they could run their tailings onto, and render their ground valueless, and this custom unrestricted would prevent junior locators from cribbing or stopping the tailings from above in any way.[9]

The principle of property development without interference prevailed, but later legislation would provide the power of eminent domain to miners for tailing disposal channels (races).

Regardless of a legal or constitutional right to a way of necessity over private property for a tailings race, mine owners with tons of tailings to move wanted timely action, not legal action. John W. Plummer, the superintendent of the Granite Mountain Mining Company in Granite, Montana, wrote to Samuel T. Hauser in Helena in 1887 to explain his options. The company needed a right of way over private property "for our tailings or tailing waters." Plummer had approached the owner hoping to buy the right of way and water rights for $6,000, but the owner wanted $8,000. Further negotiation resulted in the owner upping the ante to $8,000 plus "our relinquishment of the waters of Frost Creek." All the company wanted was "a right to flow water from our tailing yards into the waters of Flint Creek" across the lands of "Parker, and Duffy's ranches or portions thereof," and it was "willing to pay a remuneration much in excess of their value." In the final analysis, if the owner did not come around, then "the law gives us such right as we demand, but we prefer settling matters without excessive costs, and in an amicable manner."[10] A month later company president L. M. Rumley had enough of negotiation and was willing to pay $10,000 "rather than commence legal proceedings for condemnation of right of way."[11] Time was more important than money, and settlement, more efficient than litigation.[12] Certainty was equally precious. J. Cavanaugh, a Butte attorney, wrote to Edward Beattie of Helena in 1913 with a proposition to buy his placer claim for a dump "so that we will be beyond fear of molestation."[13] Certainty and efficiency went hand in hand in avoiding litigation.

Under certain circumstances, litigation was necessary, but it had hazards beyond costs. Cornelius B. Nolan, a Helena, Montana, attorney, was to assist Edward Scharnikow of Deer Lodge in a tailings trespass case, with the plaintiff, Lee Montgomery, also in the office of county sheriff. Despite the obvious advantages with the jury, Nolan had concerns about Scharnikow because he was "not satisfied with the activity that he displays in preparing his case, for it seems to me he ought to go up there and see the ground, or at least have a talk with the witnesses or determine before trial just the witnesses required, and why they are required."[14] Litigation was an uncertain thing even with adequate preparation, but it was to be avoided if at all possible.

The principle was even clearer when two mining companies in litigation retained the same law firm. In 1896 the law firm of Johnson and Johnson of Boise, Idaho, wrote to Captain James Hutchinson, the superintendent of the Trade Dollar Mining and Milling Company of Silver City, Idaho. They wanted a meeting of the minds. The Boise attorneys noted that "for some time past the DeLamar people have been complaining of the pollution of the waters of Jordan Creek by tailings from the Black Jack and Trade Dollar mines." The attorneys professed a desire to avoid litigation. They suggested that there might be some lack of knowledge of the damage caused by the tailings. Then they recommended a solution, "that the tailings from the Black Jack Mill can be impounded without much expense, but to impound the Trade Dollar tailings would be somewhat more difficult." Yet there was an engineering solution involving "the taking of a piece of the wagon road out of the bottom of Long Gulch and the building of a new road for a short distance on the side of the hill, which would be the principal expense." Finally, they remarked, "do you think this would be the better course and thus avoid a continual wrangle with your neighbor and the expense and annoyance of litigation?"[15] The lawyers exercised their powers of persuasion to keep both clients happy and paying. The important message was efficiency in compromise.[16]

Not all mine owners thought of compromise first. When the Colorado Fish and Game Commission in 1907 ordered Albert Eugene Reynolds to construct a dam and settling pond to keep the Raymond Mill tailings out of the Ohio Creek, he "argued rather belligerently that if the people of Gunnison County thought that catching fish was more important than developing mines and mills, he would halt construction of the Gold Links Mill."[17] As Jared Diamond thinks, "while denial or minimization of responsibility may be in the short-term financial interests of the mining company, it is bad for society as a whole, and it may also be bad for the long-term interests of the company itself, or the entire mining industry."[18] Three years later, the mill's new owner built the dam and ponds under threat of litigation. A less belligerent response flowed from the pen of John R. Lucas regarding the alleged tailings pollution of Rock Creek, Montana. Writing to Rutledge Parker, the forest supervisor, U.S. Forest Service, in 1913, Lucas averred that "I do know that there are just as many fish in Rock Creek today as there were 20 years ago." Further, "while the placer mining may muddy the water of the West Fork, it does not in any way interfere with the water or fish in the main stream below Gillis's ranch." The company had absolutely "no desire to pollute the waters in any way, and whatever we can do to protect the fish, we are more than anxious to do." He closed with a promise to take up the issue of "building tailings dams" with his superiors.[19]

From the late nineteenth century forward, mine operators found that tailings could be a great source of precious metals as their recovery and refining technology improved. In 1896 Robert Chester Turner of Bodie, California, wrote to J. K. Wilson of San Francisco regarding the Stonewall, its tailings, and the mine in San Diego County. Turner noted that "the mine is full of water" and values were undeterminable, but the cyanide process "could be successfully applied at Stonewall" to the tailings pile.[20] Turner was equally positive that they could make money from tailings "washed into the lake" that could be recovered "at low water. These, of course, being on the San Diego Flume Cos. ground are legally the property of that Company, but I would be glad to handle them with the other tailings."[21] Dr. Rose LaMonte Burchan wrote to G. W. Paymal, the superintendent of the Yellow Aster Mining and Milling Company of Randsburg, California, in 1918 that "the Big Dump of tailings is showing a higher average than we have counted was there. Of course this will largely depend on where they are taking the sample—those underneath nearest the Big Mill will be the highest."[22] The reason for the estimate of values was that the earliest tailings would have had the simplest technology applied to concentration and those tailings would contain the greatest values. The Parrot and Colorado tailings dump in Butte, Montana, contained an estimated 600,000 tons, 236,000 tons above water. W. N. Rossberg of the Timber Butte Milling Company told John Gillie, the manager of mines for the Anaconda Company, in 1920 that "as a large portion of the tailings lie under water it would be difficult to determine tonage at the pit."[23] Mine and mill operators were concerned first about values and the cost of recovery. The issue of groundwater pollution seldom entered the conversation. One of the reasons that it was not part of the conversation is that the Mining Law of 1872 made no provision for the disposal of tailings in an environmentally safe manner.

Domestic water consumers started that conversation. The citizens of Monarch, Montana, were victims of tailings pollution. "The waters of Belt Creek are still seriously polluted with tailings from the Cascade Silver mines and mills," H. A. Templeton wrote to Montana Attorney-General S. C. Ford in 1920. Monarch citizens "are now hauling their domestic water supply with teams from a spring two miles away," he continued.[24] Templeton also told the Montana state veterinarian that the pollution "impairs the use thereof for watering livestock" as "the amount of the mine slack and refuse is such that it leaves the water in this creek in a milky-like fluid."[25] This started the Montana attorney-general on his way to Great Falls in August 1920 seeking an injunction.

When the dimension of the problem increased, the law and politics of pollution changed. In Idaho, the mines and mills of the Coeur d'Alene District created jobs, produced almost half of the nation's silver, and dumped 72 million tons of tailings into state waters. The heavy metals and toxics ground deep into the watercourse beds, fouled the waters, and produced a Superfund site.[26] In Northern California, the miners of the Trinity, Salmon, and Klamath rivers had reached an agreement with sportsmen to protect the Klamath and its tributaries as a sporting stream. Fish were economically significant, and a lawsuit could end the mining. The agreement in 1939 was for mining to proceed without interruption between November 1 and July 1, "but after that latter date must be conducted in such a way as to prevent rolling or discoloration of the stream."[27] As late as the 1950s, the mining companies continued to insist that their dumping was in pursuit of the greater economic good. Similarly, in Montana a water-quality study reported in 1970: "For the past 80–100 years, wastes from the copper mining, milling, and smelting operations in Butte and Anaconda area have been discharged into the Clark Fork River. In the past, these wastes created conditions toxic to fish and other biological forms as far downstream as Missoula, a distance of 100 miles."[28] The custom of miners claimed by the prospectors, Long Tom operators, and corporate mining giants left its heritage first in dead fish and last in the beds of watercourses.[29] Jared Diamond has observed, "The mining industry evolved in the U.S. with an inflated sense of entitlement, a belief that it is above the rules, and a

Grubstake Cyanide Mill, Red Bluff, Montana, Ca. 1906–8.

Pages 90–93: Series of six photographs of cyanide process, ca. 1900.
Courtesy of the Pioneer Museum, Bozeman, Montana.

Mixing ore and cyanide solution.

Decanting gold in cyanide solution.

Decanting gold in cyanide solution.

Adding zinc gold dissolved in cyanide. Zinc bonds with cyanide producing a very fine gold precipitate.

Anaconda Smelter looking east to west from Athletic Field, Anaconda, Montana, 1923. Note the massive tailings field to the left of the smelter stack. Courtesy of the Montana Historical Society, Helena.

view of itself as the West's salvation—thereby illustrating the problem of values that have outlived their usefulness."[30] Arguing in the 1970s that the refuse of the past was for the good of the people fell increasingly on deaf ears.

The problems clearly stemmed from the failures of the Mining Law of 1872. Members of Congress had all of the mining district regulations before them, and some anticipated the problem of tailings disposal. Even when the environmental degradation of hydraulic mining became manifest, courts rather than Congress had to take the lead in dealing with the ecological disaster.

CHAPTER 10

HYDRAULIC MINING

By the stream, the skull and a single femur

of an agouti glistens with the sun.

Washed her by high waters, white a paper,

I want to speak what these bones tell,

what the roots of trees, hanging down from the cliff,

a half woven veil seeking lodgment in air

might say to a northern world which seems

to value only fiscal balance.

—Joseph Bruchac, "The Guachero Bird Cave"

in *Ndakinna* (2003)

Water and gold mining were joined when the first pan filled with pay dirt and water left a trace of color in the pan. Water was flumed to gravel and processed more dirt until 1853 when the invention of the penstock concentrated water at high pressure.[1] From there American invention abounded until rivers of water were run through hoses, nozzled at even higher pressure into mountains of gravel, and sluiced away downstream leaving more gold.

Washing dirt with water in 1850 was hard work. Samuel P. Spooner described the problems in an 1850 letter: "I am hearily sick of it. Hydraulicing is hard work. We can only get water night times, so are up to our knees in snowater all night keeing the course opan and have to throw out rocks the next afternon making from 16 to 18 hours a day of the hardest kind of work."[2] Mining was "something a man has to see and experience before he had any idea about it," John Downey

Early California hydraulic mining. Courtesy of the California History Section, California State Library.

penned in 1857, adding that extreme cold, starvation, inflated prices, and "inflamatory rheumatism" all went with the gamble in the Mother Lode country of California.[3]

After the invention of the penstock and the efficiency of hydraulic mining became apparent, hydraulic technology spread rapidly. Colorado miners were just as anxious as Californians to cut down those hills and process them. In "Humbig Gulch," Colorado's "hydraulicers" were "tearing up 'Mother Earth' at a fearful rate, undermining houses and removing every obstacle in their progress in searching for precious ore."[4] In 1880 Spring Creek was the "largest hydraulic mine in Black Hills," with a flume fifteen miles long, a quarter of a million dollars in equipment, and a yield of $750,000.[5] The Pearch hydraulic mine in Humboldt County, California, "during the water-season . . . is kept in operation for 24 hours per day by a crew of 10 men." The miner owner had a 1.5-mile-long flume from the Pearch and Cheney creeks supplying three giants (gooseneck nozzles on hoses that shot high-pressure water into gravel). Gold was "recovered by means of wood-block riffles in a 'Y' sluice reaching both ends of the pit and discharging to Klamath River."[6] The miner's eye was on those riffles and the amount of gold that could be gleaned therefrom. The Blue Gravel Company of Smartsville, California, in the 1860s washed 1,600,000 cubic yards of material through its sluices and used three tons of mercury to recover gold "as it passed through four miles of wooden, block-paved sluices."[7] Mercury losses downstream with the millions of tons of debris amounted to 11 to 25 percent.[8] The miner's focus was on gold recovered and mercury lost, not debris and toxic waste.

Downstream riparians saw something else. Polluted water, dead cattle, destroyed pastures, and buried private property caught their eye. Lawsuits resulted, and mining engineers went to work gathering evidence. Louis Janin was on the job in California in 1878, entering daily findings in his "Mining Debris Case" notebook:

> Bear River is evidently filling up with sediment, and this sediment is caused by the rush of water from the hydraulic claims. A striking characteristic of this sediment is the presence of mica.
>
> The sediment of "slickings" is very fine-scarce any of it gritty and must carry large percentage of clay.[9]

Janin also took a look at Wolf Creek and the "tailings from sluice at Idaho Mine. All the quartz crushed at Grass Valley flowed into Wolf Creek and the quantity was over a million tons." The Wolf Creek sediment was "washed into Bear River in the great flood of 1862, the deposit, in places, is said to have been 150 ft in depth."[10] The current situation did not look good because "the Ditch tender says that more slime and mud is being dumpt down this year than ever before; in fact that there has been a yearly increase in the amount."[11] Only an injunction would halt the onslaught on downstream private and public property.

The legal actions opened in 1879 with a Yuba County lawsuit. Legislative action followed. But the hydraulic mining industry saw the beginning of the end in a federal court injunction in 1884.[12] A Debris

Commission emerged to regulate the use of hydraulic technology, but fundamental change had arrived.

The filing of the lawsuit put the hydraulic miners onto unfamiliar ground. George Washington Cox told William Rollin Morgan in 1881 that he was building a debris dam, having "deemed it best to say nothing publicly about our Dam while the Gold Run Suit is on the boards—we want to see if we have any rights—Dam or no Dam."[13] In 1885 Cox was not optimistic about the future of hydraulic mining. "I feel we will not be allowed to hydraulic more than one more year," he wrote Morgan, "if that long." Dilatory tactics were best, such as "playing with the marshal and those sent to investigate." Yet, "if we are shut down, Scales is all we have worth a continental, and that is a gamble." In sum, "this debris matter upsets everthing."[14] Truly the lawsuit and the 1886 injunction changed enterprise, as Cox observed in 1886:

> To *do* the *right thing* is the object in my view. What is the right thing? We are right and can mine and not do damage to *anyone*. But even being right, can we win at an age when humanity is not broad enough to control and manage an affair that seems to be so easy of solution? The solution is—restrain debris which is easily done and let the now second great industry of the state go on.[15]

The Debris Commission that emerged was to administer "the right thing," and now it was for mining men to comply.

How to comply was a matter of engineering and cost. Fred C. Turner told Robert Chester Turner in 1904 that he was constructing a tailings dam of thirty-five to forty feet in height. That dam "may figure all right and may be the cheapest. I've no time to do any figuring, would be much guess work without knowing what the place is."[16] Robert Turner wrote to C. H. Mallen, the superintendent of the Brunswick Consolidated Gold Mining Company of Grass Valley, California, in 1917, telling him that "Uren can undoubtedly get the information wanted by the Debris Commission without much trouble, only tell him to be sure to make the discharge box big enough to carry the flood water of the creek as well as the regular discharge from the mill."[17] Good engineering could prevent disasters due to mountain rains. Seven weeks later Turner told Mallen that "it will not be impossible to comply with their [the Debris Commission's] requirements, but it will materially add to the cost of the [tailings] dam we have to build to do so."[18] For mining men, the bottom line of compliance could be found in the cost-benefit matrix.

The federal court injunction changed the legal landscape as well as the mining ground. William S. Chapman, a San Francisco attorney, laid it out for William R. Morgan in 1886: "We have now to show cause why we shall not be stopped from dumping into Slate Creek. Before Sawyer [federal judge], we are now in both courts and we must make the claims our defense alone. It is going to be very hard to make the thing stick for the water below the lower dam is quite muddy."[19] Although the Pioneer Mine in question looked doomed, Morgan's hydraulic mine on the Klamath River was not, because "the tailings are dumped into the Clamath River and go through a gorge into the ocean—not a foot of land every covered with slickens." Further, "no such mining scheme exists in this state, plenty of water every day in the flume—plenty of pressure— lots of room for dump—no debris question to interfere—and plenty of gold in the gravel."[20] Chapman was right. The fact of dumping in the ocean was not reached by the injunction, and hydraulic mining contin- ued well into the twentieth century.[21]

This was the only good news Morgan heard. Chapman also told Morgan in 1887 that in Amador County, the "hydraulic miners" had turned "the slickens on" agricultural lands and the farmers "complain." Chapman thought their complaints were "malicious, vindictive and mean," but "I do not really think that we will be able to win."[22] Further, to operate any hydraulic mine "probably might be held as a violation of the injunction, thereby laying the company open to a fine."[23] In 1888, George W. Cox of Oakland reported that the court had levied stiff fines on violators of the injunction and concluded, "The way things are going it is useless to attempt to do anything."[24] Cox presented a much gloomier picture in 1890:

Van Ness . . . said [about the injunction,] "The *law*, the *law*, you Can't beat the *law*, and besides who can you *trust*."

> I was about a week with the Debris Commissioners. . . .
> We went over the whole ground. They were very practical and I
> like them. I presented our side the best I could—showed them
> our dams and facilities for impounding, and that the debris was
> impounding itself.[25]

Cox later reported on the results: "In this morning's paper is a synopsis of the Debris Commissioner's report to the Secy of War. It is all *against us*. Hydraulic mining is now gone under Completely, as a *legal* proposition."[26] In the diggings, some carried on, but not without difficulty. Timothy Donahue wrote to Morgan in 1890, "We were getting along first-rate until the Spies came along and served papers on me. I had to pay two fines."[27] In 1895 Donahue reported the old ways "dead as a door nail."[28] George Cox was more philosophical about the demise of hydraulic mining, writing, "You know it is California all over. To go to bed broke and dream at least of waking up a Millionaire. So Californians have a wealth in anticipation which they much enjoy."[29]

Time did not heal the animosity that the victims of hydraulic mining and the slickens generated. Even in 1896, Timothy Donahue reported to William Morgan that "they are as bitter as ever in Marysville you cant strike a lick up there unless you have a permit and build dams that takes money and you know there is no ground there to justify you build there."[30] Quite simply, the pollution controls necessary priced the miners out of processing low-grade gravel. Mine property declined in value as a result. Robert Chester Turner, a mining engineer, described the Pittsburg Liberty Mine as "a sucked orange" to a colleague in Los Angeles in 1912.[31]

On better ground, there were opportunities. Robert Chester Turner reported to R. H. Countiss in 1917 regarding the U.S. Debris Commission regulating hydraulic mines. The commission had served notice that they had to restrain their tailings. "They want us to erect a concrete dam, which would be very expensive and I am trying to get them to authorize an earthen structure, which we could build very cheaply," he epistolized.[32] The problem with the earthen structure in the mind of the commissioners was "its temporary character," Turner told C. H. Mallen.

Further, "they say we will undoubtedly keep it up while we continue to operate the mine, but that our interest in doing so will cease in the event of our closing down the mine." Such an abandoned structure "would probably be washed out by a freshet or cloudburst."[33] The commissioners recognized the transient nature of miners and the permanent hazard of unrestrained tailings. In fact, the commissioners claimed "that 60 tons of quartz will amount to more than 27 cu. yds per day and that the reservoir created by the proposed dam will fill up in less than 854 days, the time estimated. The are undoubtedly right in this."[34] Being right was not the issue. Cost was the only issue. The company tailings dam design by the commissioners' lights was "inadequate." Given this turn of events, Turner offered that "it will not be impossible to comply with their requirements, but it will materially add to the cost of the dam we have to build to do so."[35] To do business, miners had to assume the costs of tailings dams.

In Montana the Mike Horse Mine's tailings dam was built of earth and survived the flood of 1964. After the freshet had passed, the U.S. Forest Service inspected the dam and told the Anaconda Copper Mining Company to bring it up to safety standards. Time passed, warnings were issued, excuses were offered, and nature came calling in 1975. The dam failed, and tailings, slickens, and slimes roared down the watercourse. The ash-colored waters extended their deadly wash fifteen miles downstream, wiping out 80 percent of the trout population.[36] Another abandoned mine and its tailings dam splashed into history.

The California hydraulic mining disaster was another lost opportunity for the Congress. As the federal courts clearly pointed out, mining debris impaired the navigational servitude, a national interest. Yet Congress did not revisit the Mining Law of 1872 and provide for national standards and national supervision of tailings impoundment. The sluicing went on, and the rivers filled. Worse yet, the toxic waste miners knew flowed with the tailings poisoned the water. Jared Diamond has observed, "Toxicity problems associated with mining were already recognized at Butte's giant copper mine and nearby smelter a century ago, when neighboring ranchers saw their cows dying and sued the mine's owner, Anaconda Copper Mining Company."[37] It was not just the arsenic associated with Butte's copper ore that deposited toxic waste on the ground and into the water. Cyanide and mercury were part of the gold-extraction process.

Cyanide process was old in principle and known in the United States by the early nineteenth century. There was the obvious danger of working with a toxic material, but in the nineteenth century working with a coating of oil or "coal oil" was "an effective protection for skin." If inhaled, the recommended antidote was chlorine gas, ammonia, or ether.[38] Both cyanide and the cure could be deadly. Yet cyanide caught on as a process for gold-bearing ore in the 1890s after the development of a process of treatment of ore crushed to a powder in 1885.[39] Miners around Bodie, California, erected cyanide-leaching plants about 1890 that "made it possible to leach the tailings profitably[,] and property owners down the creek" built such plants.[40] In 1897 Robert Chester Turner described how those plants got rid of waste: "Here in Bodie all solutions (cyanide, etc.) are emptied into creek which flows through town and cattle, dogs and Indians drink the water 300 yards below plants without injury."[41] "One of the first mills to successfully use the cyanide process on an operations scale" was located in Brigham, Utah.[42] Otis E. Young Jr. has observed that "cyanidation set off a gold rush" about 1890, "but this boom attracted little attention because it was devoid of what the public considers glamour. There was no prospecting except by attorneys among the dusty patents of defunct mining companies."[43] Further, cyanide was not a foolproof process. As Robert L. Spude has observed for the Bradshaw Mines of Arizona, the installation of a cyanide mill was ineffective because zinc and copper in the ore "fouled the cyanide solution."[44] What was needed was more chemistry.

In Grass Valley, California, a new cyanide plant created a stir, particularly for William Sampson, the mine's chemist and assayer. On September 6, 1903, he wrote excitedly to Edna Dahl Sampson in San Francisco, telling her that "Mr. Foote is going to put in a cynide plant out at the mill." What that meant to him was "lots more work."[45] Meanwhile, he went about the business of extracting gold. In October 1903 he found a "very rich specimen at the Central shaft . . . to rich to send to the mill so I pounded them with a mortar and pestle." Some of the specimens "were

Southern Cross Cyanide Plant, Cable, Montana, ca. 1906–8. Courtesy of the Pioneer Museum, Bozeman, Montana.

almost solid gold." He pounded them "as fine as possible, then put the broken pieces in the furnace to roast off the sulphates." His furnace was a miniature smelter for this purpose, and "when the sulphates is roasted off, I take the rock, while it is red hot, and throw it in cold water: By doing that the rock crumbles: after that we screen and pan it."[46] Sampson also used mercury to extract gold. In 1904 he reported that "we didn't have very good luck with our oil burners the other day, one of them kept getting choked, and we took the gold out of the retort before all the mercury was driven off." Recognizing the health hazard, "we tied wet towels over our mouths and didn't get any silver in our system."[47] Temperature control in processing also was a problem. On one occasion, "we got too hot a fire and melted the bottom out of the retort and all the gold went into the fire."[48] In April 1904 the cyanide plant was up and running "at the North Star," and it was "something new in the cyanide process, and if it is successful it well be a big thing."[49] The process was good for profits but hard on livestock. On April 21, 1904, Sampson supposed, "The stock

M. W. Alderson assaying
at the Southern Cross
Cyanide Mill, Cable,
Montana, ca. 1906–8.
Courtesy of the Pioneer
Museum, Bozeman,
Montana.

that got poisoned must have taken a drink from the tail race. Cyanide is one of the deadliest poisons."[50] The toxicity of cyanide was not a mystery, but again even the scientifically trained had little regard for the disposal of toxic substances.

Cyaniding continued to be popular and profitable, but more environmental questions arose over time. In 1897 Robert Chester Turner of Bodie worried more about public relations and liability than pollution: "Nevertheless, while there is no danger of contaminating [the] lake, yet there is danger of an outcry & we must make every effort to have a guarantee clause, covering the point, included in contract [to work the Stonewall tailings and dump with cyanide]."[51] In 1933 L. W. Shotwell, the superintendent of the Fort Belknap Indian Agency at Harlem, Montana, wrote to G. W. Worthington, the manager of the Little Ben Mining Company, regarding plans for a cyanide milling operation: "The Indians of this reservation expressed concern over the possible damage that might occur through the discharge of cyanide solution into the steams or the washing of tailings on the reservation." Shotwell sought an alternative, asking whether "it is possible for you without a great deal of expense, to dump your tailing and discharge solution into another gulch which leads south and away from the reservation."[52] Worthington sought legal advice and got it: "If the cyanide process results in damage, then an injunction may issue or damages may be recovered."[53] He responded by requesting a meeting with the tribal council so that he could explain his now smaller project with "retaining dams."[54]

The fact of legal liability for cyanide pollution also caused mine owners to increasingly insert no-pollution clauses in mine lease agreements. For example, the lease of the Hale and Last Chance placer claims in 1922 in Montana stated that "said water shall be returned to said channel free from all contamination by tailing or anything that might be used in or about said mill in the use of said water" and more specifically, "free from all cyanide and all other poisons, and said party of the second part is hereby forbidden to use poisons of any kind in the use of said water."[55] Lawyers hoped to use this language to insulate their client from pollution claims downstream. Law and business practice in toxics sometimes merged.

Mercury was another commonly used chemistry kit to extract gold. William Z. Walker noted in his diary on November 7, 1849, that he "cleared off fine worked with a Quicksilver machine took out 1/2 pound of gold."[56] Quicksilver was readily available in California from the New Almaden Mine, and the gold rush pushed it into increased production to meet the demand.[57] As late as the 1970s mercury was still mined in California, but its heritage was that "the Napa-Sonoma-Lake County region has hundreds of small, idle, and abandoned mercury deposits."[58]

The dawning of the environmental age and attempts to revise the Mining Law of 1872 brought the convergence of environmental concerns and the federal subsidies to mining into public view. The politics of the late twentieth century had changed from that of 1872. Yet the legacy of stream gravels from hydraulic mining and toxic waste from tailings and gold processing were embedded in the American West.

CHAPTER 11

MODERNIZING THE MINING LAW OF 1872

Imagine the earth as self-

elegy, memory articulated

into headland, stone,

volcanic ash and harder caprock, life

translated slowly into layers.

White stone against bright sky, I

can't hear the words not spoken, only know

this is memory, this/could be grief.

—Elizabeth Dodd, "At Scott's Bluff, Nebraska"

in *Archetypal Light* (2001)

In 1974 the comptroller general of the United States produced a report to Congress entitled "Modernization of 1872 Mining Law Needed to Encourage Domestic Mineral Production, Protect the Environment, and Improve Public Land Management."[1] The report was the beginning of a concerted attempt to change the mining law system. The major attack on the sacred writ of western mining came in the 1990s, and inertia prevailed again.

The comptroller general's report offered findings and conclusions to Congress. First, the Mining Law of 1872 had not encouraged mineral development. Rather, mineral claimants sat on their claims rather than developing them. In fact, of the 240 mining claims visited in four states, only one was being mined. Only three of the claims had been mined at any time. Of the ninety-three mineral patents visited, only seven were being mined, sixty-six appeared dormant, and twenty were being used for nonmining purposes. Sixty percent of the nonmining purpose uses were simply residences. Second, the comptroller general determined that the system of recording claims at county recorder's offices had resulted in a web of confused titles and interests costing mineral developers and governmental agencies dearly in clearing titles and determining parties responsible for environmental damage. Third, environmental damage on seven of the claims and nineteen of the patented claims was clear and unmitigated. Fourth, the government was not making money on mining claims or patents. Speculation in mining claims was obvious. The GAO recommended that mineral development be incentivized and that the federal government make money on mining through leasing. Further, the GAO recommended a federal exploration permit system, leasing, recording with the Department of the Interior of all claims, and authority for the secretary of the interior to grant hardship life tenancies to those living on claims.

Congress politely filed the report away and turned its energy to Watergate and a Mideastern oil embargo. The mood of the Congress and of the mining industry was grounded in inertia. Mining reform was remote except for the pesky environmental issues. Little had changed since Edward H. Peplow Jr., the executive secretary of the Arizona Mining Association, had delivered a paper on the General Mining Law in 1967. Peplow argued that the Mining Law of 1872 was designed to lure people to the West to unleash the wealth of the mineral regions. In 1967 that seemed accomplished, but Peplow saw no need to tinker with the statute:

It would not be surprising if, from the perspective of 95 years later, these laws were found to have been unrealistic and badly wanting in meeting our needs today. Quite the contrary is true. Call it unadulterated genius or blind, dumb luck, whichever you will; but one of the pleasant surprises of history is that the mining law provided so well for the needs of one of the nation's two most basic industries that mining has been able to keep pace with demands undreamed of when the law was drawn.[2]

Peplow continued by asserting that the statute's success was its ground-
ing in the free enterprise system. Another reason for the success of
the Arizona copper industry was electricity. It enabled technological
advances that made low-grade ore-processing profitable.

There were winners and losers in the free enterprise system. Peplow
noted that large corporations had prospered under the General Mining
Law of 1872 aided by electricity, chemistry, and sound corporate management. The evolution of the mining business had culled out small
operators:

> The days of the small, personal copper operation vanished. Not
> that there were not—as there still are today—droves of rugged
> individualists who dreamed of striking it rich and having the
> whole ownership for themselves. It was simply a matter of eco-
> nomic fact; individuals just could not finance the huge invest-
> ments needed to equip and operate enterprises of the magnitude
> copper mining had to be.[3]

The rugged individualistic miner, pick in hand, still symbolized a mining frontier in the midst of growing corporate mining conglomerates:

> The older properties were found by the traditional prospector,
> with his pick and his pack and his burro. Poor old Alkali Ike!
> His day is long gone, and his place has been taken by a gen-
> eration of Space-Age youngsters, geophysicists equipped with
> everything from airplanes and helicopters to highly sophisti-
> cated magnetic and electronic equipment which enable them
> to perceive metallic mineralization a thousand feet and more
> beneath the earth's surface.[4]
>
> Despite the passing of the era of the grizzled prospector,
> mining law and mining practice were doing just fine the way
> they were.

Peplow defended the status quo because to change the General
Mining Law, especially the patenting of a valid discovery, would mean

disaster. Investors would flee from the industry, and the domestic need for metals would go unmet, he protested:

> Thus I submit to you that the Mining Law of 1872—no matter what faults it may be found to have in other areas—had one magnificent asset which must be discarded under any circumstances. Over the years it has fostered the operation of the free enterprise system. It has engendered intensive research; it has promoted expansion of existing properties; and it has fostered *conservation* in the truest sense of the term—the orderly, efficient and profitable development of the natural resources of the United States for the benefit of every American.[5]

To Peplow the movement of public land to private property status was critical even if Alkali Ike was a mere memory.

Yet there were plenty of ideas afloat regarding how to improve the mining laws in the era. Robert G. Dwyer, counsel for the Anaconda Copper Mining Company, told Senator Lee Metcalf that "if the mining laws are to be saved the Industry should also advocate the abolition of the discovery pit and assessment work by a bulldozer and substitute in lieu thereof, geological, geophysical, geochemic and drilling work."[6] Dwyer wanted exploration by the corporate whiz kids to count against that pesky annual assessment work requirement. Senator Metcalf wrote to Donald W. Lindren, the president of Lindgren Exploration Company of Wayzata, Minnesota, in 1970, telling him that "there should indeed be no conflict between the exploitation of a large mineral resource and the protection of the environment." Yet practice belied theory in the Stillwater area, where "needless and inconsiderate destruction of public lands due to the exploratory actives" was evident: "This included damage to such other land uses as livestock range, wildlife, recreation, aesthetics and watershed."[7]

The *Billings Gazette* joined in the chorus regarding Anaconda and the Stillwater area. The paper reported that a group of Billings and Laurel outdoorsmen was calling for an investigation of "the proposed Anaconda development on the Stillwater River." The group said,

"Eventually we would like to expand our focus to encompass a complete review of state and federal mining laws." The group felt that "there mining laws were written for special mining interests and not in the best interests of the general public." It was clear that the sportsmen did not believe the company "assurances that no pollution would be allowed to infect the river."[8]

The concern about mineral exploration went beyond a few fly fishermen. Donald Aldrich, the executive secretary of the Montana Wildlife Federation, sent an open letter to the Montana Congressional Delegation in 1970. He stated that "accelerated exploration and locating mineral claims the past few years threaten many watersheds, timber stands, wildlife areas and scenic and historic sites." Something needed to be done. "We must have legislation immediately," he argued, "that will guarantee consideration of all values before land can be taken out of public ownership and completely desecrated." Leasing was one option, but "to ensure adequate protection from a rush to the Recorder's Office, it would be essential to have a moratorium on patenting and locating claims during the period that the legislation is being considered."[9]

Other voices spilled into legislator's ears. Gordon Whirry, the chairman of the Environmental Task Force of Bozeman, wanted federal action on "the Heddleston project near Lincoln, Montana"—the proposed open-pit mining operation by the Anaconda Company. He feared "a vast and irreversible alteration of Montana's landscape and Montanans' lives."[10] Robert J. Shotliff of Missoula declared that "most of us Montanans feel this way and will not stand by and let this state be raped by mining interests."[11] State Representative Alvin Hageman of the Stillwater County Democratic Central Committee thought mining company environmental damage "a very concerned subject in this county, and believe it can also be a big political issue in the upcoming election."[12] Politics and the environmental movement were coming together.

Senator Mike Mansfield of Montana heard the voices for environmental regulation. In 1970 he wrote to Edward P. Cliff, chief of the U.S. Forest Service:

Recently a matter has arisen in Montana and other states which is of deep concern to me and my colleague from Montana, Senator Lee Metcalf. I am alarmed at the environmental destruction which has accompanied exploratory and other mining activity on national forest lands and at the apparent inability of the Forest Service to control this development.[13]

Mansfield noted that the Forest Service was working on regulations but urged Cliff to get them in place as soon as possible.

The administrative law process dragged along apace. In 1971 Stanley Dempsey, the chairman of the Forest Service Regulations Subcommittee of the American Mining Congress Public Lands Committee, wrote to Chief Cliff commenting on the proposed Forest Service regulations. The American Mining Congress was the lobby for the industry in Washington, D.C. Dempsey argued that

many mining states now exercise considerable control over the environmental aspects of mining. If the regulations of the Forest Service and those of the states conflict, mining operators may be caught in the middle of a confusing overlap of authority. We suggest that a provision be added to the regulations permitting cooperation between Forest Service personnel and state agencies.[14]

Dempsey was also concerned about state location requirements and advocated a single federal standard as well as the preemption of state discovery work requirements. Regarding air- and water-quality standards and solid waste disposal requirements, the American Mining Congress was opposed because "they require more than compliance with applicable federal and state air quality standards." Further, any attempt to create a uniform access law was "unwise and unnecessary."[15] Uniformity could be either confusing or helpful. It depended on the circumstances or perhaps interests.

Chipping away at the edges continued. In 1974 Senator Mike Mansfield pushed the issue of strip mining of coal onto the legislative table when the Congress was looking at the Mining Law of 1872—again. On April 3, 1974, Senator Lee Metcalf addressed the North American Wildlife Conference in Denver on the issues. Metcalf told his audience that the issues were broader than mining, in that they involved the "public's resources."[16] The Mining Law of 1872 was the "only law that puts the land use decision entirely in the hands of the developer," Metcalf offered. Further, "the miner—individual or corporation—alone decides that mining development is the best use of public lands, without regard to other values. Nor are there requirements for rehabilitation."[17] Metcalf continued with an extensive history of public domain policy and Mansfield's amendment to limit coal bed exploitation. He concluded with a conservation message, telling his audience that there was "one thing Congress can never do: Congress can never regain our public resources once they are given away. Congress can never restore resources that are wasted. Congress can and must protect our public resources, for the next and succeeding generations."[18]

In addition to coal lands, the uranium craze generated by the atomic age caused others to further question the wisdom of the Mining Law of 1872. Ken Walcheck, writing in *Montana Outdoors* in 1975, asked, "How can individuals and mining firms exploit natural resources within an area supposedly dedicated to protecting natural scenery and opportunities for outdoor recreation?" The "answer lies in obsolete mining laws dating to 1872. Specifically, the mining law of 1872," he declared. Walcheck focused on the staking of 1,165 claims for twenty-three thousand acres. "Faced with this beehive of activity, the Forest Service does not have a 'big gun' to wield under federal law. It lacks authority to protect the public's interest from private exploitation of minerals," he wrote, "even if an overriding concern to save the Long Pine exists."[19]

In 1975–76 Congress revisited the issues and produced the Federal Land Policy and Management Act of 1976.[20] The statute contained two critical provisions. First, Congress gave the Bureau of Land Management the authority to create a records system. Second, Congress retained the legislative power to withdraw public land from mineral claimants by taking the power away from the executive branch.[21] The reach of the Mining Law of 1872 was limited without revising the statute itself.

In 1977, Congress passed the Surface Mining Control and Reclamation Act (Public Law 95-87) taxing working coal mines. The purpose was to create a fund for the mitigation of surface damage to mined lands. In practice, the dollars went to states via the Office of Surface Mining Reclamation and Enforcement. By the 1990s the coal lands tax dollars were diverted to the West for the purpose of mitigating the environmental damage created since 1849.[22]

With the Surface Mining Control and Reclamation Act on the books, the Mining Law of 1872 was moving closer to the center of the crosshairs. Senator Lee Metcalf wrote to David Knoyle in 1977 that he would "do everything I can to enact revisions of the 1872 Mining Act so that the same general protections afforded in the national strip mining bill can be extended to areas of hard rock mining." The cause was the environment, and Montana had the best examples of why such reclamation provisions were critical. Metcalf observed that "the situation in Butte is a particularly sad one because the very industry which has kept the town alive well be the one which consumes and destroys it."[23] The toxic soil, the polluted water table, and the toxic Berkeley Pit constantly filling with toxic water were only part of the problem, but clearly the most visible part.

Senator Metcalf knew that the issues at stake went to jobs as well as to the environment. He wrote to Mrs. Ray Farrey of Townsend that

> as for Montana's economy, that is also a serious matter. Our history has been one of boom-and-bust economies of extractive industries. We must weigh the values of a traditionally one-shot timber-mining process against those values which are lost or diminished: watershed protection, wildlife habitat, tourist attraction, recreation and others. The latter also contribute to our economy.[24]

Metcalf also knew that American values and the Montana mind-set were not on the same page in the 1970s. He told the chief of the Economic

Geology Division of the Montana Bureau of Mines and Geology in 1977 that national values rather than Treasure State thinking must prevail when it came to wilderness. He wrote,

> Your argument is a familiar one. Although certain mineral activities are permitted in wilderness areas, the overall effect is to diminish exploitation. It follows that jobs and availability of minerals are indeed affected by wilderness designation.
>
> However, recognition and admission of these facts do not necessarily make wilderness undesirable. The key point to keep in mind is that the public is owner of all Federal Lands and has thus far been willing to pay the necessary price to keep pristine a small percentage of those lands. Wilderness decisions are made by Congress in full public view and have been largely acceptable to the American people. Put another way, the "trade-off" which you deplore is viewed otherwise by a majority of Americans.[25]

The future of Montana's economy was no longer tied to extractive enterprise, and wilderness held the prospects for future economic and aesthetic gain.

Morris K. Udall of Arizona told the American Mining Congress on January 25, 1977, that the Mining Law of 1872 should be repealed and a federal leasing system put in its place. R. B. Olson, Anamax Mining Company counsel, thought that ill-advised. Such a move would pitch the country into dependency on foreign minerals. Rather than abolition, Olson suggested a recommendation to the Public Land Law Review Commission of 1970 of "a system . . . which incorporates the desirable features of a location-patent system and a leasing system."[26] Tinkering was better than abolition.

Senator Howard W. Cannon of Nevada expressed concerns about all the changes in the works. "Considerable controversy has developed in regard to proposed Bureau of Land Management regulations on surface mining activities," Cannon reported in February 1977. "The mining industry in Nevada and other western states feel strongly threatened by bonding and planning requirements. The small prospector, in particular, may be put out of business by these regulations," he warned. The Alkali Ike who was gone the decade before still walked Nevada's public lands according to Cannon. Metcalf replied that the BLM regulations were only the start and that he wanted "to review all mining practices on public lands with an eye to revision of the 1872 Mining Law."[27] Metcalf knew that the small prospector had faded into myth. He also knew that "reform" of the Mining Law of 1872 could "benefit industry as well as society."[28] Yet as 1977 closed Metcalf was not optimistic about "reform of the 1872 Mining Law." He reported to Robert L. Varner of Utica, Montana, that "a combination of factors make prospects dim for the 95th Congress. The workload is extremely heavy; Congressman Udall, Chairman of the House Interior Committee, has bowed to heavy pressure in Arizona and compromised his position on reform." Finally, "there is so much controversy surrounding the issue that more than a year would probably be required even under the best circumstances."[29] Unfortunately for mining law reform, its champion, Lee Metcalf, passed away in Helena, Montana, on January 12, 1978.

The environmental movement was chipping away at the edges of the Mining Law of 1872. Mining interests resisted but learned political and practical lessons on how to deal with Congress and how to comply with environmental statutes, regulations, and litigation. Although it did not deal with the Mining Law of 1872 specifically, Congress did pass significant environmental statutes that applied to the mining industry. The Clean Air Act Amendments of 1970 established uniform, national standards identifying a wide range of pollutants and sources. In 1972 Congress passed the Clean Water Act to protect fish, shellfish, and wildlife as well as water recreation. Lawmakers thought they could rid the nation of all pollution discharges by 1985. In combination, these federal statutes further armed state and federal regulators with law to curtail mining and smelting pollution.

CHAPTER 12

Environmental Law in the
Age of Aquarius

I saw all over the desert what human hands had left:

strip mining left a pulverized mountain of debris.

—Julia Stein, "This Land" in *Walker Woman* (2002)

Miners did not see the environmental law revolution coming, and until Anaconda's smelter closed, many thought public relations and politics would continue to solve their legal problems.[1] Miners gathered in conventions and admired their accomplishments rather than reading Aldo Leopold's *A Sand County Almanac* (1948), Rachel L. Carson's *Silent Spring* (1962), or Barry Commoner's *The Closing Circle* (1971). The Clean Air Act of 1963 gave the federal government enforcement power over air pollution, and the Water Quality Act of 1965 gave similar authority over water pollution on interstate waters. Mining interests watched, but they had defeated the Justice Department before and mining was, after all, a needed industry. When the Clean Air Act was amended in 1967 and 1970, smelter interests saw the return of the smoke wars of the turn of the century. When President Nixon signed the National Environmental Policy Act of 1969 into law on January 1, 1970, the Age of Aquarius had matured into Earth Day celebrations and a full-scale attack on polluters, including those patriot prospectors of the American West.[2] On July 8, 1971, Republican Bob Mathias introduced H.R. 9661 calling for "the California Desert National Conservation Area."[3] Three weeks later Republican Congressman Jerry Pettis put H.R. 10305 in the hopper, calling for an 11-million-acre national conservation area.[4] Despite the fact that Congress had not amended or repealed the sacred Mining Law of 1872, the nation's lawmakers had confronted

Anaconda Copper Mining Company's "New Works," constructed with a high stack to offset air pollution litigation of the Deer Lodge Valley farmers and ranchers. Courtesy of the Montana Historical Society, Helena.

environmental pollution head-on, and that included the practices of mining corporations in the West.

If the miners missed what was going on in Washington, D.C., they could hardly avoid the dramatic political shift to green in Montana, the home of Anaconda Copper Mining Company. In the winter 1970 edition of the *Montana Business Quarterly* K. Ross Toole, a University of Montana history professor, challenged people to stop the pollution. He reviewed the Butte air pollution disaster of 1889–1891, the *Bliss* case of the Deer Lodge Valley farmers of 1911, and the 1957–58 Missoula pulp plant's water and air pollution. The tired explanations of industry did not clear the air of the "yellowish-gray, vile-smelling smog."[5] Toole asserted that

> clean air, clean water, wilderness areas, and beautiful country-sides are not "bonuses" any longer. America is running out of these commodities—and fast. It *is* trite, but man does not live by bread alone and no planner should forget it. The "quality of life" may not attract industry, but neither should industry be solicited which destroys the quality of life.[6]

In addition, Toole contended with economists and their cost-benefit analyses. Putting a price on aesthetics was one thing, but knowing that "the number of deaths from lung cancer in the Anaconda area is 29 times greater than in the Gallatin Valley . . . and 12 times greater than the national average" was beyond economic models.[7]

The people of Montana had an interest in health that transcended jobs, Toole argued. The land, water, and air were part of a public trust the people must manage wisely. The solutions were classic: "But, as Cassius said, 'the fault lies not in our stars, but in ourselves.' And, therefore, it is correctable. Perhaps the ultimate strength of man lies in some capacity to look into himself and out at the world—and change things. That, at least, is our best hope—and it may well be our last."[8] Toole challenged the people of the last best place to change, and he was not alone.

Toole's message was not the only missive for environmental control. The Northern Plains Resource Council published *The Plains Truth*, telling Montanans of the massive strip mining of coal planned for Colstrip and the proposed dam on the Upper Yellowstone River.[9] Environmental activists in Missoula formed Gals against Smog and Pollution to demand legislative reform, and activists in Helena created the Environmental Information Center to educate voters on the need for regulation.[10] Voters responded and sent a new breed of legislator to Helena who created the Montana Environmental Quality Council in 1971, a Utilities Siting Act in 1973 to regulate power plants, and a flurry of 1975 statutes including coal mining reclamation, re-registration of all water rights, a moratorium on Yellowstone River development, and the

K. Ross Toole, ca. 1956.
Courtesy of the Montana
Historical Society,
Helena.

highest coal severance tax in the nation.[11] These legislators also passed
the Metal Mine Reclamation Act of 1971 and the Opencut Mining Act
of 1973.[12] The former law created a permit system for mining, and the
latter, an application procedure for the open-cut mining of benton-
ite, clay, scoria, phosphate rock, and gravel. As Jared Diamond has
observed, despite the 1971 law, mining "companies discovered that they
could extract the valuable ore and then just declare bankruptcy before
going to the expense of cleaning up."[13] Montana was in the regulation
and reclamation game. Montana would not be alone.

The legislative action in Washington, D.C., and Montana was mir-
rored in other states. Colorado passed the Colorado Open Mining Land
Reclamation Act of 1973 and the Mined Land Reclamation Act of 1976,
putting reclamation and environmental regulation on the books.[14] Idaho
put the Idaho Surface Mining Act and the Idaho Placer and Dredge
Mining Protection Act in the statute book in 1977.[15] California's attack on
pollution was broadly based and historically grounded in intermittent

statutory attention to the environment.[16] In 1969 the Clean Water Act or Porter-Cologne Water Quality Control Act and the Surface Mining and Reclamation Act of 1975 put regulation into the mining business. Under the 1969 statute the State Water Resources Control Board issued extensive regulations regarding the discharge of mining wastes to land, known as chapter 15 regulations. The board created a three-tiered mine waste classification system, design standards, monitoring requirements, and other regulations for waste piles, surface impoundments, and tailings ponds. Nine Regional Water Quality Control Boards implemented the regulations.[17] The California legislature also passed an Endangered Species Act in 1970, the San Francisco Bay Conservation and Development Commission Act in 1969, the Wild and Scenic Rivers Act in 1972, and the Coastal Act in 1976.[18] The legislative turn to regulation caused mining men to turn to lawyers and training to maneuver in the new administrative law maze.

Just as Julia Stein's eye caught the waste piles in Death Valley and linguistically turned image into poetry, so too geographer William L. Graf saw the arroyos and gullies of Central City, Colorado, as mining's geomorphic heritage. Writing in the 1979 *Annals of the Association of American Geographers*, Graf determined that "the major impact of mining on stream systems of the Central City Mining District was the initiation of stream entrenchment."[19] Mining necessitated lumber, and "the timber was exhausted by 1863," resulting in accelerated "erosion of slopes" and stream entrenchment "up to 21 feet deep into Quaternary valley fills that are silt-sand debris from nearby slopes."[20] Landscape alteration from mining piled waste up and cut trenches down. A quarter century later, Richard V. Francavigilia surveyed the mining West and found altered landscapes varying in form due to technology, management philosophy, and weathering. The mining past and present leave mining landscapes.[21]

Reclamation could level that ground, but miners needed instruction. Mining publications like the *Mining Congress Journal* increased the number of articles on the environment.[22] Mining conventions had sessions on environmental regulation. The Institute on Mineral Resources Permitting sponsored by the Rocky Mountain Mineral Law

Foundation in Tucson in March 1981 offered fourteen paper sessions. Peter Keppler's paper on the mineral permitting process focusing on responsible mining management was significant in its time and tone. Keppler observed that

> the list of federal environmental protection statutes seems endless: The National Environmental Policy Act, Clean Water Act, Federal Water Pollution Control Act, Safe Drinking Water Act, Toxic Substances Control Act, Resource Conservation and Recovery Act, Surface Mining Control and Reclamation Act, and the reams of regulations issued pursuant to each of them, place great responsibilities and burdens on mineral resources companies, as well as other industries. Concurrent state and local laws and regulations deepen the murky waters one must navigate to be permitted to construct and operate a mine. Today, most mining companies understand the concern behind these laws and the importance our society places on clean air, clean water, and aesthetically pleasing vistas. It is understood that there is no longer any tolerance for unfettered mineral development; instead the challenge to protect the environment goes along with the responsibility to produce the raw materials needed by our society.[23]

Keppler went on to explain how American Metal Climax, Inc. (AMAX) was conducting an "Experiment in Ecology" in developing its Henderson molybdenum deposit in central Colorado. AMAX used its experience with the Climax Mine in 1967 to go to the U.S. Forest Service and environmentalists to plan the mining operation with the environment in mind. Keppler emphasized that "AMAX was genuinely concerned about ecological matters and did not treat the Experiment as simply a public relations tool designed to gain favor for the company by making token appeasement to environmental groups."[24] For example, their tailings disposal area was fourteen miles away from the mine, on the other side of the Continental Divide, and served by a railway tunnel nine and one-half miles long. The Environmental Impact Statement contained broadly based assessments of flora and fauna. Private lands purchased for mining use were opened to the public for hunting and fishing.[25] Coordinated efforts with regulatory agencies and environmental groups coupled with "honest dealing with concerned parties will usually bring about the desired result," Keppler concluded.[26] The message was clear. Miners needed to get their operations in order, get ahead of the regulatory deadlines, consult with environmentalists, and start mining in full compliance.

The irony of Keppler's advice was that in 1981 AMAX was in economic trouble due to the world market in molybdenum. Company warehouses were filled with concentrate. AMAX stopped hiring in December 1980 and in 1982 folded major operations, putting Leadville into a depression.[27] The even greater irony was the fate of AMAX's plans to open a molybdenum mine near Mount Emmons and Crested Butte, Colorado.

Crested Butte was a coal-mining town until the 1950s, when it converted to the recreation business. In the 1970s AMAX announced its plans to develop a molybdenum mine near Mount Emmons. Molybdenum was AMAX's game, and its record for environmental sensitivity and community consultation was established.[28] Regardless of AMAX's record, community meetings turned into shouting matches and clearly drawn images of tailings piles, unregulated growth, and thousands of outsiders working for the company. AMAX promised an environmental and cultural paradise, but the environmentalists and NIMBY advocates prevailed. Crested Butte remained a ski resort free of the mining debris and miners' now negative references in the new green world.[29] The clear message was that jobs and strategic metal mining were less important than environmental quality. The trout and the slopes would be safe for recreational dollars.

Following the AMAX lead, but with greater success, the Viceroy Gold Corporation of Las Vegas, Nevada, a subsidiary of Viceroy Resources Corporation of Vancouver, British Columbia, opened exploration of the Hart Mining District in eastern San Bernardino County, California, and extending into Clark County, Nevada, in the 1980s. Starting in 1985 the company located over eight hundred claims, bought claims, and negotiated royalty agreements with claim owners.[30] Viceroy purchased the Walking Box Ranch in 1989 to get ahead of environmental concerns regarding the impact of the mine on tortoises. It agreed to replace ten thousand plastic claim posts with wooden stakes to eliminate the problem of birds, lizards, and mammals getting trapped inside the claim pipes. Viceroy agreed with the Nature Conservancy to establish a 45,000- to 60,000-acre tract for tortoise preservation on the Walking Box Ranch. It also relocated roads, posted reclamation bonds, agreed to revegetate at its expense clay pits it mined for leach pads, erected cyanide tanks to protect wildlife, installed monitoring wells, provided free commuter service for employees to protect tortoises, and agreed to continuing employee education to assure wildlife and cultural resources protection.[31] Further, when it came to the California Desert Protection Act boundaries, Viceroy was not included in the wilderness designation to allow mining.[32] The concerted efforts of Viceroy staff, environmental consultants, and environmental organizations resulted in an accord on conservation, reclamation, and habitat protection that allowed mining to start.

Whether of Crested Butte or Viceroy's Castle Mountain Mine, the public had a growing awareness of the legal and environmental status of mining. Buried in a story entitled "Mine Law Is Pure Gold to Speculators" in the May 22, 1989, edition of the *Los Angeles Times*, staff writers Louis Sahagun and Mark A. Stein noted the Audubon Society's concern about a tailings pond at the proposed Castle Mountain Mine (actually a cyanide heap leach pond). The concern was that migratory birds would think it water instead of poison and die as a result. Sahagun and Stein also noted the Wilderness Society's concern for groundwater and the effect on wildlife in the Mojave Desert. Yet the bulk of the story was about the General Mining Law of 1872 and how locators could stake claims for minimal costs, patent claims just ahead of urbanization, and rip off the public. "Most often," they wrote, "those real estate speculators accused of abusing the mining law are small-time operators–sometimes miners whose aggregate business grew into building-supply company and then branched out into residential or commercial development."[33] The abuses were becoming more public.

Other abuses emerged in the 1980s, but these were about governmental regulation. The U.S. Supreme Court in three cases in 1987 took up the balance between private property rights and governmental regulation of land use. The question was when had the government gone too far and a constitutional taking of private property under the Fifth Amendment to the U.S. Constitution taken place. The first case involved the 1966 Pennsylvania Subsidence Act aimed at the coal-mining industry. The Court upheld the statute as falling under the police power of the state to protect the public interest in health, the environment, and public protection from a nuisance. The second case involved a Los Angeles ordinance that prohibited the development of private property designated a flood protection area, and the Court held that it constituted a taking and ordered that compensation be paid. The third case, again in California, involved the Coastal Commission and the need to provide an essential and rational nexus between a regulator condition and the development-caused problem.[34] If these cases gave miners any legal hope of lifting the regulatory burden, the U.S. Supreme Court gave them and local regulators guidance in *California Coastal Commission v. Granite Rock* (1987).[35]

The Granite Rock owned land adjacent to Mount Pico Blanco in California's Big Sur region and between 1959 and 1980 conducted investigations of white limestone deposits. Granite Rock also held mining claims adjacent to its private property on federal land. Deciding to develop the deposit on federal land, Granite Rock worked with the U.S. Forest Service in arriving at a plan to mine the deposit. The Forest Service proposed modifications to the plan, and Granite Rock complied, resulting in Forest Service approval of the plan. The same California Coastal Commission whose regulations of beach house alterations resulted in a landmark takings decision discussed above required a coastal development permit of Granite Rock despite the Forest Service–approved plan.

Before determining the permit conditions, Granite Rock and the American mining industry went to court to challenge the permit requirement. The argument was that the General Mining Law of 1872 preempted the state regulatory law. The most important question involved in the case was whether states could regulate a miner's use of a claim or more pointedly whether a state regulatory body could trump the sacred right of a claimant to burrow in the earth. The Court held that the General Mining Law of 1872 did not preempt state regulation imposing a reasonable environmental regulation.

Importantly, the way Granite Rock and the mining industry posed the question helped the U.S. Supreme Court answer the question. Granite Rock argued that the permit, even if it was an environmental regulation, had the potential of prohibiting mining per se, a federal purpose enshrined in the 1872 statute. If the California Coastal Commission could trump an approved Forest Service plan, then there was a conflict between state and federal law and the Court had to find a federal preemption. Given the timing of the court action, the Coastal Commission had not issued its regulatory conditions, and only the abstract permit power was before the Court. Such an abstraction did not afford the Court any basis for determining whether the regulatory conditions would, in fact, prohibit the mining of limestone. Sandra Day O'Connor, a Stanford-educated Arizona lawyer, judge, and legislator, told Granite Rock that the state was not determining the basic uses of federal land but, rather, seeking to regulate a given mining use. That regulation would require that mining be conducted "in a more environmentally sensitive and resource-protective fashion."[36] The state snout was clearly protruding under the miner's tent.

The Mining Law of 1872 was not a shield from state regulation of mining practice, and federal statutory development meant that mining industry practices had to comply with federal regulations. It was clear that mining had entered a regulatory regime despite the fact that the Mining Law of 1872 stood without congressional revision or repeal. How long would Congress sit on the sidelines of the Mining Law of 1872 revision?

CHAPTER 13

A FRONTAL ATTACK
ON THE MINING LAW OF 1872

It is too easy for me

to feel my identity giving away, just as the soft cement

rolls off the conveyor belt and into the river, where

the ducks have done their breeding,

    and the whole family

has gathered to gaze, though it seems that the water

may have lost most of its meaning in direct proportion

    to our loss of memory. . . .

—Brian Young, "A Chatterbox in the Aspirin Trees"
in *The Full Night Still in the Street Water* (2003)

One hundred forty years after the California gold rush and 117 years after the passage of the Mining Law of 1872, the U.S. General Accounting Office issued a report calling for the revision of the venerable General Mining Law. Another political firestorm swept the West. Alkali Ike, the small prospector of nineteenth-century mythology, joined with corporate whiz kids grinding out data. The mining statistics in the hands of lobbyists slowly buried congressional reform, but incremental change again found its way westward.

The GAO's 1989 report contained little new information on the impact of the Mining Law of 1872 but reminded legislators why change was needed. In 1986 the federal government sold seventeen thousand acres of public land by the patent system for $42,500. Weeks later these Alkali Ikes sold their patented mineral lands to major oil companies for

$37,000,000.[1] In addition to the dollars involved, the House had requested and the GAO had investigated the annual work requirement.

The GAO summarized the legislative history of the General Mining Law of 1872 and noted changes in the statute. First, Congress had removed the fuel minerals such as coal, gas, and oil from coverage and created alternative systems. Second, Congress had removed the common-variety minerals such as sand and gravel from coverage. Finally, Congress and the president had withdrawn from mineral exploitation 727 million acres of public land for wilderness areas and national parks. Most telling, however, was the fact that "various proposals have been made to amend the act's hardrock minerals patent and annual work provisions, but none of them have been enacted."[2] The patent and work requirements had done nothing to bring about mineral claim development.

The Mining Law of 1872 also appeared out of step with recent federal legislation. The GAO reported that

> the patent provisions of the Mining Law of 1872 clearly run counter to other national natural resource policies and legislation. The Federal Land Policy and Management Act of 1976 (FLPMA) provides that, in general, public lands should remain under federal ownership and be managed for the benefit of all users (multiple use) as well as for future generations (sustained yield). However, mining claim holders can gain title to federal lands by patenting their claims, thereby precluding future public use of these lands.[3]

Patented claims impeded the effective management of abutting federal lands and barred federal control of incompatible development of those patented lands. What had happened was simple: patented claims were private property, and if the government wanted it, the government would have to take it by eminent domain. The Fifth Amendment to the U.S. Constitution required payment for the private property. Mineral patentees had government to hold up if it wanted to acquire their property for a public purpose.

One kind of development that galled environmentalists and

reformers was the patented claim converted into profitable nonmineral enterprise, with the federal government not receiving a single copper cent. The GAO referenced ski resorts in Keystone and Breckenridge, Colorado.[4]

The GAO reminded Congress that this was not its first report. In 1974 the GAO had found that the 1872 Mining Law did not provide a system for determining the number and location of claims, ensure mineral development, give the federal government a fair market return on the minerals extracted from the public domain, or protect the federal lands from degradation. FLPMA had addressed some of these concerns in 1976. Claim and annual work affidavits were now filed with the Bureau of Land Management, and that agency now knew where the claims were located. Less effectively addressed, GAO claimed, were fair market value returns and environmental protection. In 1979 the GAO returned to the issue and again called for fair market value returns and the abolition of the patenting system.[5]

The GAO also revisited its findings regarding the annual work requirement and recommended that it be replaced with a payment system directly to the federal government. In 1974 the GAO found that "237 of the 240 claims we reviewed showed no evidence that mineral extraction had ever taken place, and on 146 of the claims, no evidence of development work existed."[6] Verification of work by the Forest Service or the BLM was an inefficient use of their resources. "While the mining community generally recognizes that many claim holders certify that they have met the annual requirement without ever performing the work, it would be difficult to differentiate between work certified but not done and work done that cannot be verified," the GAO concluded.[7] Further, where bulldozers did work, in particular, the disturbance of land was significant. The disturbance did nothing to develop the claim in most cases.[8] GAO and the Congressional Budget Office in a 1988 report favored an annual fee paid in to the federal Treasury.[9] GAO warned that such a provision might start a stampede to patent claims to avoid paying the fee.

It did not take long for the press to pick up the story. On May 22, 1989, the *Los Angeles Times* ran a series entitled "Public Land, Private

Profit: Inside the Bureau of Land Management." The second in the series focused on the Mining Law of 1872 and the GAO report. The *Times* opened "Mine Law Is Pure Gold to Speculators" with a story of a Tonopah, Nevada, miner who used the Mining Law of 1872 to stake a claim where the federal government wanted to develop a nuclear waste dump. His $500 investment yielded $249,500 from a federal buyout of his claim. Further, "growing concern about the appropriateness of the pick-and-shovel General Mining Law in an era of satellite-image prospecting is encouraging a congressional debate over how best to reform— or rewrite one of the nation's most basic economic and environmental regulations."[10] As the Tonopah miner made clear: "If you're legal in filing a claim and do everything by the [book], no body can stop you. The law protects the little man." Those little guys were staking thousands of claims outside resort communities, particularly Las Vegas and Laughlin, Nevada. They were doing what miners of the nineteenth century were doing, locating claims adjacent to paying mines hoping to leverage mine owners into paying them off to expand their operations. Now twentieth-century Alkali Ikes were staking anything to await community development in their direction. Neither locators of the nineteenth or twentieth centuries intended to develop a mine. The *Times* also cited the GAO example of a $42,500 patented claim turned into a $34 million sale to oil companies as an example of the abuse of the statute. Conflicts with other federal policies and statutes also graced the story. Environmental degradation was another unintended consequence of the General Mining Law. Regardless, Keith Knoblock of the American Mining Congress (AMC) was quoted in opposition to any change in the law. "Our fear is if it is opened up, we'll end up with a mineral-leasing system for hardrock mining," he said. The greatest impact of such change, Knoblock predicted, would be on small miners.

The *San Francisco Chronicle* found one of those small miners. Dan Sagaser was a seventy-eight-year-old miner living in a cabin he built in the Siskiyou National Forest on his mining claim. Now he was being evicted under the 1976 Federal Land Policy Management Act's requirement that small-scale ("mom-and-pop") miners be put out of the national forests. Speaking of the Mining Law of 1872, Sagaser said that "to us, it was like the Constitution. We believed in it. We invested our lives in it. Now they say it doesn't count anymore. I don't understand it."[11] Although Sagaser did not understand what had happened, Congress did and saw that mining operators in national forests had been abused for decades by vacation home builders, hunters, fishermen, and small miners. All had erected structures for their use whether they mined or not, and all in the name of the sacred Mining Law of 1872.

Whether a mom-and-pop operation or an Alkali Ike prospector, the little miner, just like the family farmer that agribusiness likes to parade out for legislators, was seldom seen until legislation prompted industry action. But the GAO report was followed by a flurry of legislation, and the mining press picked up on the threat, the need for unity, and the job of educating the public. The *National Inholders News* of Sonoma, California, in its November–December 1987 edition trumpeted that the "Cranson Wilderness Bill (S-7) threaten[ed] mining['s] largest withdrawal in the history of the lower 48 states." The paper found "Dick and Anna Singer, a mom-and-pop prospecting team" who had made a "world class discovery" enabled by the Mining Law of 1872. On page 8 of that edition, Don Fife told readers that the "Mining Law is America's Secret Weapon against the Soviets," who intended to dominate the world strategic mineral supply.[12]

In Denver, the *Mining Record*'s January 3, 1990, edition celebrated one hundred years of publication. The paper had moved from a mining stock daily to a weekly and even a bimonthly in the 1960s. In 1990 it was a weekly with thirty-five thousand subscribers and a comprehensive coverage of the mining industry. In 1990 it had plenty of political news to print. Beyond the news of a century of mining news, the *Mining Record* had a good deal of good news to report. Miners were to assemble in Denver to "sharpen environmental skills" by attending seminars and workshops. John Gromley, representing the Colorado Mining Association, offered that "our industry has a new ethic and a continuing commitment to the environment. Since we do business under environmental controls, we constantly seek better ways to solve environmental problems."[13]

In Brawley, California, the Gold Fields Operating Company reported another environmental advance in the form of a gold heap leach pond cover. The *Mining Record* reported that "Mesuite has been very aggressive in its program to discourage birds from the gold solution ponds." Before the pond cover, the company had used "multi-colored pennant flags, propane cannons, electronic bird distress signals and methodical inspection" to reduce bird fatalities caused by cyanide poisoning.[14] In Washington, D.C., Secretary of the Interior Manuel Lujan Jr. reported that 1989 marked another banner year for miners, with a 5 percent increase over 1988, marking the third year of recovery for the industry since the 1982–86 slump.[15]

There was disturbing news as well. The California Mining Association and the Desert Conservation Institute, a mining industry education program, were battling environmentalists in California. The California Desert Protection Act contained in H.R. 780 and S. 11 threatened to close the California deserts to mining.[16] Hearings in Beverly Hills in February 1990 demonstrated the power of the mining lobby. Opponents wearing orange caps and sporting orange placards jammed the hall at Beverly Hills High School to shout their opposition to the bills. The arguments were familiar. Closing the deserts to mining would affect the supply of valuable minerals. Shortages of aggregates would affect infrastructure. Cutting mining would mean unemployment. Private property rights would be impaired.[17] The mining industry deployed all the usual tactics Jared Diamond has noted as the "usual resistive strategies, such as denying the reality of toxic effects, funding local citizens' support groups to state their case, proposing cheaper solutions than those proposed by the government, and so on."[18] Mining was under attack. The Sierra Club reported on the event, noting that Congressman Mel Levine "pointed out that the bill would close only three working mines."[19] The orange people appeared at a San Diego hearing where Senator Barbara Boxer "was stellar in her support of the Bill" and "the 'Orange People' were buffoons," according to Peter Teague.[20]

John A. Knebel, the president of the AMC, made the attack theme explicit at the National Wilderness Conference in Salt Lake City. Knebel told the audience that "the Environmental Left seems hellbent on turning this whole country into its own private wilderness playground." His evidence was that 90 million acres of public lands had been placed off-limits to mining. Further, environmentalist propaganda offered that the mining industry had "never spent one red cent for pollution abatement." That was dead wrong, Knebel maintained, citing statistics showing that the mineral-processing industry had spent heavily on pollution control technology.[21] That fact needed to be communicated to the public.

The U.S. Bureau of Mines pitched in to educate the public. The Earth Day displays in twelve cities told mining's story clustered around three themes. First, minerals were hidden treasures represented by photographs of spectacular ore specimens. Second, the mining industry was meeting our mineral needs. Graphics and postcards for distribution pushed the concept that minerals were crucial in our economy and the nation was dependent on foreign countries for some minerals. Finally, the Bureau of Mines was in the forefront of environmental protection. Its mineral land assessment program preserved "access to land containing mineral resources while protecting environmentally sensitive areas." The bureau was also conducting research on acid mine drainage and had won awards for its efforts. The bureau also was working with the Environmental Protection Agency on Superfund sites and other mining contamination areas. The story concluded: "The Bureau of Mines hopes that this Earth Day effort will, in at least a small way, communicate the message that we all depend on minerals to sustain our lifestyle and we can produce minerals while preserving important environmental values."[22] Education in action at the sites of environmental disasters contained two messages. First, the Bureau of Mines was a mining industry support group. Second, the bureau was working to clean up the mess the industry left behind. The images were certainly not all positive.

William Grannell, the executive director of the Western States Public Lands Coalition (WSPLC), a broadly based lobby for mining, oil and gas, lumber companies, and cattlemen, saw the negative writing on the wall. The Big Five made up of the Sierra Club, the Audubon Society, Nature's Conservancy, the National Wildlife Federation, and the Wilderness Society was ganging up on multiple-use industries on the public domain. They wanted the public domain to be "pristine parks" without development. Grannell observed that on their agenda is the 1872 Mining Law and many more restrictions to public lands access. They have convinced Senator Bumpers to introduce a strong anti-mining law. And, this year, they have the support of congressman Nick Joe Rahall, who chairs the Interior Committee Subcommittee on Mining, to offer a rewrite of the mining law. Be assured the pressure will be on Congress to produce tough new laws.[23]

The mining industry needed to organize and ally with the other users of the public domain to stop the environmentalists. Grannell's organization had created the "People for the West" to organize such a campaign and produce a petition to Congress signed by a million people to stop the Big Five. Grannell's lobby had already fought the spotted owl campaign in Oregon to save the timber industry and Oregon jobs. They won concessions by putting pressure on the Oregon Congressional Delegation, forcing a "timber summit" and winning legislative concessions.

Mining could do the same job, and Grannell's organization had a plan. It would target "five western states, where congressional delegations need to have a stronger voice in support of natural resource development." Then it "will rally vocal community groups to support the industry and retention of sensible mining laws." WSPLC would contact people in cities affected by a "no-mining" policy and rally them to the cause. Finally, it would educate the people "throughout the west" regarding mining's positive contributions to the economy and regarding the costs of a "no-mining" policy. Most importantly, "from you who are reading this article, the campaign needs more than just good wishes to make it work. It needs your financial support." With dollars and organization, the Big Five could be stopped.[24]

The campaign rolled on. In June Nevada Governor Bob Miller "in a strongly worded-letter" told the Nevada Congressional Delegation to oppose the BLM-proposed $100 per claim rental fee as a substitute for the annual work requirement. He argued that "the removal of the assessment work requirement retards the diligent development of minerals and enhances the opportunity for nonresident speculators to abuse the Mining Law."[25] Three of four members of the Nevada Congressional

Delegation opposed "changes proposed for the 1872 Mining Law." Senator Harry Reid called the claim rental fee a "tax hike" that would not benefit Nevada. He declared that "prospectors, miners and Nevada should not be penalized when there are other ways to lower the deficit."[26] The "T" word carried political potential.

More than the 1872 Mining Law was at stake. The Mountain States Legal Foundation (MSLF), another public domain users defense fund, attacked the Superfund, arguing that it was unconstitutional on the grounds of a violation of due process of law, that it was an ex post facto statute, and that it unconstitutionally took private property. The MSLF also thought the statute violated the separation of powers doctrine.[27] MSLF declared a major victory over the National Wildlife Federation (NWF) in a case involving the BLM's review of land withdrawals and classifications. The U.S. Supreme Court had declared that NWF did not have standing to bring the suit, and William Perry Pendley, the president and chief legal officer of the foundation, trumpeted that

> after nearly five years, the management of the public lands of the west has been returned to the American people. Since this law-suit was filed in 1985, 180 million acres of public land—an area the size of the states of Texas, Vermont, and New Hampshire combined—was controlled by the courts and by the environ-mental organization that brought the suit. As a result, western-ers were denied the ability to use this vast area for work and for recreation. Also tied up in the lawsuit were 1,000 oil and gas leases, 7,000 mining claims and hundreds of other applications for use of the public lands by neighboring landowners, small towns, and other rightful users of the public land.[28]

For the reading public, the announcement seemed spectacular. For law-yers it was just another standing case, and for users on those 180 million acres, most never noticed the fact of the lawsuit's existence.

In May 1990 the New Mexico Mining Association corralled Representatives Nick Rahall, Bill Richardson, and Steve Schiff in Albuquerque. Richardson of New Mexico arranged the meeting so miners could make their views clear to Rahall: "Rahall told the industry representatives that his views on the mining law were still evolving and that he was still very much open to comments and criticisms from the mining industry." He told them he would be holding hearings on his bill in September and that his bill was not a leasing bill and contained no royalty provisions. The New Mexico miners were concerned that once it was on the floor of the House of Representative, the House members could turn it into a runaway bill detrimental to mining interests: "Rahall committed to the group that as bill sponsor and floor manager, he could control the process and would kill the bill should it take an unfavorable course." On specifics, miners did not like the discretion given to land managers under a permit system, the role of state and local governments in the process, user fees, rental fees, and environmental reclamation bonding; "Rahall took notes of each of the concerns and said again that he was not locked in on any provision of the bill."[29] These themes of opposition to change found increased data and rhetoric when hearings started in Washington, D.C.

More legislation stirred the mining lobby. The American Mining Congress strongly opposed a moratorium on the patenting of mining claims approved by the House Interior Appropriations Subcommittee. AMC President John A. Knebel argued that any moratorium "would create chaos with respect to good faith patent applications whose applications are now pending." Knebel told senators that the Mining Law of 1872 was a land-tenure law that had accommodated "dramatic changes in mineral requirements and market conditions for 117 years."[30] Those miners around Las Vegas and ski resorts were in accord with those sentiments.

The Mountain States Legal Foundation went after the National Park Service and the U.S. Forest Service for allegedly silencing the U.S. Bureau of Mines and its request to address the Greater Yellowstone Coordinating Committee (GYCC) at its August 1990 meeting in Helena, Montana. William Perry Pendley, the president and chief legal officer of the foundation, said, "The GYCC told the U.S. Bureau of Mines experts not to bother coming, that it didn't want to learn of the mineral potential of the millions of acres which the GYCC wants to lock up." Pendley also noted that "the GYCC apparently made a similar decision not to invite the U.S. Geological Survey, which possesses unique expertise on the location of oil and gas resources." These wrongheaded decisions would ultimately hurt "the American consumer."[31] The MSLF clearly insinuated that government agencies had barred other government agencies favorable to mining interests from the free flow of information needed to make informed decisions.

The American Mining Congress took a similar angle in criticizing the *Washington Post*'s position on the Mining Law of 1872. Accusations of "disregard for the stringent environmental standards" by a mining corporation were false, President John Knebel retorted. In fact, the company had agreed to more than "80 specific environmental requirements" and posted a reclamation bond of $1.5 million. Moreover, the article totally ignored the fact that the mine produced 150 jobs in a small Nevada town and "has added significantly to the economic well-being of that formerly economically depressed area."[32] The environment and jobs were linked at the political level. It was another AMC effort to get all of the facts before the mining public.

In September 1990 the California Mining Association was gearing up for testimony before the House Subcommittee on Mining and Natural Resources. Bill Tilden, the chairman of the Lands and Minerals Committee, previewed his testimony for the readers of *California Mining*. Nick J. Rahall's "Mineral Exploration and Development Act of 1990" created a rental fee with expenditure requirements to maintain and develop a mining claim. It also eliminated the patenting of surface rights and nonprecious metals from the list of minerals qualifying for location. Tilden offered that

> one of the major considerations is the value of this legislation against the abandonment of the Mining Law of 1872. That law has been amended many times. It seems that the positive aspects of Rep. Rahall's bill could be incorporated into an amendment of the current law and avoid unnecessary confusion and re-definition of activities which work well now through the Mining Law.[33]

Tilden also argued that the absence of a patenting provision and a standardized forty-acre claim format would deter miners from finding clay, talc, gypsum, and other critical minerals needed by industry and create a nightmare of confusion over conflicting claims. Yet the most unfortunate part of the bill was the requirement that a full Environmental Impact Statement be approved. This comprehensive land-use planning system clearly indicated that the "primary consideration" was given to the environment and not to "mineral development." Further, with the creation of a new statute, miners would "face another century of precedent-setting case law to define it."[34] Tilden pushed the deterrent aspects of change with the consequent loss of mineral resources. He was not the first to indicate that statutory change of any kind would lead to legal uncertainty due to litigation.

While Tilden was off jousting with environmentalists in Washington, California miners had problems of their own in Sacramento. Assemblyman Tom Hayden and Attorney-General John Van de Kamp were pushing "the Environmental Protection Act of 1990." Glenn Rouse, the executive director of the California Mining Association, called the initiative a challenge to "economic survival." Certainly the environment needs protection, Rouse maintained, "but we believe issues should be approached with scientific documentation and singular focus. Not with a helter-skelter, one-size-fits-all initiative."[35] There was more in the structure of the bureaucracy:

What seriously shakes those of us who speak for our industry is the factor of the unknown entity. A monstrous agency with the ability arbitrarily to halt a project—at any stage and regardless of the investment. And at its helm, a "czar" with virtually no accountability for his or her enforcement of this broad-based mandate and no criteria to hold this powerful position.[36]

The initiative attacked industry by allowing the state to take ancient redwood stands by eminent domain, cutting carbon dioxide emissions, requiring secondary sewage treatment, giving fish and wildlife priority over agriculture in terms of water supply, banning chlorofluorocarbons in automobile air conditioners, prohibiting certain pesticides in agriculture, and requiring testing of imported food. This parade of horribles was a call to companies to educate their employees on the dangers of the initiative.

The good news was that the first California teacher manuals were set for teacher training in 1991. The California Mining Association was following the lead of the Nevada Mining Association and the Nevada Department of Mining in holding teacher conferences and putting money into training and scholarships for teachers and students.[37]

Even more disturbing were the efforts of Congress to go after other aspects of mining in addition to the sacred writ of 1872. The Lead Exposure Reduction Act of 1990 was another shot at the industry: "AMC and its member companies are very concerned over the potential for adverse consequences posed by this bill." John A. Knebel wrote a strongly worded letter to the Senate, indicating, "AMC is particularly concerned by any legislative approach that singles out lead, or any other substance, for special treatment where the overall legislative intent is to protect the public health from risks posed by toxic substances."[38] Just another shot over the bow, but the AMC took all such legislation seriously.

Even more seriously in September 1990 were the hearings on the Mineral Exploration and Development Act of 1990. David W. Delcour, the vice president of Amax Mineral Resources Company and chairman of the AMC Public Lands Committee, went to Capitol Hill and spoke against any change. First, the bill failed to include discovery as a basis for a mineral right on the public lands. Second, the requirement of up to $6,400 expended on a forty-acre claim was too expensive. Third, a new statute would breed litigation. Delcour declared that "one of the reasons the existing Mining Law works so well is the fact that practically every imaginable aspect of it has been interpreted by the courts" and a new statute would foster "litigation brought by those who seek to reduce sharply the availability of public lands for mineral development purposes."[39] Finally, the bill put too great a burden on the Department of the Interior to administer the program. The bottom line was that absolutely no change was needed and any change would cost the taxpayers dearly.

Another GAO report surfaced amid the turmoil focused on unauthorized activities on hard-rock claims. The GAO visited fifty-nine sites and found that thirty-three had "unauthorized residences, non-mining commercial operations, illegal activities or speculative activities." The GAO recommended a holding fee, and the Department of the Interior agreed with the approach. The U.S. Forest Service opposed the concept on the ground that a fee would not eliminate the abuse. Further, the Forest Service thought that enforcement of existing laws could eliminate the abusing claimants and their shacks. AMC agreed with the Forest Service on this one.[40]

Meanwhile, mining communities were moving away from the extractive industry. Idaho's "Silver Valley" was a "Superfund" site laced with arsenic, cadmium, lead, and other toxic materials dumped on the land by the smelters. Kellogg, Silverton, and Wallace, Idaho, had turned to tourism. Aspen, Colorado, was now a ski resort. Crested Butte, Colorado, had moved from coal-mining town to ski resort. Park City, Utah's, silver mining past was featured on postcards, and its present was as a resort city. The boom and bust of mining moved to mining museums, gondolas for tourists and skiers, and commemorative markers of mine disasters of the past for tourists to view.[41]

While tourists poured dollars into Idaho, Jack Lyman, the executive director of the Idaho Mining Association, was in Washington testifying regarding the Rahall bill. He warned that the bill would compromise "our ability to compete in world markets and to produce the raw materials which fuel the nation's economy." Further, a new law "would limit access to public lands for mineral exploration and would jeopardize the whole body of case law which establishes property rights under the law."[42]

The American Mining Congress representative also was testifying in Senate hearings against S. 1126 sponsored by Dale Bumpers of Arkansas. Stanley Dempsey, the chairman of Royal Gold, Inc., and a member of the AMC Public Lands Committee, argued against the 8 percent royalty rate on minerals. Rather than taxes, Dempsey urged the Senate Subcommittee on Mineral Resources Development and Production to focus on more exploration, more discoveries of strategic and critical materials, more jobs, and more national wealth. Dempsey concluded that "the present system of making hard minerals available as reward for discovery, and their development by individuals and firms operating in a free market system is working well and should be retained."[43] Dempsey's argument was absolutely congruent with the 140 years of no taxes on mining, particularly hard-rock mining.

William Tilden made the trek from California to Washington and reported on the House hearings. Ralph Nader was there and called the Mining Law of 1872 a "give away program" and recommended a leasing program. Nader opposed the bill because it did not go far enough. Tilden testified against the bill and the repeal of the Mining Law of 1872. The only thing he saw positive about it was the rental fee for claims. Rahall announced, at the end of the hearings, that "he would review and fine-tune the bill for introduction at the next Congress."[44] Round one went to the miners.

Meanwhile, the Bureau of Land Management had been busy. In 1990 the BLM announced a new policy of requiring mandatory reclamation bonds for exploration and mining operations. This $1,000 per acre exploration and $2,000 per acre mining bonding requirement would be in place during the current rule-making process. All existing operations had one year to comply, and cyanide operations had until January 1, 1992, to post their bonds.[45] Now it was reclamation by rule, not statute. The environment of mining law was changing.

The changing environment provoked thoughtful response. Mark Anderson, the president of the Northwest Mining Association, saw the Middle East crisis over oil as a catalyst for change because the public was aware of the need for a national energy policy. The Endangered Species Act had given the spotted owl icon status and locked up countless acres to the timber industry. This had caused many to see that a balance was needed, and from this awareness a new mineral policy might emerge. Anderson declared that

> we can't live without natural resources. Minerals are the building blocks of our society. Natural resources—those things that come from the ground—are the source of new wealth. We need to develop a government and public understanding that the

pipeline to mineral production will also create a panic if cut. We
need policy that will reach out twenty or fifty years to properly
plan for mineral supply. We need access to public lands, and
we need to know we will be able to operate with a reasonable
prospect of a profit.[46]

The significant theme of certainty in mining coupled with supply was
evident.

A September 8, 1990, conference in Bend, Oregon, looked to find
certainty in the interests of miners and government compliance agencies. The Oregon Department of Geology and Mineral Industries, the
Oregon Department of Environmental Quality, the Oregon Department
of Fish and Wildlife, the U.S. Forest Service, and the U.S. Bureau of
Land Management sponsored the conference. The Northwest Mining
Association was the private organization facilitating the planning of
the conference and helped to arrange for speakers. Keith Droste, the
director of acquisitions for FMC Gold Company in Denver, and Tom
Albanese, the chief operating officer of NERCO Mining Company, out-
lined the regulations as well as the costs of each step in the exploration, production, reclamation, and closure process. John Mitchell, the
chief economist for the Portland-based U.S. Bancorp, explained the
economic value of mining jobs in timber-dependent southeast Oregon.
A Northern Plains Resource Council member told the audience that
communities needed to organize before the first mining drill went into
the ground. John Fitzpatrick, the director of community and governmental affairs for Pegasus Gold Corporation, assured people that the
new mining companies were on the side of mitigation, community welfare, and jobs. Other speakers touched on a variety of topics, but the
idea of a "town hall" approach to dialogue on important issues facing
mining and the environment was evident.[47]

The concept of dialogue was not as clear at the American Mining
Congress 1990 annual convention in New Orleans. Milton Ward,
AMC chairman, declared that "there never has been a time when we
haven't had challenges in this changing world of mining, and if we're
going to make progress, we'll have to have change." The question was

the direction of that change. Charles F. Barber, the former chairman of Asarco Incorporated, saw two major challenges: access to public lands and environmental protection. The attack on the Mining Law of 1872, the "heart and soul" of hard-rock mining, was an attack on access. Environmental protection law was in place, and mining had responded, but environmentalists wanted to heap on new layers of regulations. Mining must work within the legal framework but improve its public image. "Honesty and credibility lie at the base of acceptability. Our greatest challenge is to communicate industry's role in the creation of wealth," Barber maintained.[48] More than compliance with law was required. Mining needed a public image, and it must educate the public regarding its role in society.

The atmosphere in Denver was quite different when Colorado Mining Association (CMA) members gathered. They were particularly angry about the proposed $100 per claim holding fee, labeling it a "regressive tax levied on claimholders without regard to the value of their claims." Even though the Senate Energy and Natural Resources Committee had considered the proposed fee and rejected it on a 9–9 vote, a CMA spokesperson told miners that it would find new life in the next Congress. Charles Melbye, the chairman of the CMA, wrote in a letter to the Colorado Congressional Delegation that the "small miners and junior exploration companies find most of the deposits in the U.S. and then bring them to major companies for development and mining." The $100 per claim was an "additional burden" the small miner could not bear. Further, the mining industry already paid its fair share to government through filing fees and special severance taxes. Instead of taxing the small miner to death, government should balance its budget with "a genuine downsizing of the federal government." New mining fees and royalty payments threatened the future of mining, Melbye maintained.[49] Alkali Ike was an endangered species if government imposed such a crushing burden.

If $100 looked devastating to hard-rock miners, Congress had something in store for the large and small air polluters alike. The *Wall Street Journal* announced that a clean air bill had passed a Congress anxious to get it on the books before Election Day in November 1990. "With a cost to industry of as much as $25 billion annually, the mammoth bill to clear the skies of smog, acid rain and toxic factory fumes has earned praise from both industry and environmental interests that have battled for a decade over reducing air pollution," the *Journal* declared.[50] Even the local dry cleaner and gas station operator, the Alkali Ikes of small business America, had to comply. Chlorofluorocarbon producers were on a hit list for extermination in the twenty-first century. The environment of business was changing to protect the air in America.

While environmentalists hailed the passage of the bill, Senator Alan Cranston's California Desert Protection Act bit the dust. Cranston withdrew the bill after withering fire from mining interests, the desert recreation folks, and the Department of Defense. Bill Tilden, the chairman of the Desert Conservation Institute, said, "It was not politicking. It was not partisan. The California Desert Protection Act was simply bad legislation." Tilden also indicated that the Desert Conservation Institute had asked the U.S. Bureau of Mines to conduct a study of the eight million acres Cranston wanted to lock up. The Bureau of Mines study found that S. 11/H.R. 780 would cost $2 billion to San Bernardino County alone as well as twenty-three hundred jobs and $620 million in personal earnings and taxes. The Department of Defense thought that the bill would lock up precious desert lands from future military training use. Regardless, Tilden warned that Cranston would be back in 1991 and "we must be ready to confront and defeat it."[51] As we remember from the Washington hearing on the Rahall bill, Tilden wore a different hat at the time. When the desert was at stake, Tilden was representing a desert institute.

The environmentalist attack in South Dakota took the initiative path, but this political solution failed. In 1990 voters gave the environmentalists "the third defeat of anti-mining initiatives in South Dakota in the last four years." James A. Anderson, the president and chief executive officer of MinVen Gold Corporation, said that "the defeat of the initiative is a significant vote of confidence by the public for the responsible mining practices now employed by the various companies" in South Dakota and "the regulatory authorities which help supervise the mining industry."[52] The combination of environmental compliance and public education seemed to be working.

Mining companies were solving environmental problems and reducing their exposure to regulatory sanction and public disdain. To eliminate wildlife deaths at its tailings pond, the McCoy/Cove Mine in Battle Mountain, Nevada, installed a new treatment plant necessitating a three-week shutdown and loss of gold production.[53] Wharf Resources solved one of its problems at South Dakota's largest heap leach gold-mining facility by using hydrogen peroxide and copper to neutralize spent ore and was experimenting with biological methods to similarly meet state standards. In addition, a 1989 environmental assessment mandated by the South Dakota legislature was in the process of evaluating environmental impact.[54] The Lincoln Project fifty miles east-southeast of Sacramento, California, was proceeding through the permit process and within environmental assessment regulatory parameters. The *Mining Record* reported that "early on, environmental considerations were recognized and the approach used in permitting, to minimize lead time and avoid duplication, involved a staged study which allows an Environmental Impact Statement to start as the underground test work is in process."[55] As a result the original Environmental Impact Statement could be updated as the final mining plan evolved. Simply, mining corporations were dealing with the new regulatory environment and continuing to mine with environmental considerations in mind.

This did not mean that the industry did not see demons lurking about in the land. Michael Doyle, the president of the Nevada Mining Association, declared the Environmental Protection Agency "the Witch of the East" for its attempt to label mine wastes as hazardous and requiring treatment. A report had recommended that hard-rock mining wastes be tested and disposed of under the Resource Conservation and Recovery Act, but with EPA jurisdiction. Jim Arnold, the chairman of the Nevada Mining Association Environmental Committee, told delegates to the Nevada Mining Association convention in Las Vegas that they were "in a battle for our lives."[56] The imagery was ironic because the yellow brick road only led back to Kansas.

Thomas S. Hendricks, from the neighboring state of Colorado, was in Washington, D.C., telling U.S. senators to leave the Mining Law of 1872 alone. Hendricks, the founder and owner of the Hendricks Mining

Company, also told senators that any royalty fee would put small miners out of business.[57]

Miners in Spokane at the Northwest Mining Association heard the same message. Richard J. Kehmeirer, the vice president of exploration for the Atlas Corporation, recommended unity, public education, and cash conservation. One of the challenges for small mining companies was that both environmental activists and miners needed cash to stay the course of environmental regulation. The Castle Mountain Mine of San Bernardino County, California, was cited for its three-million-dollar expenditure in the permit process.[58] Andrew Leach of Klohn Leonoff, Inc., told the convention faithful that "the mining industry is extremely responsive to environmental concerns and has made enormous strides in achieving environmental objectives, but meeting those objective will become more and more complex in the next decade." Leach singled out the Pegasus Gold Corporation operation at Anaconda, Montana, because of its "award-winning open pit gold operation." Pegasus "went out of their way to be sensitive to the environment." Further, "they were able to succeed despite the fact that the access road passed through an elk wintering ground." Pat Gochnour of the Brohm Mining Corporation of Deadwood, South Dakota, explained the permitting process and some innovative ways mining companies had approached the process. Gochnour observed that "I can remember 10 years ago when these issues didn't get much attention. Now, these sessions draw tremendous attendance."[59] Times and the environmental regulatory atmosphere had clearly changed the focus of miners.

Off the mining record, the voting public saw another mining industry. All of the testimony in Congress and public education put mining into the public eye, but not necessarily with the industry's spin. The *Los Angeles Times* ran a December 18, 1990, story entitled "You'll Find Welfare in Them Thar Hills." Daniel Akst wrote that the minerals-mining industry was "a business so addicted to government handouts that it apparently can barely lift a shovel without taxpayer help." Mining was "a mighty industry built on dazzling natural abundance and unbridled domestic growth. It was blessed with sweetheart legislation and enjoyed a degree of worldwide pre-eminence." The problem was that it "resisted innovation, relying instead on its ability to extract private profit at public expense, especially by ignoring the cost of the environmental degradation that it had a habit of leaving behind." The 1980s had pitched the industry into restructuring, but it had emerged "a scaled-down but profitable $30-billion-a-year business that seems to lack the will—and possibly the wherewithal—to invest in its own future." The Mining Law of 1872 was the foundation for this welfare mentality.

Efforts to change the Mining Law of 1872 had produced a great deal of data. "A group lobbying to change the law guesses" that "$4 billion a year" in mining revenue flowed from the public domain: "Even the American Mining Congress, the trade and lobbying group, admits that most known metallic mineral reserves in the West are on U.S. property." Regarding the bill of Senator Bumpers, the "8%-royalty plan," it "died in Congress." But it seemed to have life for the next session: "Agast, the industry says that exacting payment for the minerals will hurt the competitiveness of U.S. mining companies and that tampering with the law will let environmentalists change it somehow so they can tie the miners up in litigation." Akst offered that "no property owner in his right mind would buy that."

In context, Akst told the reading public that "before you get mad at the miners—and we're not talking about the odd grizzled prospector here, although they're also to blame—remember that the industry isn't unusually greedy in all this." Subsidized farmers, broadcasters, and homeowners were equally feeding at the public trough.[60]

The frontal attack on the Mining Law of 1872 stalled in Congress, and the mining industry was working to defeat the "Witch of the East" while accommodating environmental regulation just as the local dry cleaner was installing air pollution equipment. Twenty years after the first Earth Day, mining continued, but with an eye to permitting, Environmental Impact Statements, abatement, mitigation, and reclamation. It was a new vocabulary but one that miners acquired as a second language.

CHAPTER 14

THE CONTINUING ATTACK
ON THE MINING LAW OF 1872

Someone of theirs has died, perhaps

they have lost their jobs in the offices,

in the hospitals, in the elevators

in the mines,

human beings suffer stubbornly wounded

and there are protests and weeping everywhere:

while the stars flow within an endless river

there is much weeping at the windows,

the thresholds are worn away by the weeping,

the bedrooms are soaked by the weeping

that comes wave-shaped to bite the carpets.

—Pablo Neruda, "Ode to Federico Garcia Lorca"
in *The Poetry of Pablo Neruda* (2003)

The first round of congressional testimony on the repeal of the Mining Law of 1872, the imposition of royalties for mining on the public domain, and the California Desert Protection Act had gone to the mining lobby. Legislation was taken off the table, but 1991 was another year. The miners used persistence and the tear in the corner of Alkali Ike's eye to argue against change. Meanwhile the mining education program continued.

The Colorado Mining Association (CMA) was quick to get the ear of Secretary of the Interior Lujan. David R. Cole, the president of CMA, told Secretary Lujan that "an onerous burden is being placed on the mining industry by the Federal government through several requirements while at the same time some in Congress are proposing repeal of the Mining Law itself." Rahall's bill had been reintroduced, and the Bumpers bill was expected in the Senate with "a new royalty provision in addition to a ten-fold increase in holding fees for mining claims." Cole told Lujan that "the fee and royalty provisions applicable to public lands threaten both small and large mining and exploration companies." Further, "smaller miners account for a substantial share of exploration investment, while major companies provide the greatest share of production from the most efficient operations." Stephen D. Alfers, CMA counsel and chairman of the CMA Mining Law Review Committee, argued that with legislation "virtually eliminating private tenure of mineral lands, inhibiting project financing of public lands, adding exorbitant holding costs, and creating new expenses associated with administrative delays," miners would be deterred from looking for minerals on the public domain.[1] The miners wanted to get ahead of the legislation and make certain that their message was clear in administration minds.

The Environmental Protection Agency, which some called the "Witch of the East," was working on mine waste rules. The EPA announced that it was developing mine waste rules under the nonhazardous title of the Resource Conservation and Recovery Act, Subtitle D. The EPA program in its final form would be administered by state compliance agencies.[2]

Information increased apace. A study commissioned by the Utah Association of Counties saw light in the form of a Dr. George Leaming of the Western Economic Analysis Center of Marana, Arizona, report. In response to a bill to withdraw more land for wilderness, the report listed a parade of horribles. The withdrawal of 3.2 million acres of federal land in fourteen Utah counties would hurt hunters, families, children, the elderly, and the physically impaired. Cattle would be banned, and mining, prevented. Personal income would fall $1.75 billion, and 93,600 jobs would be lost. Sales would dive by $6.87 billion per year, and tax revenues would be off $595 million. The Wilderness

Impact Research Foundation thought the report understated the real economic impact.[3]

Round two of hearings on bills to repeal the Mining Law of 1872 opened in April 1991. Hearings on Rahall's H.R. 3866, the "Mineral Exploration and Development Act of 1990," were held in Denver and Reno. Bill Tilden, the chairman of the California Mining Association's Lands and Minerals Committee, thought that the bill was a particular threat to California because of the state's status as the nation's leading producer in the area of industrial commodities.[4] The California Mining Association (CMA) also awarded reclamation excellence prizes in three categories: "Excellence in Reclamation Best Reclamation, Best Second Use of Mined Land and Reclamation Revegetative Plan." The awarded were to showcase innovative and effective reclamation plans. Viceroy Gold Corporation's Castle Mountain Project won the "Best Reclamation" award.[5] The CMA annual meeting made two themes clear. First, opposition to any changes in the Mining Law of 1872 was fixed in the matrix of rhetoric. The rhetoric focused on industrial metals and materials rather than California's number one mining interest—*gold*. Second, the CMA recognized that the environmental movement was a fixture of mining and that miners needed models. Viceroy's rerouting of a road to spare the California desert tortoise, waterfowl protection at the cyanide ponds, and revegetation were clear signals that affirmative environmental responses were now part of mining. The revegetation plan of Teichert Aggregates–Coors/Fong and Muller was even more indicative of where the industry was moving. Without prompting, an aggregates company had offered to revegetate Cache Creek and had gone to the Audubon Society and other environmental protection organizations with the plan. The result was that when it went to the county board of supervisors with the plan, the Audubon Society and a past president of the Sierra Club testified in favor of the plan. Randy Sater of Teichert Aggregates put it simply: "We saw no reason why not to proceed. It was an opportunity for mining to do something positive for the creek."[6] California mining had come a long way indeed from the days of hydraulic mining dumping millions of tons of aggregates into California's watercourses.

When the Reno hearings opened, the "People for the West" rallied for the Mining Law of 1872 and against the Rahall bill. Bob Filler, the general manager of the Gold Fields' Mesquite Mine, told *California Mining* that the Mining Law of 1872 was critical for the exploration of the public domain by risk takers like Dick and Anna Singer, the prospectors who convinced Gold Fields of the value of their claim. Without the claims and patenting features of the Mining Law of 1872, the Singer family and Gold Fields would never have been able to open the Mesquite Mine, and its million ounces of gold would have remain locked up in the ground.[7] *California Mining* also announced that the first Minerals Education Conference was slated for August on the campus of California State University, Sacramento.[8] On the education front, Gold Fields held an open house at the Mesquite Mine in conjunction with the hearings and drew two thousand visitors. One feature of the mine tour was the "Overlook Trail," a cooperative venture of Gold Fields and the Bureau of Land Management.[9] Opposition and education again were linked. Cooperation with federal agencies was as clear as the trail and overlook plaque telling visitors of the splendor of the desert.

Despite the threat in Washington, California gold miners were doing well. The BLM reported that 1990 gold production was up 47 percent over 1989 production. Gold miners paid $45,040,000 in mineral lease and permit fees of the $51,415,000 total of 1990. BLM forked over half of that to the state and $10.6 million to California counties. In addition, major environmental protection measures were in the works or in place.[10] The facts demonstrated that mining was paying its fair share.

John Colvin, the manager of corporate lands for U.S. Borax and Chemical Corporation, was testifying against the Rahall bill. He told *California Mining* that the "industry's position was effectively packaged" and "clearly described the results on public lands should the legislation pass." Colvin told the House Subcommittee on Mining and Natural Resources that Rahall's excessive rental and diligence fees would discourage small miners. Further, the bill did not contain secure land tenure or guaranteed access provisions, eliminated the right of self-initiation in the claim process, and gave administrative agencies too much discretion. Colvin said, "The bill ignores completely the mineral discovery requirement of the present Mining Law, which is the backbone of the self-initiation concept for mineral exploration and development on federal lands." Further, the Mining Law of 1872 was "proven and enhanced by over 100 years of case law and administrative action." Colvin conceded that the Mining Law of 1872 was increasingly under attack, but he understood that proponents were conceding that there was not much hope of passing the bill this year "but they are looking toward next year."[11] Again, the themes were clear. Alkali Ike would be out of business. Mining had no certainty without the discovery, claim, and patent triangle. Any change in the Mining Law of 1872 would throw case law out the window. Miners would take their business to foreign countries.

Education continued in Sacramento, with 118 teachers crowding into classrooms to learn about mining. Teachers wrote evaluations at the end of the conference and wanted more next year. One wrote, "Critics and environmentalists have a lot to say about the destructive forces going on in mining. I think this is your turn to shine." Teachers learned how to pan gold and took a daylong tour of Homestake's McLaughlin Mine conducted by Ray Krauss, the environmental director. The message was now planted. Whether it would germinate in the public schools remained to be seen.[12]

While mineral education spread, the BLM was drafting rules for cyanide operations, known as the "Cyanide Management Plan." The BLM was in the administrative law pipeline. The rules required the "best management practices" for biological risks, hydrology, leach pads, liners for leach pads and tailings piles, wildlife protection, monitoring, and reporting. Reclamation bonding was required for all cyanide facilities on public lands.[13] The regulatory regime continued to deal with gold-mining operations despite the gridlock in hearings on the Mining Law of 1872.

Miners also were working to stop bills dealing with desert lands. Fears that the East Mojave Desert would become a national monument, off-limits to mining, spurred "non-stop appointments and briefings" with members of Congress and their staff. It was another flank attack on mining, but the industry counterattack was organized.[14] With the lobby going great guns in the halls of Congress, the public spent more time wondering about the impact of the Gulf War and taxes.

California's budget woes turned Governor Pete Wilson to the sales tax, and Nevada wondered whether the gambling tax could sustain government's insatiable appetite for revenue. Nevada was in the midst of a gold-mining boom in 1991, producing 50.9 percent of U.S. gold, but more was needed to fill the coffers of government. The *Wall Street Journal* suggested that "Nevada's future prosperity, once gambling cools off, may rest on maintaining an environment that fosters private-sector expansion. Some believe this entails public expenditures such as the mining program at the University of Nevada–Reno."[15] Those gold dollars BLM reported in California would be doubly welcome in Nevada.

In 1990 Thomas Hendricks was in Washington telling lawmakers to keep their hands off the Mining Law of 1872. In September 1991 he was the subject of a *Wall Street Journal* story. Tom was a "bearded, soft-spoken 42-year old" who operated the Cross Gold Mine at the 9,700-foot level. Tom had dropped out of the University of Colorado to pursue his boyhood dream of searching for gold. He started the quest in 1971, "but the world he knew is disappearing." Many of the mining companies were now in the hands of "big foreign companies." Further, "environmental legislation has raised the hurdles for mining." Tom was Alkali Ike, but in the high country rather than the Arizona desert.

The future was clouded. "The last straw for Mr. Hendricks and the few others like him may be a bill now pending before Congress that could drastically change the cost structure of mining in the U.S. The Mining Law of 1872" was under assault: "The law has almost always had critics who thought that that was far too sweet a deal. And as the benefits started flowing to larger and larger companies over the years, the criticism reached a claims." U.S. Senator from Colorado Ben Nighthorse Campbell, a long-term supporter of mining, said, "They get the gold, and we get the shaft." Further, the abuses, including holding up the government to prevent mining, were now very public. The Rahall and Bumpers bills now in Congress targeted the abuses and the free lunch mining had enjoyed for over a century.

The passage of a bill ending the old mining system "could mean the end of the line for Mr. Hendricks and his kind, the lone-wolf prospectors who were so much a part of the lore of the West." Hans Von Michaelis, a Denver mining consultant, saw a bigger picture: "In America today, the farther away you get from where the real work is done, the more money you make. Tom is trying to buck that trend." Phillip Burgess, the president of the Center for the New West in Denver, said that "the mining industry has gone through a metamorphosis from low-tech to high-tech industry, and that means more production with fewer people. From an economic point of view, that's a success story. But it's a disaster from a political point of view because there are fewer people with a stake in the industry."[16] Burgess perhaps counted the eight hundred who rallied in Reno in 1991 rather than the eighty thousand in the mines of Butte in the nineteenth century.

The fight against mining law change and the California Desert Protection Act continued.[17] Hearings on the California Desert Protection Act drew plenty of testimony, and opponents dressed in "STOP S. 21" T-shirts.[18] In 1992 compromise legislation was also on the table in hearings in Washington, D.C.[19] By fall 1992 the legislative process was whittling away at the Bumpers bill.[20] John A. Knebel, the president of the American Mining Congress, announced that the amendments "represent a significant change in the Mining Law." The American Mining Congress supported the change, and Knebel thanked supporters. Senators Harry Reid of Nevada and Pete Domenici of New Mexico had offered amendments that required payment of fair market value for the land surface when receiving a patent and reversion of land title for patented mining claims if any unauthorized or unapproved use takes place. Self-initiation was safe. Another amendment required that all lands patented after the date of enactment be subject to federal reclamation standards. The long-sacred $100 annual assessment work fell to a $100 annual fee per claim. Senator Dale Bumpers tried to have the Senate delete the amendments but lost on a 52–44 vote. Bumpers also lost on a one-year moratorium on issuing or even processing patents to mining claims. Nick Rahall's 1991 bill was now the Mineral Exploration Act of 1992, and it made it out of the House Interior and Insular Affairs Committee.[21] While the mining industry was educating Congress, the second annual Mineral Education Conference drew ninety-five teachers from around California for further enlightenment.[22] Procedural barriers slowed Senator Alan Cranston's California Desert Protection Act in the Senate.[23] Mining's political allies were helping the cause.

Partisan politics were paying off. Cranston's Desert Protection Act died in committee. *California Mining* thanked Republican Senator John Seymour for playing "a major role in blocking action on the Desert Protection Act." Senator Seymour announced that "real men and women live in the desert. They work there, raise their families there, and they matter. Senator Cranston sold them out and Mrs. Feinstein would do the same." Feinstein was challenging Seymour in the next election, and Congresswoman Barbara Boxer was running for Cranston's soon vacant seat.[24] Although miners could be jubilant about the demise of the Cranston Bill, the BLM was proposing stricter rules for the non-mining use of unpatented claims.[25] Republican Senator Larry Craig of Idaho put S. 755 into the legislative pipeline representing a mining industry approach to reform.[26] The legislative process was the inertia the industry needed.

Yet the administrative process was slowing mining and was growing in complexity. In February 1992 Manhattan Mineral applied for an exploration permit on its patented claims in the Sweet Grass Hills of Montana. The BLM received the application for permit and a storm of protest. A coalition of American Indians, ranchers, environmentalists, and historic preservationists pushed the BLM into an extensive study of the area. The protest expanded to demands that the Department of the Interior keep leaseholder miners out of the area as well. It turned out that the area was a spiritual area for several tribes, contained an archaeological site of great interest, and drained onto and into surface and groundwater sources for ranchers. BLM told Manhattan Mineral that it needed an Environmental Impact Statement simply to explore its property. Such a requirement may have been a first for the BLM. For Curly Bear Wagner of the Blackfeet Nation, it was a way to stop the desecration of a sacred shrine.[27] American Indians were also in Congress asking for amendments to the American Indian Religious

Freedom Act of 1978 to give them power to stop such trampling on sacred sites.[28]

In Congress now U.S. Senator Diane Feinstein reintroduced S. 21, the California Desert Protection Act, with revisions including the removal of a 31,000-acre tract owned by Viceroy Resources to allow it to continue its gold-mining operations. Bill Tilden wanted a properly structured bill, and Margaret Allender said, "We had hoped she would be more responsive to working toward a consensus, but she was direct in saying the bill was an election mandate and a campaign pledge. She also said she was interested in hearing about well-documented issues and proposals."[29] Both were part of an institute fostering education regarding California mining.

Education was a dangerous thing. In the same issue of *California Mining* that reported on the meeting with Senator Feinstein, a report on the Sacramento River cleanup plan unveiled an EPA $54 million plan to reduce the flow from the Iron Mountain Mine into the Sacramento River. As usual, "the EPA Superfund may help pay for the corrective action, but possible court action could require prior owners, including ICI (ICI Americas, formerly the Staufer Chemical Company), to pay all or part of the costs."[30] The *Los Angeles Times* saw a "witches' brew of acid waste, copper, zinc, cadmium, and other chemicals." This was in a "surreal world of Iron Mountain, creeks run a brilliant red, sterile from high doses of heavy metals. Dark-green water, as caustic as battery acid, pours from underground caverns and poisoned springs bubble up from the ground as if from a steaming caldron." It was "the largest toxic waste site in the West, responsible for killing hundreds of thousands of fish, depleting one of the state's most important fisheries and posing a threat to the state's water supply in the Sacramento River." It was not a new problem: "Dating back to 1899, there have been countless fish kills in the river below Iron Mountain." The booming copper town of Keswick also had a smelter that "destroyed the vegetation for miles around." The environmental damage resulted in a federal court injunction shutting down the smelter in 1907. Yet mining continued: "The miners dug huge caverns inside the mountain, some of them large enough to hold a 20-story office building. Before mining operations were halted in 1963, they also cut off the top of the mountain, leaving a large crater at the summit." That crater and those tunnels produced the environmental disaster. The EPA Superfund response was "an interim plan, designed to prevent a major spill during the next 30 years and buy time for scientists to come up with a more permanent solution." Ted Arman, the president of Iron Mountain Mines, Inc., told the miner's side of the story. He objected to the whole idea and told the *Los Angeles Times* that the government should ignore the cleanup work and allow the resumption of mining. "It is not an environmental hazard," Arman said: "That has been propagated by the state, the EPA and everyone else. . . . They made up a big thing about fish kills. It's not true about fish kills."[31] The Wicked Witch of the West ran red and green into the waters of the West. Demogorgon was at work.

Miners now asked Washington for a balanced approach to legislation. California miners went to State Department of Conservation Director Ed Heidig with their concerns about the Feinstein bill. Comprehensive review of the desert area was under way to get at the facts of the matter.[32] The California Mining Association appealed to President Clinton for a balanced approach to land management.[33] Five women joined a forty-four-member delegation of miners who went to Washington to lobby against the Rehall and Bumpers bills. Donna Rollar, a blaster and drill operator at the Mesquite Mine, and Helen Warwick, a mining engineer for Gold Fields' Mesquite Mine, also made their position clear to Senator Feinstein's office regarding the California Desert Protection Act.[34]

While mining women lobbied against locking up the desert to mining, American Indians and environmental interest groups found common ground against the expansion of the Pegasus gold mine in the Little Rockies. Pegasus Gold, Inc., a Canadian company, had been in the Little Rockies north of the Missouri River in central Montana since 1979. In 1993 they wanted to expand their operation from four hundred to one thousand acres. The Assiniboine and Gros Ventre tribes considered the Little Rockies a sacred site, and the mined area drained through the Fort Belknap Reservation. Issues of American Indian religious sites and water quality merged when BLM test wells detected increased acidity.

Environmentalists and tribal leaders had lost an attempt to halt expansion of the mine in 1990, but now there was evidence of sulfide pollution. The Mineral Policy Center and Red Thunder, Inc., were now linked in opposition to further expansion. John Fitzpatrick, a Pegasus representative, told a Montana State Senate committee that the expansion did not affect any tribal sacred sites and told the *High Country News* that the Mineral Policy Center merely existed "to repeal the 1872 Mining Law." Virgil McConnell Sr., a tribal elder, asked the company and BLM "to hold off until a full cultural survey is done. Otherwise, Pegasus will just pay somebody to come in and say nothing's there."[35] The concept of a negative declaration was creeping into the discourse over environmental compliance.

Gender also was on the agenda. The "Women in Mining" group that lobbied Congress against the Bumpers and Rahall bills was the first wave. California Mining Association President Carolyn Clark led a "fast-paced information blitz" in Washington. Clark found legislators clearly impressed by the first wave. She observed that "mining has the image of a male, two-piece blue suit type raping the land." Now "for the first time, legislators heard from women working at mine operations who were paid well to drive trucks and could support their children on what they earned." These women "were real people who got their attention. The CEO's brought another point of view. It was a perfect complement."[36] The "blitz" had rolled out surprise weapons.

The blitz in Washington paralleled a slower offensive offshore. The *Wall Street Journal* noted that U.S. mining corporations were moving south and finding that permits to mine took a day compared with the months or years in the States. "As existing mines play out, the companies are leaving the U.S. with the blessing, if not open encouragement, of the Clinton administration and Congress, which are proposing even stiffer environmental regulations and new royalties on metals on public lands," the *Journal* reported. Looking at the situation in Washington state and Bolivia, the environmental record was quite a contrast. Environmental groups stalled exploration and mining at every turn in Washington, but in Bolivia mining corporations were lauded for their environmental record. Philip Hocker, the president of the Mineral

Policy Center, agreed that the big U.S. and Canadian companies generally followed good environmental practices abroad. Yet he remained
"skeptical of smaller companies, especially those with bad environmental records in the U.S."[37]

Those pesky polluting prospectors and their small company succes-
sors grew larger in the discourse over mining law reform. The Mineral
Policy Center released its "Burden of Gilt" report outlining a century of
environmental damage caused by mining. The Mineral Resource Alliance
piggybacked on a news conference called by California Congressman
George Miller and Mineral Policy Center President Phi Hocker in
Washington, D.C. The alliance offered a rebuttal focused on present
environmental records of mining company stewardship and potential
lost jobs. In the last analysis, the alliance favored "environmentally sensitive and responsible mining operations and consistent enforcement of
regulations."[38] The discourse now included balanced enforcement in a
regulatory world.

On July 17, 1993, tribal leaders joined environmentalists from the
Mineral Policy Center and the Montana Environmental Information
Center in a four-mile walk to demonstrate against the Pegasus Gold
Mine expansion. The Fort Belknap Reservation representatives
included Red Thunder and Island Mountain Protectors. Three Indian
spiritual leaders offered prayers and spoke with television and local
newspaper media. Keeper of the Gros Ventre Flat Pipe said that the
miners "don't realize what they are doing. They are hollow men."[39] The
spirits of the mountains did not move the miners, but the Indians and
environmentalists hoped an Environmental Impact Statement would
halt their movement.

News of mining disasters past and present dotted the western news.
The Crystal River of Colorado ran black from time to time because of
coal mining.[40] A million tons of arsenic- and lead-laden tailings graced
Triumph, Idaho, bringing out a Superfund designation.[41] Awareness
increased as mining reform measures inched through Congress.

By autumn the California Desert Protection Act had moved
through the Senate Energy and Natural Resources Committee with
eleven changes. Yet Bill Tilden, the chairman of the Desert Conservation

Institute, expressed disappointment that the recommendations of reducing the protected acreage by six hundred thousand acres were rejected in favor of a mere thirty thousand acres. Tilden maintained that the mining industry did not oppose desert protection. Rather, it wanted a balanced approach with environmental and economic factors protected.[42]

While lobbyists were working their magic in Washington, miners on the ground were painting a new picture of Alkali Ike. Congress had changed the mandatory annual work assessment into a $100 per claim rental fee administered by the BLM. August 31, 1993, was the deadline for paying the fee. By the fall, the numbers were in, and the claims now abandoned were astounding except to miners. Nevada claim holders abandoned 140,000 claims. In Idaho twenty-six thousand of fifty-seven thousand claims fell to nonpayment. In sum, 480,000 of about one million claims were now open for location by others.[43] Reaction to the deflation of claims was mixed. Bill Mote, the executive director of the Northwest Mining Association, saw "serious mining shortages in the future." Patricia Holmberg, the president of the Independent Miners' Association, offered that "the reform is a disaster for small miners." Despite the fact that the law exempts miners with fewer than ten claims, Holmberg said that small miners held more than ten claims and it was simply a matter of "whether a family is going to have food on the table." Glenn Miller, a professor of environmental and resource sciences at the University of Nevada, Reno, thought the fee was "a good first step." He offered that "miners have always had an unbelievable free ride: free administration, free land, free minerals. If the land is worth anything to them, they should be willing to pay the fee."[44] Elden Hughes of the San Francisco Sierra Club e-mailed Rose Strickland and others in November 1992, observing that "Robert Sanregret, Exec. Dir. Of National Assoc. of Mining Districts . . . [his] statement is a very candid admission that the $100 assessment work was never being done."[45] Common knowledge in some quarters was public knowledge as the locations were again public lands. If miners would pay the $100 fee, perhaps they would pay a royalty.

The royalty loomed larger when the House of Representatives voted 316–108 on the Rahall bill. That bill called for an 8 percent royalty on the gross production of mines, abolished the patenting of claims, created reclamation standards, and gave administrative agencies the power to declare portions of public lands off-limits based on suitability for mining. The bill went to a House–Senate Conference Committee to reconcile differences with a Senate bill calling for a 2 percent royalty on net profits, continued patenting at market prices, and a reclamation fund for abandoned mines.[46]

Eight western governors called for "reasonable and fair" mining law reform in 1994. The American Mining Congress thought the Rahall bill would have a "devastating impact" on mining and supported Larry Craig's Senate bill. An economic study of both bills projected the loss of forty-nine hundred jobs under the Senate version and a massive loss of forty-four thousand jobs under the House bill. The economic loss in the twelve western states was $129 million versus $1.2 billion in lost wages.[47] U.S. Senator Harry Reid of Nevada sat on the Conference Committee and worked to dispel myths about hard-rock mining. Mining paid its fair share of taxes without any reform. Only three-tenths of 1 percent of public lands had been patented. Finally, "companies adhere to stringent reclamation and resource protection laws." Reid anticipated that 1994 would be a year of decision on mining law and the issues would be resolved "once and for all this year."[48]

Meanwhile, concerns about mining pollution of various kinds continued to surface. The Peabody Western Coal Company was suspected of drying up the Moenkopi Wash on the Hopi Reservation in Arizona.[49] Kennecott Copper's Brigham Canyon Mine in Utah was producing $400–600 million in profits but was slated for the Superfund because of massive environmental pollution caused by its copper-mining and smelting operations. Kennecott was spending about $80 million per year to clean up past pollution and contain present groundwater pollution.[50] Gold mines in northeastern Nevada were sucking the aquifer dry, and the BLM was working with companies to mitigate problems.[51] The Andalex Resources Company proposed a massive coal mine on Utah's Kaiparowits Plateau trucking seven tons per day out through the Glen Canyon National Recreation Area, the Paiute Reservation, and Cedar City.[52] Montana's Golden Sunlight Mine spilled forty-five tons of

arsenic-laden slurry. Golden Sunlight spokesman Paul Dale specu-
lated that it happened "sometime last fall or this spring." The spill was
discovered by state and federal inspectors on June 20, 1994, and they
cited the company for not reporting the spill.[53] Open-pit gold-mining
operations created "destroyed habitat, fouled streams, de-watered
aquifers and horizon lines rebuilt as tailings piles."[54] Atlantic Richfield
Company and the state of Montana were busy under the Superfund
cleaning up mine wastes and tailings piles in Anaconda.[55] The Northern
Plains Resource Council took out a full-page advertisement in Helena,
Montana's, *Independent Record* entitled "Poisoning Montana's Precious
Water: Porkbarrel Senator Burns Will Inflict 1872 Mining Disaster on
Montana Taxpayers!"[56] The proposed New World Mine near Yellowstone
Park, the Seven-Up Pete Joint Venture near Lincoln, and the Zortman-
Landusky Mine in north-central Montana all posed potential envi-
ronmental disasters.[57] The *New York Times*, the Greater Yellowstone
Coalition, Yellowstone Park personnel, and the Montana Environmental
Information Center (MEIC) all opposed the proposed mine operation
because, as Jim Jensen of the MEIC put it, "the proposal by Crown Butte
is so unrealistic, puts that whole area in such risk from the tailings pond,
that no rational person would allow them to mine there."[58] The Phelps
Dodge Mining Company and Canyon Resources Corporation joint
venture near Lincoln, Montana, posed the threat of an environmental
disaster for the Blackfoot River.[59] A Colorado jury awarded Globeville
residents $28 million for 106 years of cadmium pollution. Asarco, Inc.,
filed a notice of appeal, and Macon Cowles, attorney for the 567 residents,
commented that "it never ceases to amaze me how Asarco goes to the
wall on every single issue to avoid cleaning up the neighborhood. They
could have settled this case for a fraction of what it's ending up costing
them."[60] Meanwhile in Butte, Montana, the Superfund spending to clean
up put millions of dollars into the economy and cut unemployment by
almost 14 percent. The cleanup was a "multi-generational" affair because
Butte's pollution was "massive."[61] Mining interests and environmentalists
continued to push the agenda for reform and regulation in print.

In Washington the political process continued. The *Wall Street
Journal* questioned the need for reform and argued that "privatizing the

vast federal tracts in the West is nearly always a good thing."[62] Conference Committee inertia became evident. On September 30, 1994, the *Independent Record* declared that "mining reform is dead." Senator Bennett Johnston of Louisiana said that "he no longer has hopes for a bill acceptable to mining interests and Western Senators." Johnston noted that he had gained the support of American Barrick, but the mining lobby put "tremendous pressure" on the mining company to retreat. Representative George Miller of California "accused the mining companies of stonewalling and pressuring Western senators into opposing whatever bill came out of the discussions." Jack Gerard, speaking for the Mineral Resources Alliance, demurred, telling reporters that the mining industry wanted a reform law in 1994 but was unwilling to accept some provisions of the proposed law.[63] The *High Country News* also passed the news on to its environmentally sensitive readers, quoting Nevada Senator Harry Reid saying, "It's dead." The *News* blamed the mining companies in Nevada for Reid caving "in to them." Politics in the West were at stake, and the Democrats did not want Republicans to state that Democrats had declared war on western jobs.[64] Superfund reform measures suffered the same fate.[65] The Mining Law of 1872 and the mining lobby stood the test of politics.

Yet, while the celebrations continued in mining organizations, the Senate on April 13, 1994, sent the California Desert Protection Act to the House on a vote of 69–29. The House sent it to President Clinton's desk for signature. The law designated 3.5 million acres of the California desert as wilderness under the administrative authority of the Bureau of Land Management. It also added 1.2 million acres to the Death Valley National Monument and designated it a national park. The law created a 1.4-million-acre Mojave National Preserve and designated Death Valley, Joshua Tree, and Mojave as national park wilderness in addition to transferring 20,500 acres of BLM land to California for the expansion of the Red Rock Canyon State Park. The *Los Angeles Daily News* reported that "the desert bill was unique from some previous wilderness legislation in that it does not prohibit all mining."[66] This sounded like good news to mining interests, but there was more. The act recognized preexisting claims in the desert, "but before digging can begin, mining companies must show there are abundant deposits below the surface. Even if there are, mining companies will be prohibited from using any mechanized equipment to extract ore."[67] Mining sources noted that mining was now on a pick, shovel, and mule basis. Alkali Ike was now the only reality to mine in a wilderness area under the law. The Sierra Club celebrated the passage of the law: "When President Clinton signed the [California Desert Protection Act] into law on Halloween, the event crowned a legislative struggle that began in 1986, the year the Sierra Club persuaded California Senator Alan Cranston to introduce the bill."[68] The triumph for the Sierra Club was even greater because the great pumpkin was now joined with the Witch of the East.

The Mining Law of 1872 survived a genuine attempt at change, but the mining industry was under further pressure to change its ways. The regulatory regime, the sacred places movement, and litigation even outside the parameters of the Mining Law of 1872 were closing in on the mining companies. In Wisconsin, we will see how they came together.

CHAPTER 15

BADGER STATE BATTLE FOR MINING

The sole true Something—This! In Limbo's Den

It frightens Ghosts, as here Ghosts frighten men.

Thence cross'd unseiz'd—and shall some fated hour

Be pulverise by Demogorgon's power,

And given as poison to annihilated souls—

Even now it shrinks them—they shrink in as Moles

(Nature's mute monks, live mandrakes of the ground)

Creep back from Light—then listen for its sound;—

See but to dread, and dread they know not why—

The natural alien of their negative eye.

—Samuel Taylor Coleridge, "Limbo"
in *The Poems of Samuel Taylor Coleridge* (1961)

In 1990 an Environmental Impact Statement regarding the development of a mine near Ladysmith, Wisconsin, started a movement against mining in the state that ended in the purchase of a mine by the American Indian tribes most affected by the venture. The thirty-two-acre open-pit operation seemed innocent enough, disturbing a mere 181 acres, but when the tribes, wildlife interest organizations, the state legislature and governor, the Sierra Club and Earth First, and the media were involved, the mine was hardly innocent. The mining company tried to educate the public and the legislature. The tribes and their allies did the same. The process brought to the surface all of the problems with mining and faced by the mining industry. This was not a fight with the Mining

Law of 1872 or any mythical miner. This was a fight over mining itself and the reach of the regulatory regime, the power of sacred places, and the place of state agencies, particularly the legislature, in the matrix that had become the mining enterprise in the late twentieth century.[1]

The Flambeau Mining Company, a wholly owned subsidiary of the Kennecott Corporation, wanted to extract copper and gold from a deposit it owned. The open pit was projected to be thirty-two acres and would be 140 feet from the Flambeau River, a trout stream of regional note. The ore crush was to be thirteen hundred tons per day and shipped out of state. Low-sulfur waste rock was destined for a forty-acre waste pile north of the pit. High-sulfur waste rock had a twenty-seven-acre lined stockpile to call home. A wastewater treatment plant with an eight hundred-gallons-per-minute capacity stood ready to treat runoff and groundwater inflow of the stockpiles. If the heavens should open, the pit was the destination for any deluge. Six years after the pit yielded its bounty, the mining company was to move all the glacial overburden and soils back to their prior place and replant the area in grasses and trees. A 7.5-acre wetland would emerge at the end of the reclaimed pit, and all would be well in Ladysmith. The employment picture enhanced by mine construction and mine operations would return to the usual depressing profile, but town coffers would now be filled with tax money from the mine and its employees. So said the Final Environmental Impact Statement of 184 pages.[2] The reclaimed mine would be so much a part of nature that it hardly stood a chance of becoming part of the travel page or the Wisconsin Tour of Mines.[3]

The Flambeau Mine did not escape the notice of environmentalists. Flambeau Summer organized a July protest that attracted over four hundred people, with thirty occupying the mining ground. Police moved in and arrested demonstrators.[4] Two days later the Flambeau Mining Company started a fencing project, and Flambeau Summer was meeting in Ladysmith to plan its next move.[5] Flambeau Summer requested a supplemental environmental review of the project and moved demonstrators into the path of the fence project. Arrests again followed. The chairman of the Lac Courte Oreilles Wisconsin Chippewa Band asked for a supplemental Environmental Impact Statement (EIS) based on the endangered and threatened species on the site. Chairman Gaiashkibos further demanded that all licenses and permits by suspended while the review was conducted.[6] The state denied the request to suspend the licenses and permits but promised to consider a revised EIS. Chairman Gaiashkibos met the denial with a statement that three endangered species had been discovered on the site since the permits had been issued early in 1991. The species were the purple warty-back clam, the bullhead clam, and the snake-tailed dragonfly.[7] On July 12, 1991, Governor Tommy Thompson vetoed a bill that would have banned mining in state forests, parks, and other lands managed by the Department of Natural Resources. Thompson thought that there were circumstances where mining could go forward. Representative Spencer Black of Madison, the chairman of the Assembly Natural Resources Committee, commented that "as a result of this veto, it would be legal to mine in the Chippewa Flowage."[8] The political lines were scratched under the capitol dome in Madison. Democrats demanded a mining ban, and the Republican governor said no.

The public pattern was set. Protesters camped out at the doorstep of the office of the Department of Natural Resources and at the mine site.[9] Mining companies spent money for lobbyists and media advertisements. Spencer Black commented that "this is typical of environmental battles. They're trying to spend a lot of money to be able to mine with weak environmental regulations."[10] On August 2, 1991, the Department of Natural Resources decided to order a supplemental EIS but did not halt preliminary work at the Ladysmith site. The Sierra Club saw this as a ploy in light of the Sierra Club–Chippewa Band lawsuit filed in Dane County.[11] Dane County Circuit Court Judge George Northrup enjoined work at the site on August 29, 1991, because of its probable impact on endangered species on the site and in the Flambeau River.[12] The company appealed.[13] Flambeau Mining told the press that the injunction would cost the area fifty jobs. Roscoe Churchill of Ladysmith, an opponent of the mine, regretted the loss of jobs but opined that "I don't see this as a big boon if the price is the Flambeau River."[14] Meanwhile, the legislature was blasting studies that found economic benefits flowing from mining and passing bills to deny mining permits to companies or operations convicted of more than one felony involving environmental violations.[15]

The administrative process ground along, and in 1993 the Flambeau Mine opened for business. All the studies were in, and the permits, issued. Yet Roscoe Churchill said, "I've looked at a lot of sulfide mines. If this is going to be environmentally safe, then it's going to make history—because there has never been a safe sulfide mine." Further, "to put this in an unlined pit 50 steps from the Flambeau River . . . is insane."[16] Meanwhile, the legislature was busy with mining bills "aimed squarely at the Kennecott mine in northern Wisconsin."[17]

Despite the protests and in light of the success of the Ladysmith mine, Exxon Coal and Minerals joined with Rio Algom, Ltd., of Canada in a joint venture entitled the Crandon Mining Company to open a zinc and copper mine nine miles southwest of Crandon. The Sierra Club promised a "good fight" over the mine.[18] American Indian tribes quickly joined the fight. Chairman Gaiashkibos thought that Rio Algom brought a poor reputation to Wisconsin based on its environmental damage in Canada. Tom Maulson, Lac du Flambeau Chippewa chairman, said that "our elders tell us that when our grandfathers ceded these lands to the U.S., it was our understanding that we were allowing our mother (earth) to be disturbed only as deep as the plow could turn over." Arlyn Ackley, the chair of the Mole Lake Sokaogon Chippewa, told the press that Exxon and Rio Algom "demonstrated their arrogance" by announcing their mining plans without consulting the tribes.[19] The writing again was on the wall.

American Indians and sports fishing organizations joined in opposition. Other environmental interest groups quickly added their voices in opposition. The tribes and the sports fishing groups were recent enemies over spearfishing but now saw the Wolf River as sacred for different reasons.[20] The filing of notice to seek permits in February 1994 started the administrative process.[21] On March 14, 1994, members of many Wisconsin tribes demonstrated at the state capitol building in Madison. The Gray Panthers, Greenpeace, the American Indian Movement, the Watershed Alliance toward Environmental Responsibility, and other groups joined in the demonstration. The sound of drumming and traditional "honor songs" could be heard throughout the capitol square area as the demonstrators marched down Webster Street to Department of Natural Resources (DNR) headquarters.[22] In April the "Exxon mine" was on the agenda of the statewide Conservation Congress.[23] The Conservation Congress, normally a hunting and fishing interest organization, voted overwhelmingly in favor of tight environmental restrictions on mining.[24] The Menominee and Oneida tribes pledged support of mining opposition. Oneida Tribal Chairwoman Deborah Doxtator said that "the acid mining issue is the most detrimental to the next seven generations. We are always looking to the future, to the next seven generations."[25] The Oneida and Menominee were downstream of the mine. Hearings on the mine opened in April, with the voices of hundreds in opposition and J. Wiley Bragg, Exxon's public relations expert, with supporters of mining and jobs.[26] Over the media blitz, hearings began.[27]

While the administrative process proceeded, the public was taking sides. In 1996 ninety-two of three hundred candidates for the state legislature signed a pledge to support a moratorium on mining.[28] Editorials drew strong letters to the editor. The letters consistently blamed mining for failures of responsibility and the Republican Party for insincerity about environmental protection.[29] The Environmental Protection Agency and the DNR argued over environmental assessments and plans.[30] A plan to pump wastewater thirty-eight miles to the Wisconsin River raised the hackles of counties, villages, and towns along the route. The plan kept wastewater out of the Wolf River but resulted in numerous resolutions opposing the mine per se.[31] On the mining ground, the Nashville town board moved to an agreement to allow mining.[32]

Amid the Crandon Mine controversy, news drifted in from Ladysmith. The Flambeau Mining Company's open-pit mine was doing fine. Even Roscoe Churchill said the company was doing a good job on water quality. Others felt that the economic boom promised had not materialized, tax revenues were understated, and the company was reaping a bonanza.[33] As the 1996 elections neared, mining and environmental quality became a litmus test for candidates.[34]

With the election behind them, politicians, environmental activists, and mining interests turned to the business. Water-quality implications of mining bothered the Lower Wisconsin State River Board just as much as water levels in adjoining lakes and streams concerned the DNR.[35] Legislators continued work on a mining moratorium, while the Sierra Club took aim at Governor Thompson's environmental plan.[36] The issues or at least symbolism moved in the media, ranging from appropriating Green Bay Packers garb as antimining statements to television advertisements with Crandon residents supporting the mine.[37] Mining moratorium as a political issue moved to center stage.[38] Mining and environmental groups put out information on mining. Advocates of mining cited mines with great environmental records including the Flambeau Mine.[39] Environmentalists cited the opposite.[40] A senate subcommittee reported the moratorium bill out on a party-line vote: "The moratorium would deny permits to companies that cannot cite a hard-rock mine that operated safely in geology similar to Wisconsin's for 10 years and has also been closed for ten years without polluting ground or surface waters."[41] Some thought the bar for mining to be set at an impossible height.[42] Others thought it would not close the Crandon Mine.[43] The senate approved the bill 29–3 after Republicans narrowed the definition of *pollution*.[44] Governor Thompson characterized the bill as a mining ban but would wait to see what emerged from the Republican assembly.[45]

If politics were hot in Madison, they were boiling in Nashville, Wisconsin. Ten people were seeking the five elective jobs in the town, and antimining candidates made their credentials clear. After a recount, the antimining candidates swept into office.[46] Politics as usual in a small town was a thing of the past, yet some wanted local folks to just let economics take its course.[47]

Local people getting local jobs from mining were clearly a thing of the past. By summer Earth First demonstrators from New England, Montana, and California and People for Wisconsin, a private property advocacy organization like the People for the West, squared off in the Badger State. Demonstrations and arrests followed.[48] Editorials and letters to the editor debated whether this was a Wisconsin issue or a national issue due to the Earth First demonstration.[49] The small town mine was now an urgent message on the Internet.

In August the Crandon Mine won a major victory in the administrative process. The Army Corps of Engineers determined that its proposed interbasin transfer of water from the Crandon Mine to the Wisconsin River was not illegal.[50] The Crandon Mining Company increased its lobby spending to almost $100,000 per month and turned up the PR budget. Antimining folks turned up the rhetoric and the data and focused on the legislature.[51] The administrative process ground on the Department of Natural Resources.[52] The legislature took a recess, but the new year had the moratorium bill still in the assembly.

On January 8, 1998, Keith Reopelle of Environmental Decade presented Representative Spencer Black, a Madison Democrat and sponsor of the moratorium bill, with a two-foot-high stack of petitions signed by forty thousand people in support of the bill. The bill required any company wanting to mine in Wisconsin to cite a similar mine that had been operated safely for ten years and closed for another ten years without causing pollution.[53] Essentially a company would have to go to the record of western mining for evidence that it could mine in Wisconsin. The public was also writing letters and responding to polls with generally negative attitudes about mining.[54] University of Wisconsin Professor of Rural Sociology Bill Freudenberg opined that Crandon Mine economic projections were not reliable because of worldwide zinc prices. The boom-and-bust cycle of mining was the future of any Crandon Mine.[55]

The legislative process and lobbying activity continued apace. The momentum of "an energized coalition of Native Americans, conservationists, hunters, anglers and environmentalists" had the mining moratorium bill on the verge of passage in the Republican assembly.[56] The DNR announced the appointment of a Crandon Mine advisory panel to seek "the best science."[57] Meanwhile assembly Republicans amended the bill, and it passed 75–21, sending it back to the senate. Environmentalists cried foul.[58] The bill as passed was a signal to Exxon. It sold out and moved out.[59] Lobbyists turned their attention to the Wisconsin senate.[60] Rio Algom, the Canadian mining firm, dropped Crandon Mining as a name and created Nicolet Mineral, with a "new approach" and a new president looking "forward to listening and talking with our neighbors to build and operate a mine that will be a model of environmental stewardship."[61] Politics continued to work toward compromise, and on

February 4, 1998, the assembly sent a revised senate version to Governor Thompson. The bill retained the ten-year-plus-ten-year provision but changed the proof level of nonpollution for a decade after closure to "significant environmental pollution."[62] What was significant was for rule makers and courts to decide.

With the bill on his desk, Governor Thompson had to decide whether to sign it or veto it. The Republican assembly sent him the bill with a 90–6 vote. Popular organizations as well as environmental and tribal interests called for his signature. Thompson responded by signing at an Earth Day celebration.[63] But the cheering did not stop on Earth Day. There was work to be done.

The Crandon Mine was now Nicolet Mineral Company, and it had a new idea to eliminate the pipeline to the Wisconsin River and the pollution of the Wolf River. It would seal the mine site with a concrete grout.[64] The pipeline had expanded the coalition in opposition to mining.[65] The coalition now turned to the DNR to put rules in place to implement the law. The DNR simply stated that it was busy working on the EIS for the mine and would get to the rules later.[66] Environmentalists were in court trying to stop the pipeline and in the press reminding the public of the threat from the Nicolet Minerals plans and gimmicks.[67]

Rule making found a rest in Limbo's den, and in September 1999 a legal petition visited the DNR asking for rule making after eighteen months of inertia.[68] The Flambeau Mine closed in 1997, and in 1999 people were taking stock. Yes, there were a few jobs and $27 million in taxes paid, but those sulfide rocks were now back in the unlined mine hole. The question was whether those sulfides emerged as acid and polluted the Flambeau River.[69] In 1999 leaching pollutants appeared in monitoring wells, and environmentalists cried foul. Jana Murphy, the Flambeau Mining Company environmental and reclamation manager, and Larry Lynch of DNR agreed that the effluents existed, that they were expected, and that they were so minimal that they posed absolutely no threat to the river due to dilution. The Sierra Club and Wisconsin's Environmental Decade representatives saw the inevitable mine acids that pollute surface water and groundwater.[70] The Kennecott Minerals Company saw the poster child for environmentally sensitive mining in the new century.

Kennecott argued that this was the model mine. It had eleven operating permits from the DNR with two hundred special conditions. DNR regulated its operation, monitored it, and visited the mine. All the terms and conditions had been met. Three-fourths of the jobs went to local residents while the mine operated, and over $10 million in state and local taxes went back to local communities. Monitoring demonstrated no adverse effect on air quality, groundwater quality, or the Flambeau River. The company donated $500,000 to build the Rusk County Community Library and reclaimed the site. In conclusion, the "mine successfully operated without any violations, citations or complaints" and was a good corporate citizen.[71] Others looked at the economic reality of the mine and thought its promise far greater than the reality on the local scene.[72]

With the Flambeau Mine in its evidentiary pocket, Nicolet Minerals in 2000 continued through the administrative process. The 2000 EPA Toxic Release Inventory included hard-rock mining companies for the first time in eleven years. The worst offenders were in Nevada with 1.3 billion pounds of toxic waste, Arizona with 1.1 billion pounds, Utah with 459 million pounds, and Alaska with 306 million pounds.[73] Groundwater pollution questions slowed the permit process for Nicolet Minerals, but it was actively recruiting supporters including Ducks Unlimited and working out local agreements.[74]

The local agreements ran afoul of the interests of both parties, and the proposed use of cyanide in minerals processing put Nicolet Minerals back in state politics.[75] Montana had passed a cyanide ban in 1998, and it had withstood several legal and political tests. The Summitville Mine disaster in 1992 had killed aquatic life for seventeen miles downstream in Colorado. A January 2000 cyanide spill in Romania had wiped out 250 miles of the Danube and made national television. The public was aware of the dangers.[76] Regardless, the administrative process ground ahead, and the Environmental Impact Statement was in sight.[77]

In 2002 the suggestion that the state buy the mine emerged, and talks started. The tribes and environmentalists liked the idea of state lands closed to mining.[78] Opposition focused on the cost of purchase and loss of tax revenues.[79] Proponents saw a Wolf River headwaters playground

Wisconsin Governor
James Doyle. Courtesy
the Offices of Governor
James Doyes.

for generations of people.[80] The purchase quickly became the Wolf River Headwaters Protection Purchase and a partnership of the state and the opponents of the Crandon Mine.[81] Appraisers were busy fixing a price for the mine and its environs.[82] The state balked at the $51.2–94 million price tag.[83] When the talks folded, BHP Billiton, the Australian company that operated Nicolet Minerals Company, pulled out of the project and looked for a buyer, citing the "Wisconsin brick wall" against allowing mining at Crandon.[84] The fact that companies had come and gone still left mining a possibility as the administrative process continued.

As BHP Billiton exited, the Northern Wisconsin Resources Group entered as the new owner.[85] The newly elected governor, Jim Doyle, shut down Governor Thompson's Wisconsin Science Advisory Council on Metallic Mining, whose work was to identify environmentally safe technologies for mining.[86] Republicans and mining interests cried foul, while environmentalists continued to complain about the mine's impact.[87] Yet the permit and EIS process continued.

While the legal system continued in its contentious and complex way, the tribes had been busy. The new owners had made an offer in July.[88] Intense negotiations resulted in a deal in October. The Sokaogon Mole Lake Chippewa and the Forest County Potawatomi were buying the company out for $16.5 million funded by Potawatomi gaming and a loan to the Mole Lake Band.[89] Dale Alberts, the president of Nicolet Mineral for seven years, thought the buyout signaled "the end of mining in the state."[90] The day before Halloween 2003 the tribes withdrew the mining permit application. Glenn Reynolds, an attorney for the Mole Lake Band and now projects manager for Nicolet Minerals, signed the letter to the DNR. What was corporate ravaging of mother earth was now part of a tribal sovereignty fight and another example of tribal pride.[91] Just as the gaming struggle had empowered the tribes, now their strength and resolve were equally clear.[92] In February 2004 the tribes were honored at the annual conference of the Wisconsin Stewardship Network at University of Wisconsin–Stevens Point. Governor Jim Doyle handed out statues to tribal representatives commemorating the historic purchase.[93]

Hard-rock mining in Wisconsin had triumphed in Ladysmith and generated enough political angst to enable a mining moratorium. Mining was more than the Mining Law of 1872. It was part of a changing political matrix energized by environmental concerns and a mining history of environmental disasters throughout the West. The politics and shifting coalitions that generated national attempts to change the Mining Law of 1872 and to ban new mining in California's deserts came together in Wisconsin. Just as Montana had banned cyanide usage in mining in the state, Wisconsin had put one mine in native hands and handed the industry a moratorium. In doing so, another example of state action to curtail mining was on the books.

CONCLUSION

It wallowed in its water-bed; it burrowed,

    heaved and swung;

It gnawed its way ahead with grunts and sighs;

Its bill of fare was rock and sand; the tailings

    were its dung;

It glared around with fierce electric eyes.

Full fifty buckets crammed its maw;

    it bellowed out for more;

It looked like some great monster in the gloom.

—Robert Service, "The Prospector"
in *Collected Poems of Robert Service* (1940)

The 1990s gave the nation a glimpse of American mining in the debates over the revision of the Mining Law of 1872, cyanide disasters and a ban, and the Ladysmith mine. What was reality? Was mining Demogorgon seeking environmental victims with its insatiable maw? Was mining an environmentally sensitive industry complying with the statutes of the environmental age and merely seeking to do business? Politically, the mining industry was astute enough to thwart efforts to repeal the sacred Mining Law of 1872, but it was unable to stop a cyanide ban in Montana, the Treasure State, or preserve the Crandon Mine in the Dairy State. The images and realities varied in time and space across the West.

Both change and inertia were clearly visible after the demise of the Rahall bill in Congress. The mining industry lobbyists had discovered public relations and the reality of environmental regulations. Jon Christensen noted in 1995 that

> the most visible sign of . . . change is industry PR. Mining companies that not so long ago wouldn't even pay lip service to environmental values are producing videos and glossy publications touting their environmental policies and reclamation work. Industry conferences focus on the environment and feature some of mining's toughest critics. And mining journals are filled with stories and ads promoting the industry's green deeds.[1]

He also reported that Kennecott had agreed to pay $1 million, in addition to a 3 percent hard-rock royalty, to the federal government as part of a deal to expand an existing gold and silver operation in Alaska.[2] This was the same Kennecott Company working the Ladysmith mine in Wisconsin. Meanwhile, an abandoned cyanide mill poisoned the water wells of Pony, Montana, and the residents blamed Montana regulators for allowing the operation in the first place.[3] A commentary in the *Los Angeles Times* offered that the Summitville gold mine in Colorado had taken $6 million in gold from the earth, destroyed seventeen miles of the Alamosa River, and now claimed compensation from the federal government because its cyanide heap had been declared a Superfund site. The claim was part of the private property rights regime focused on takings under the Fifth Amendment that requires that government pay for property it takes by eminent domain.[4] To the author, this was part of "a crazy scenario."[5]

In the Panamint Valley of California the Timbisha Shoshone were trying to stop the Briggs Mine of Canyon Resources Corporation of Colorado. The tribe was "newly empowered by provisions of the California Desert Protection Act" and concerned about the potential destruction of culturally significant sites. The tribe also indicated that "government officials . . . never consulted with them about the project." Frederick Marr of California Indian Legal Services indicated that the potential future reservation of the tribe was at the mine site. Pauline Esteves, a Timbisha Tribal Council member and chair of the tribe's Historic Preservation Committee, indicated that "a hot springs near the mining site was a traditional tribal healing place and that there were also tribal burial sites in the area."[6] The connection of the tribes to the land was now a significant part of the process.[7]

The courts continued to be another venue for mining controversies. Noranda Inc. was still trying to open the New World Mine adjacent to Yellowstone Park, and environmentalists were in federal court forcing the company to get permits and to remediate existing pollution.[8] Other legal venues also saw action. The farmers of Okanogan County, Washington, were pushing for a zoning ordinance to limit the Battle Mountain Gold Company mine to twelve hours per day of operation to abate the noise.[9] The Environmental Protection Agency was still negotiating with Atlantic Richfield and Montana Resources to forge a consent decree for work on the Berkeley Pit in Butte, Montana.[10] Dead geese floating in the Berkeley Pit brought journalistic note ranging from the *High Country News* to *Harper's Magazine*.[11]

Floating fowl was terrible, but a sneak attack on Yellowstone Park was calamity. The New World Mine near Cooke City, Montana, was "at the top of the list of external threats to the park." The mine was two and one-half miles from the northeast boundary of the park and was projected to produce 11 million tons of sulfide tailings. Noranda Inc.'s Crown Butte Mines subsidiary proposed to backfill the mine's shafts with tailings and submerge the remainder in a huge containment pond lined with clay and plastic. Park Superintendent Michael V. Finley said, "The public is supposed to believe we can put a potential acid slurry in an envelope and keep it there forever—gimme a break."[12] The mine stirred environmental groups to action. Senator Dale Bumpers of Arkansas introduced the Yellowstone Protection Act of 1996 to protect the park from the mine.[13] The Alkali Ikes, mining's icon for the small miner, of Montana were also busy applying for "310 permits" to dig forty pits, up to ten cubic yards' worth on the Yellowstone River at Yankee Jim Canyon. Three couples wanted to run the contents through a sluice box as part of prospecting for gold. Fishermen and environmentalists saw that as "a Pandora's box."

The Greater Yellowstone Coalition saw backhoes and roads cut into the land. One of the couples had already applied to dredge upstream under the Mining Law of 1872 but had lost in the permit process.[14] Whether for big operations or small prospecting plans, the environmental issues within the administrative process were the same.

The New World Mine drew national attention because of the threat to Yellowstone Park. As a result, the Forest Service hired an outside consulting firm to review the draft Environmental Impact Statement (EIS).[15] In Congress, the rhetoric was reminiscent of the fight over the Rahall and Bumpers bills. Montana Senator Conrad Burns called Senator Bumpers an outsider butting into Montana business: "I think it's a perfect example of what's wrong with Washington today that a senator with no ties to the West would come in at the last minute and try to derail that (EIS) process."[16] The draft EIS projected minimal water, air, noise, or scenic pollution from the mine.[17] Politics proceeded, but the Clinton administration pursued a land swap to close the New World Mine and end the threat. Noranda was to receive $65 million in public land in return for the mine. Beth Norcrossm of American Rivers, a Washington, D.C., environmental group, said that "this sends a very very loud signal to the mining industry and to the American public that there are simply some places that are unfit for mining."[18] Ray Ring of Bozeman had a different message: "Whoever comes up with the most monstrous mining proposal gets the best deal."[19] Jeanne Hum of La Mirada, California, concluded that "the controversy generated by the proposed New World Mine has demonstrated that Congress needs to reform the 1872 Mining Law."[20] The New World Mine controversy left a variety of public messages. But the issue would not settle down, as negotiations on the land swap ran into a private property snag.[21]

The New World Mine was not Montana's only controversial mine project. The proposed Rock Creek Mine near Noxon and the McDonald Mine near Lincoln drew heavy fire from environmentalists because of potential pollution. The McDonald Mine threatened the Blackfoot River, "a mythic river" in Montana trout circles.[22] A 1994 mining claim moratorium in Montana's Sweet Grass Hills was extended for two more years in 1996, and the Bureau of Land Management banned all new claims on federal lands in the Sweet Grass Hills for twenty years. The central concern was groundwater pollution and the desecration of American Indian sacred sites.[23] A patenting moratorium in 1996 put that phase of the Mining Law of 1872 on hold and was part of a larger effort to reform the General Mining Law itself.[24] Similar problem mines in New Mexico and Wyoming drew local, state, and federal attention.[25] The mineral-processing industry in Utah set national records for air pollution.[26] The continuing problem of environmental pollution dogged the industry.

Yet there were clear signs of change. In 1998 Asarco, Inc., settled cases with the U.S. Department of Justice and the EPA, agreeing to pay fines and clean up sites in Arizona and Montana: "The EPA said that two settlements, filed in U.S. District Courts in Montana and Arizona, make Asarco the first company to agree to establish a court-enforced environmental-management system applying to all of its operations across the country."[27] The Homestake Mining Company's McLaughlin Mine in Northern California was winning the praises of the Sierra Club and the Soil Conservation Society for its operation. Ray Krauss, the mine's manager of environmental affairs, took a proactive approach to clean three abandoned mercury mines on the property rather than arguing with compliance agencies regarding the source of mercury pollution. Krauss moved cattle off the eleven thousand-acre site and avoided conflict with ranchers. He collected baseline data on the site and demonstrated environmental progress, including native oak trees growing on waste dumps, tailings slurry piped four and one-half miles to a less threatening location, and waste rock dumps with clay caps to prevent sulfide leaching. Even the Mineral Policy Center gave the mine a positive rating.[28]

Unfortunately, problem mines continued to draw legal and political fire. In 1998 a Montana initiative banning cyanide process for new mines moved forward and into law.[29] The supporters focused on the Lincoln mine and its potential to pollute the Blackfoot River. The images of the Summitville cyanide disaster in Colorado were clear in the public mind.[30] Mines in Oregon, Washington, and Idaho also posed threats.[31] In Washington, American Indians formed the Colville

Indian Environmental Protection Alliance to oppose hard-rock mining on tribal lands. Business Council Chairman Joe Pakootas rejected mining on tribal lands, saying, "You know we talk about seven generations in the future." Mining was "good for today, not tomorrow." The tribe filed lawsuits against state and federal agencies to stop the Crown Jewel Mine.[32] *Reclamation* became a watchword for the industry, and new technologies helped the industry restore what problem mines had destroyed.[33]

As the twentieth century closed, so did some mines. Environmental advocacy groups kept up the pressure. The Mineral Policy Center released *Six Mines, Six Mishaps: Six Case Studies of What's Wrong with Federal and State Hardrock Mining Regulations and Recommendations for Reform.* The report detailed the environmental damage of the six offenders and recommended federal mine acid drainage regulations, mine inspection, bonding, and reclamation.[34] The impact of the Montana cyanide ban forced layoffs at the McDonald Mine, and the Montana Mining Association consisted of a single employee, Jill Andrews, its executive director. Andrews commented on the situation and said, "Environmental organizations have to have an enemy in order to raise money. The mining industry has been their poster child for years. When we're gone, they'll find some other industry to destroy."[35] The Asarco Black Cloud Mine in Leadville, Colorado, brought up its last car of ore and closed.[36] The U.S. Department of Justice negotiated the eviction of the Pene Mining Company from the Westwater Canyon of the Colorado River in Utah. Mine manager Ron Pene thought he had been "backed into a corner by the Department of Justice armed with lies, mistruth and fabricated documentation."[37] The federal government notified the Battle Mountain Gold Company that it was shutting down its Crown Jewel Mine operation in the Okanogan Highlands of Washington on the grounds of alleged violation of the Mining Law of 1872 mill site provisions.[38] The federal government moved to limit the reach of the General Mining Law, and state action curtailed cyanide use.

The new century witnessed more of the same. Some of mining's past was gone. The smelter smokestacks in Murray, Utah, came down.[39] Butte,

Montana, remembered its mining past and hoped for more tourism in the twenty-first century.[40] Environmental groups questioned water tests of the Cripple Creek and Victor Mine near Victor, Colorado. Compliance agency personnel thought the discharges of zinc and cyanide were within state law limits but left final determination to the judge in the case.[41] A court ruling in Helena required Golden Sunlight Mine near Whitehall to totally reclaim its mine site. Judge Thomas C. Honzel told the Montana Department of Environmental Quality it had started with the wrong premise under the state constitution and Metal Mine Reclamation Act. The judge said, "There is nothing in the constitution or the statute which allows a reclamation decision to be based on . . . whether a mine operator will make a profit. Yet this is the premise [Department of Environmental Quality] started with."[42] Historically, the judge repudiated the premise Anaconda and the federal government had used in the early twentieth century that allowed the company to continue its practices. It was a new century, and Montana had new law. Colorado also considered new law, a cyanide ban, because of the Summitville Mine disaster.[43] Summitville, now abandoned and its company bankrupt, became a clean up for tax-payers. Summitville is an example of the practice Jared Diamond has described: "Companies discovered that they could extract the valuable ore and then just declare bankruptcy before going to the expense of cleaning up."[44] Without substantial bonds for cleanup expenses, mining companies continued old practices.

Summitville was not the only abandoned mine disaster waiting to happen. The McLaren Tailings on the Soda Butte Creek near Cooke City, Montana, turned the creek red and killed all aquatic life. Its acid, arsenic, iron, copper, lead, and zinc flowed toward Yellowstone Park.[45] In New Mexico a molybdenum mine's effluents had turned the Red River blue.[46] People died in Libby, Montana, because of a vermiculite mine.[47] Cut-and-run small operations still left environmental degradation behind in Montana.[48] In Arizona a pumice mine closed after a coalition of thirteen tribes, federal agencies, and the Sierra Club reached an agreement with Arizona Tufflite, Inc. Under the agreement the mine closed in six months and engaged in a five-year reclamation project. The federal buyout pleased tribal leaders. Hopi Tribal Chairman Wayne Taylor proclaimed in a drizzle that "the kachinas are happy. They're bringing rain to show their appreciation."[49] Acid mine drainage into the Sacramento River still plagued California.[50] Yet the Stillwater Mining Company still successfully mined palladium at the headwaters of the Boulder and Stillwater rivers in Montana's Beartooth Mountain country. Aimee Boulanger of the Mineral Policy Center applauded a "sustainable, environmentally sound and community supportive mine," and Stillwater may have started a "new paradigm here."[51] Regardless of the progress at one mine, the industry still made the number one toxic polluter on the 2000 EPA Toxics Release Inventory.[52]

January 20, 2000, ushered two new factors into the mining matrix. The Bureau of Land Management's 3,809 regulations requiring mine bonding and granting agency discretion to bar mining that would harm wildlife habitats or scenic beauty hit the *Federal Register*. George H. W. Bush took the oath as president of the United States and quickly pulled regulations not yet published in the *Federal Register* and delayed those published from going into effect for sixty days.[53] In March, Secretary of the Department of the Interior Gale Norton announced a full review of the new regulations. Watered-down regulations resulted.[54] The anticipated mining boom then began.[55] Gale Norton reversed the denial of the Glamis Imperial Mine in California that threatened a Quechan Tribe's sacred region. Preston Arrowweed, a tribal singer, said that "for us, it's our past that's being destroyed. They want to kill the area just for its gold. Is gold more important than religion?"[56] Yet state reclamation law in New Mexico brought mining industry representatives and environmental compliance officials to the table.[57]

Superfund dollars flowed into treatment, reclamation, and research, but all of that turned on money. In Idaho Springs, Colorado, the Argo Tunnel still belched out 250–300 gallons of acid per minute. A treatment plant handled the problem at $1 million per year of Superfund money, but in 2009 the taxpayers of Colorado will pay for the state's mining legacy.[58] The Bunker Hill Superfund site in Idaho covered twenty-one square miles. The projected final cost of clean up for the site stood at $1.4 billion.[59] Eureka, Utah, made the Superfund list in September 2002, and contractors started to remove the top eighteen inches of lead-saturated soil as part of reclamation.[60] In Washington, the number of polluted sites told a tale of administrative focus. Under the Clinton administration, an average of seventy-six Superfund sites reached cleanup status per year. President Bush's first year witnessed forty-eight, and under the Environmental Protection Agency's Christine Todd Whitman, the numbers declined further.[61] In Montana, the state had spent $700,000 to clean up the Pony mill site in the Tobacco Root Mountains. The story rang familiar: "Cyanide from the mill reached the groundwater, polluting a well and a spring. By 1991, the company went broke and the owners just walked away, leaving the state with a mess to clean up."[62] In the Cabinet Mountains, the U.S. Forest Service and the Montana Department of Environmental Quality gave Sterling Mining Company approval to drill an evaluation tunnel. This decision followed fourteen years of controversy, studies, and paperwork. Rock Creek Mine threatened the Clark Fork River, said environmental groups, and the U.S. Fish and Wildlife Service expressed concerns about grizzly habitat. That concern matured into a withdrawal of its biological opinion, forcing the Forest Service to pull its approval.[63] Not unexpectedly, the controversy went to court. On March 28, 2005, U.S. District Judge Donald Molloy threw out a 2003 U.S. Fish and Wildlife Service biological opinion and ruled that mining threatened grizzly bear and bull trout habitat. Environmentalists also filed in state court to challenge the issuance of a water discharge permit.[64] Litigation so detrimental to mining interests under the Mining Law of 1872 continued under state and federal environmental law and regulations.

The paperwork wars continued. In Congress, Nick Rahall introduced the Native American Sacred Lands Act to protect all sacred lands against mining and other activities that could cause significant damage to the lands.[65] Money, Congress, and mining interests kept issues before the public.

Coal mining also caught the attention of the public. The Black Thunder Mine in northeast Wyoming put out nine hundred truckloads per day and 68 million tons of coal in 2001, using computer models to reclaim the land as it mined the seam.[66] Zoning districts in Montana were suggested as a means to stop coal-bed methane development.[67]

Environmentalists worked to halt a coal mine in Lila Canyon near Price, Utah.[68] Issues of ground- and surface water pollution surfaced around such projects.

The Bush administration rollbacks of the Clinton era ignited concern from environmentalists and politicians. In Democratic California, the legislature passed, and Governor Gray Davis signed, legislation requiring mining companies to fully reclaim mine sites and to fully backfill mine pits. The target was the Glamis Gold Mine on a sacred Quechan Indian site.[69] The Quechan continued their fight in court and their alliance with the National Trust for Historic Preservation.[70] Interior Department Secretary Gale Norton and Utah Governor Mike Leavitt signed a deal allowing the state to claim old mining roads authorized under the Mining Law of 1866, a provision repealed in 1976 that preserved existing road claims. This move trumped efforts to have vast tracts declared wilderness and off-limits to SUVs and miners.[71] Secretary Norton also reversed the mill site ruling to create more jobs in the West.[72]

While Secretary Norton worked her administrative ways, the problems of coal mines, surface degradation, periodic disaster, and reclamation caught the public eye. The *Wall Street Journal* told its readers what people in coal country had known for decades: legislative fixes had not worked.[73] Ian Frazier recounted the 2000 coal mine sludge dam disaster in Kentucky.[74] The New World Mine land swap was finalized without consultation with the Northern Cheyenne. Gail Small of Native Action called it "a classic case of environmental racism." The tribe was in court and at the bargaining table with the miners.[75] Wyoming stood as the top coal-mining state, but was it economically sustainable?[76]

The question of economic development represented the magic four-letter word: jobs. Putting the question another way, more people in the West wondered whether short-term jobs are worth the long-term costs of mining. The economic equation for miners became the cost of environmental controls, permitting, and studies. Alkali Ike simply did not think in those terms, but we are in the twenty-first century, not the nineteenth.

In the twenty-first century, mining corporations entered a new business environment. Near South Pass, Wyoming, the Fremont Gold Corporation is exploring for gold within sight of the South Pass National Historic Landmark. Environmentalists and historic preservationists object. Fremont's exploration had to wait until the end of the sage grouse nesting season under its Bureau of Land Management permit.[77] Resolution Copper Company, a subsidiary of Rio Tinto Company (United Kingdom) and Broken Hill Proprietary Company Ltd. (Australia), is working on a legislative land exchange to mine copper near Superior, Arizona. The deal would end the Oak Flat Campground's existence, avoid an Environmental Impact Statement under the National Environmental Policy Act, and overturn an executive order withdrawing the land from mining. Rock climbers and environmentalists find cause for concern.[78] Amid the new regulatory regime, mining has accommodated and adapted.

The mining industry today does not hide from history and the continuing costs of cleaning up the mining legacy. Mining companies have choices. They can operate like the McLaughlin Mine or the Ladysmith mine with clear environmental plans, safeguards, and management commitment to vigilance. They can cut and run the small miner way in little tracts or Summitville proportions. The mining industry is not a monolith, despite political victories to kill off the Rahall bill to end the reign of the Mining Law of 1872.

Environmental action organizations are not united any more than all the tribes of this nation, but coalitions have demonstrated their effectiveness. From their perspective, environmental regulation has made its impact clear. What is far from clear is whether industry, tribal, and environmental interests can find areas of coexistence.

The operative language of mining law changed in the late twentieth century. Annual work requirements of $100 per year became a simple fee of $100 per year, resulting in hundreds of thousands of claims becoming public land for lack of a fee. *Moratorium* crept into the vocabulary as state and federal law halted aspects of the Mining Law of 1872. Wilderness designations took on a legal meaning that put mining off those lands and closed them for exploitation. Mining companies had to research sacred ground issues and negotiate for tribal consent to explore or mine. Mitigation and reclamation became requirements rather than something only the rust-belt industry had obligations to fulfill. The abuses of the location and patenting process still need to be addressed.[79] Mining communities need to find new reasons for existing such as tourism. Whether in Butte, Montana, or Mineral Point, Wisconsin, the lure of mining's past continues to draw people in search of public history sites.[80]

The battles in Congress continue. Congressman Richard Pombo, Republican of California, attached a measure to the Deficit Reduction Act of 2005 to lift the ten-year-old moratorium on the patenting process. The provision in November 2005 went to House–Senate negotiators, and environmental interest groups opposed the provisions as another landgrab.[81] John Leshy, a solicitor for the Department of the Interior from 1993 to 2000 and acknowledged mining law expert, expressed concern that the opaque language in the measure could lead to opening withdrawn areas like the New World Mine.[82] The Pombo provisions stimulated new journalistic interest in mining. The *Albuquerque Journal* ran a story entitled "Got $2.50? Get Yourself an Acre: Old Law Makes Fed Land a Steal," reminding readers that the patenting process allows federal land to go for a pittance. The story reviewed lands patented in Aspen, Colorado, and Park City Utah for ski resorts, and in Phoenix "a luxury hotel sits on part of an area a businessman patented in 1970 for $153 and later sold for $400,000."[83] The Santa Fe *New Mexican* published an October 17, 2005, story, noting that the Department of the Interior acknowledged that lands "companies had patented for mining were used for private, commercial development, such as at the ski reports of Aspen, Breckenridge, Keystone and Telluride in Colorado and Park City in Utah."[84] Yet another unintended consequence of the Mining Law of 1872 may be playing out in New Mexico, as Amigos Bravos formed the Mine All Mine, the Citizen's Mining Company, and staked ten claims in northern New Mexico on two hundred acres in the Santa Fe National Forest. It plans to stake another fifty claims covering one thousand acres to prevent mining on environmentally sensitive soil.[85] Whether mining or environmental interest groups prevail in this congressional public policy struggle or on the ground remains to be seen.

The tenacity of inertia regarding the Mining Law of 1872 and the vision of an environmentally cured western landscape that respects both nature and the sacred places of American Indians are up for grabs. Many of the symbols of the mining past are disappearing. Only the massive chimney remains in Anaconda, Montana, and the Anaconda Copper Mining Company's works are confined to photographs. In 2006 Asarco continued to dismantle the East Helena smelter works.[86] Yet the industry contests state regulation such as a proposed Montana rule requiring "new mine operators to show that water treatment related to mine operations would be complete within two years of a mine's closure."[87] Another company, Northern Resource Group, gifted $8 million back to the Mole Lake Chippewa after the tribe made its final $8 million payment on a mortgage held by the mining company. The Mole Lake Chippewa had borrowed the money to pay for its half of the Crandon Mine and used its casino revenues to honor its debt. Tribal leader Tony Phillippe said the gift "flabbergasted" tribal leaders but reflected, "They decided, I think, it might be good publicity to show they were helping out this tribe that actually won the war. We fought tooth and nail on this for 28 years."[88] In Congress in 2007 Nick Rahall and Jim Costa introduced H.R. 2262, the Hardrock Mining and Reclamation Act of 2007.[89] The battlefronts are local and national. The future of the West is at stake, and only an informed public can determine what lies ahead. The act passed 244 to 166 and is now in the Senate.[90]

Notes

Introduction

1. Jared Diamond, *Collapse: How Societies Choose to Fail or Succeed* (New York: Viking Penguin, Inc., 2005), p. 462.

2. Ibid., pp. 461–62.

3. Duane A. Smith, *Mining America: The Industry and the Environment, 1800–1980* (Lawrence: University Press of Kansas, 1987).

4. Diary of William Z. Walker, MSS SC 969, Harold B. Lee Library, Brigham Young University, pp. 135–37.

5. Diamond, *Collapse*, p. 38.

6. Ann Scales, *Legal Feminism: Activism, Lawyering, and Legal Theory* (New York: New York University Press, 2006), p. 108.

Chapter 1

1. *An Act to promote the Development of the Mining Resources of the United States*, ch. 152, 42d Cong., 2d sess., 1872, pp. 91–96.

2. Jared Diamond, *Collapse: How Societies Choose to Fail or Succeed* (New York: Viking Penguin, Inc., 2005), p. 462.

Chapter 2

1. John Phillip Reid, *Constitutional History of the American Revolution*, 4 vols. (Madison: University of Wisconsin Press, 1986, 1987, 1991, 1993).

2. William T. Parry, *All Veins, Lodes, and Ledges throughout Their Entire Depth: Geology and the Apex Law in Utah Mines* (Salt Lake City: University of Utah Press, 2004), p. 9.

3. Stevens to Abbey Stevens, December 12, 1849, MSS, Milton B. Stevens Collection, Box 1, Huntington Library.

4. The Diary of Gordon C. Cone, 1849–50, p. 179, at http://memory.loc.gov/cgi-bin/query/r?ammem/upbover:@field(DOCID+@lit(dia103611)), accessed May 30, 2003.

5. Johnson to Johnson, December 28, 1850, Johnson Family Papers, MSS, Huntington Library.

6. Root to Dear Sister Nelli, April 15, 1862, Enoch Root Letters, 1858–63, MSS, Huntington Library.

7. Root to Aunt Mary, April 30, 1862, ibid.

8. Clark to Brother Stanford, December 30, 1864, Henry Harmon Clark Papers, MSS, Box 1, Montana Historical Society. On Montana's experience also see Jeffrey J. Safford, *The Mechanics of Optimism: Mining Companies, Technology, and the Hot Springs Gold Rush, Montana Territory* (Niwot: University Press of Colorado, 2004).

9. Clark to Brother Stanford, August 23, 1865, Henry Harmon Clark Papers, MSS, Box 1, Montana Historical Society.

10. Ibid.

11. Hedges to Parents, September 13, 1865, Cornelius Hedges Family Papers, MSS, Box 1, Montana Historical Society.

12. Clark to William G. Clark, December 3, 1868, Clark Family Correspondence, 1852–69, MSS, Box 1, Huntington Library.

13. Hutch Stevens to Matilda Stevens Cooper, August 26, 1893, Hutch Stevens Papers, MSS, Box 1, Huntington Library.

14. Hutch Stevens to Cooper, June 3, 1894, ibid.

15. Hutch Stevens to Cooper, May 19, 1895, ibid.

16. Hutch Stevens to Cooper, September 6, 1896, ibid.

17. Hutch Stevens to Cooper, January 27, 1907, Box 2, ibid.

18. Peter C. Stevens to Matilda Stevens Cooper, December 26, 1907, ibid.

19. Peter C. Stevens to Cooper, March 12, 1908, ibid.

20. Peter C. Stevens to Cooper, May 3, 1908, ibid.

21. McKee to Keating, December 10, 1879, Nevada Mining Companies Collection, MSS, Box 2, Huntington Library.

22. Oscanyan to Turner, October 28, 1910, Bailey Willis Collection, MSS, Box 1, Huntington Library.

23. Pomeroy to Smith, January 9, 1929, Northern Belle Extension Mining Company of Candelaria, Nevada Papers, MSS, Huntington Library. Also see Hugh A. Shamberger, *Story of Candelaria and Its Neighbors* (Reno: U.S. Geological Survey and the Nevada Department of Conservation and Resources, 1978).

24. Barbour to Collins, February 12, 1937, Philip R. Barbour Papers, MSS, Box 19, Montana Historical Society.

25. Charles Wallace Miller Jr., *Stake Your Claim! The Tale of America's Enduring Mining Laws* (Tucson: Westernlore Press, 1991), pp. 24–25.

26. Otis E. Young Jr., *Western Mining: An Informal Account of Precious-Metal Prospecting, Placering, Lode Mining, and Milling on the American Frontier from Spanish Times to 1893* (Norman: University of Oklahoma Press, 1970), p. 112.

27. Diary of James Henry Morley, August 9, 1862, MSS, Montana Historical Society.

28. Ibid., September 8, 1862.

29. Ibid., December 21, 1862.

30. Ibid., February 8, 1863, and April 26, 1863.

31. Records of Lincoln Gulch, Territory of Montana, 1865–79, MSS, Box 1, Montana Historical Society.

32. A folkmoot in Saxon law was an assemblage of people for a judicial purpose to hear and decide a dispute in their village.

33. Ryan to Keating, March 27, 1879, MSS, Box 2, Nevada Mining Companies Collection, Huntington Library.

34. James J. Sinnott, *History of Sierra County*, vol. 3 (Volcano: California Traveler, Inc., 1975), p. 159.

Chapter 3

1. Charles Wallace Miller Jr., *Stake Your Claim! The Tale of America's Enduring Mining Laws* (Tucson: Westernlore Press, 1991), pp. 65–76; Russell Elliott, *Servant of Power: A Political Biography of William M. Stewart* (Reno: University of Nevada Press, 1983), pp. 53–55. On Higby, see Gordon Morris Bakken, *Practicing Law in Frontier California* (Lincoln: University of Nebraska Press, 1991), pp. 103–9.

2. Miller, *Stake Your Claim!* p. 66.

3. Ibid.

4. Ibid, pp. 66–67.

5. *Congressional Globe*, 38th Cong., 1st sess., 1864, p. 1696.

6. Miller, *Stake Your Claim!* p. 67.

7. Ibid., p. 68.

8. Gordon Morris Bakken, "American Mining Law and the Environment: The Western Experience," *Western Legal History* 1 (Summer/Fall 1988): 221–22.

9. *Congressional Globe*, 39th Cong., 1st sess., 1866, pp. 3225–29.

10. Miller, *Stake Your Claim!* p. 79.

11. Ibid., pp. 79–80.

12. *Congressional Globe*, 39th Cong., 1st sess., 1866, p. 3236.

13. Bakken, "American Mining Law and the Environment," p. 222.

14. *Congressional Globe*, 42d Cong., 2d sess., 1870, pp. 532–35.

15. *Congressional Globe*, 39th Cong., 1st sess., 1866, p. 3226.

16. *Sparrow v. Strong*, 70 U.S. (3 Wallace) 97 (1865).

17. Harvey N. Gardiner, *Mining among the Clouds: The Mosquito Range and the Origins of Colorado's Silver Boom* (Denver: Colorado Historical Society Press, 2002), pp. 32–38.

18. Harrison Burns Reminiscence, 1864–65, MSS, Box 1, Montana Historical Society, p. 71.

19. Ibid., p. 73.

20. *Laws of Montana Territory, 1864–65*, pp. 400–401 and 327–29.

21. Ibid., pp. 327–29, sec. 3.

22. Ibid., sec. 8.

23. *Laws of Montana Territory, Codified Statutes, 7th Session, 1871–72*, ch. 45, pp. 522–25.

24. George M. Lubick, "Cornelius Hedges: The Montana Years, 1864–1907" Ph.D. dissertation (University of Toledo, 1974), p. 63.

25. Ibid., p. 69.

26. "Memoirs of William H. Hunt," William H. Hunt Papers, MSS, Box 1, Montana Historical Society, p. 69.

27. Decius S. Wade, "Necessity for Codification: Paper Read Before the Helena Bar Association, April 5, 1895" (Helena: Williams and Sons Printers and Stationers, 1895), in Wade Family Papers, MSS, Box 2, Montana Historical Society, p. 10.

28. Ibid., p. 11.

29. Robert Chester Turner to W. H. Oscanyan, October 14, 1914, Robert Chester Turner Collection, MSS, Box 2, Huntington Library.

30. Gordon to Corvin, February 10, 1955, Nevada Porphyry Gold Mining Company Papers, MSS, Box 2, Huntington Library.

31. Jared Diamond, *Collapse: How Societies Choose to Fail or Succeed* (New York: Viking Penguin, Inc., 2005), p. 38.

32. See generally Isaac F. Marcosson, *Anaconda* (New York: Dodd, Mead and Company, 1957).

33. Diamond, *Collapse*, p. 37.

Chapter 4

1. This problem of the lack of law books and precedents also confronted the bar with problems of reasoning from analogy as well as local law. See Gordon Morris

Bakken, *Practicing Law in Frontier California* (Lincoln: University of Nebraska Press, 1991), pp. 33–50.

2. *The Bear River and Auburn Water and Mining Co. v. New York Mining Co.*, 8 Cal. 327, 332 (1857).

3. Ibid.

4. Ibid.

5. Ibid., 333.

6. Ibid., 334.

7. Gordon Morris Bakken, "American Mining Law and the Environment: The Western Experience," *Western Legal History* 1 (Summer/Fall 1988): 212–14.

8. *Robertson v. Smith*, 1 Montana 410, 415 (1871).

9. Ibid., 418.

10. *Chambers v. Harrington*, 111 U.S. 350, 353 (1883).

11. Ibid.

12. James Willard Hurst, *Law and the Conditions of Freedom in the Nineteenth-Century United States* (Madison: University of Wisconsin Press, 1956), p. 25.

13. Bakken, "American Mining Law and the Environment," p. 227.

14. Ibid.

15. Eliot Lord, *Comstock Mining and Miners*, Monograph #4 (Washington, D.C.: U.S. Geological Survey, 1883), pp. 97–108, 131–80.

16. *Mining Co. v. Tarbet*, 98 U.S. 463 (1878).

17. *Iron Silver Mining Co. v. Cheesman*, 8 F. 297, 301 (C.C.D. Colo. 1881).

18. *Iron Silver Mining Co. v. Cheesman*, 116 U.S. 529, 533 (1885).

19. *Larkin v. Upton*, 144 U.S. 16, 23 (1891).

20. Bakken, "American Mining Law and the Environment," pp. 228–29.

CHAPTER 5

1. Otis E. Young Jr., *Western Mining* (Norman: University of Oklahoma Press, 1970), p. 31.

2. Wilkin to McDonald, October 22, 1879, Sierra Nevada Mining Company Papers, MSS, Box 1, Huntington Library.

3. Aulbach to Hawley, July 27, 1897, James H. Hawley Collection, MSS, Correspondence 1897, Folder A-Au, Idaho State Historical Society.

4. Aulbach to Heyburn, August 20, 1897, ibid.

5. Heyburn to Hawley, October 1, 1897, ibid.

6. McIrwin to Brown, October 24, 1897, Folder M, ibid..

7. Kenneth Baxter Ragsdale, *Quicksilver: Terlingua and the Chisos Mining Company* (College Station: Texas A&M University Press, 1976), pp. 213–23.

8. See C. B. Glasscock, *The War of the Copper Kings* (New York: Grosset and Dunlap, 1935); Michael Malone, *The Battle for Butte: Mining and Politics on the Northern Frontier* (Seattle: University of Washington Press, 1981).

9. Livermore to Stevens, June 29, 1868, James D. Lomas Papers, MSS, Box 1, Montana Historical Society. Lomas was a Virginia City attorney and mining investor in the 1860s.

10. Nolan to Showers, November 9, 1895, Cornelius B. Nolan Family Papers, MSS, Box 1, Montana Historical Society.

11. A trespass is an injury to property, here mineralized ground, as well as the rights of the claim owner involving an unlawful entry on the claim holder's location. Conversion is the unauthorized exercise of a right of ownership of the ore as well as the alteration of the condition of the owner's location. Taking the ore from the location permanently deprived the owner of valuable property.

12. Martin to Bell and Bell, July 14, 1853, MSS, HM56918, Huntington Library.

13. McKee to Leonard Redfield, June 25, 1856, Leonard Redfield Collection, MSS, Box 1, Huntington Library.

14. Charles Camden, *An Autobiography* (San Francisco: Philopolis Press, 1916), p. 165.

15. Corbiere to William R. Morgan, March 22, 1853, William Rollin Morgan Collection, MSS, Box 1, Huntington Library.

16. Bowen to Mills, July 29, 1866, MSS, Huntington Library.

17. "The Boom Suppressed," *Helena Independent Record*, May 15, 1887, in Philip R. Barbour Papers, Real Estate Clipping File, MSS, Box 8, Montana Historical Society.

18. Donohue to Morgan, June 9, 1896, William R. Morgan Collection, MSS, Box 1, Huntington Library.

19. Donohue to Morgan, August 14, 1899, ibid.

20. Anderson to McElroy, April 9, 1962, Montana Attorney-General Subject Files, MSS, Box 69, Montana Historical Society.

21. Marshall Sprague, *Money Mountain: The Story of Cripple Creek Gold* (Boston: Little, Brown and Co., 1953), p. 45.

22. Contract of October 2, 1860, Mining Papers of the Blue Wing Quartz Mine, Selim Woodworth Collection, MSS, Box 4, Huntington Library.

23. Roberts to Garvin, October 11, 1880, Stephen Roberts Letterbooks, MSS, vol. 2, Bancroft Library.

24. Chumasero and Chadwick to Dear Gones, July 4, 1879, Chumasero and Chadwick Papers, MSS, Box 1, Montana Historical Society.

25. Esler to Holter, August 11, 1889, Anton M. Holter Papers, MSS, Box 93, Montana Historical Society.

26. Esler to Holter, September 29, 1889, ibid.

27. Ester to J. C. McGinn, October 20, 1889, ibid.

28. Cook to Whitney, January 10, 1862, Sierra Nevada Mining Company Papers, MSS, Box 1, Huntington Library.

29. Stewart to Trustees of the Sierra Nevada Silver Mining Company of San Francisco, July 17, 1862, ibid.

30. Nolan to Stevens, June 2, 1890, Cornelius B. Nolan Family Papers, MSS, Box 1, Montana Historical Society.

31. Ringeling to Field, August 17, 1890, Hope Mining Company of St. Louis Collection, MSS, Box 4, Montana Historical Society.

32. Maddox to Power, December 6, 1900, Thomas C. Power Papers, MSS, Box 385, Montana Historical Society.

33. Power to Maddox, December 14, 1900, ibid.

34. Nolan to Sullivan, September 26, 1905, Cornelius B. Nolan Family Papers, MSS, Box 4, Montana Historical Society.

35. Nolan to Tegen, August 21, 1905, ibid. Even where experienced prospectors located mines, their location descriptions could be ambiguous. Witness M. F. Sullivan's description of two claims he "located" for Idaho attorneys:

> I have located you both claim[s] described as follows: Commencing at Point 100 yards South west from what is know as the first White Sulphur spring thence running East 600 feet to Mammoth West line thence northerly 1500 feet prolele with Mammoth thence West 600 feet–South 1500. So you can pickout youre names, the discovery is in the South West corner. The other discovery situated about 100 yards south west of lone ceder spring thence running north 1500 feet thence East 600 feet–South 1500 feet west to discovery. I have posted notice on the warm Spring creek ditch also and return the copy.

Sullivan to Hawley and Reves, Blackfoot, Idaho, June 8, 1890, James H. Hawley Collection, MSS, Correspondence Box 1889–1891, Folder S, Idaho State Historical Society. Where on each spring the point of beginning might be situated is a good question.

36. Corette to MacDonald, January 15, 1915, Corette Letterpress Book, Corette and Corette Records, MSS, Box 1, Montana Historical Society. Other abstract and

title opinions are contained in the letterpress book, and as late as 1944 the firm was continuing to issue such title opinions. See Corette and Corette Records, MSS, Box 11, Montana Historical Society.

37. Van Dam to Snyder, October 22, 1934, Combination Metals Reduction Company Papers, MSS, Manuscript Division, Special Collections, MS 493, Box 4, University of Utah Marriott Library.

38. Frank J. Huggins Correspondence, 1853–1863, MSS, Bancroft Library.

39. Gordon Morris Bakken, *Practicing Law in Frontier California* (Lincoln: University of Nebraska Press, 1991), pp. 72–82.

40. Countiss to Turner, December 22, 1915, Robert C. Turner Collection, MSS, Box 1, Huntington Library.

41. Walsh to Power, June 3, 1922, Thomas C. Power Papers, MSS, Box 395, Montana Historical Society.

42. Walsh to Rhys, January 12, 1925, Box 416ibid.

43. Rhys to Walsh and Nagle, January 15, 1925, ibid.

44. Smith to Henry H. Markham, January 16, 1897, Henry Harrison Markham Collection, MSS, Box 16, Huntington Library.

45. Schuyler Journal of 1914, Brigadier-General Walter Scribner Schuyler Papers, MSS, Huntington Library, p. 74.

46. Ibid., p. 139.

47. Martin to William P. Stuart (Phoenix), March 7, 1938, William Plato Stuart Papers, MSS, Box 9, Arizona Collection, Hayden Library, Arizona State University.

48. Smith to Alfred B. Summers, December 31, 1906, Alfred B. Summers Papers, MSS, Box 1, Huntington Library.

49. Gibbs, Poland Mine Diary, MSS, October 8, 1932, entry, Arizona Collection, Hayden Library, Arizona State University.

50. Watts to Hayden, February 23, 1950, Senator Carl T. Hayden Papers, MSS, Box 53, Folder 7, Arizona Collection, Arizona State University.

51. *Arizona Gazette* clipping of December 17, 1883, Charles Baldwin Genung File, Hayden Pioneer Biographical File, Arizona Collection, Arizona State University.

52. Williams to Hayden, August 30, 1967, Senator Carl T. Hayden Papers, MSS, Box 336, Folder 9, Arizona Collection, Arizona State University.

53. Secretary of the Interior to Hayden, December 5, 1967, ibid.

54. During national depressions, misery loved company; as John E. Corette of Butte, Montana, told William J. Taaffee on March 20, 1931:

> The business depression there is nothing compared to the business depression here. You probably know that before the crash copper was selling at

eighteen cents per pound, and that today it is selling at ten cents, with no market. Our mines are practically closed, as our products are copper, silver and zinc, and the price for those products is so low, and in addition there is such a small market, that we are probably going through a harder period of depression than any other section of the country. (Corette and Corette Records, MSS, Box 2, Montana Historical Society)

55. Johnson to Haviland, July 9, 1931, I. B. Mining Company Records, MSS, Box 2, Montana Historical Society. Location work was that necessary to attest to a discovery of a valuable mineral. Representation work was the $100 per year of work required by federal law to maintain rights in the claim. Failure to perform and record the work opened the claim to relocating or "jumping."

56. Pope and Smith to Lancaster, March 6, 1936, Black Pine Silver Mines, Inc., Records, MSS, Box 5, Montana Historical Society.

57. Lancaster to Pope and Smith, March 11, 1936, ibid.

58. Edgar McClure, President of Black Pine Silver Mining Company, to J. D. Matthews and Co., August 29, 1933, Box 1, ibid.

59. Nevada Porphyry Gold Mining Co. to Michal, June 25, 1938, Nevada Porphyry Gold Mining Co. Collection, MSS, Box 11, Huntington Library.

60. Clark to Hauser, January 4, 1894, Samuel T. Hauser Papers, MSS, Box 23, Montana Historical Society.

61. Congressman Metcalf's Statement to the House Interior Committee's Mines and Mining Subcommittee, July 18, 1958, Lee Melcalf Papers, MSS, Box 394, Montana Historical Society.

62. Melcalf to William Booth, February 25, 1958, Box 371, ibid.

63. Dichter to Metcalf, July 31, 1963, Box 395, ibid.

64. Chumasero and Chadwick to Drummond, November 25, 1873, Chumasero and Chadwick Papers, MSS, Letterpress Book, 1869–74, Box 1, Montana Historical Society.

65. Smith to Henry Harrison Markham, January 16, 1897, and December 12, 1897, Henry Harrison Markham Collection, MSS, Box 16, Huntington Library.

66. *Report XVIII of the State Mineralogist*, vol. 18 (Sacramento: State Mineralogist, January 1922), pp. 22–23.

67. Evans to Hobbins, June 21, 1927, Anton M. Holter Papers, MSS, Box 92, Montana Historical Society.

68. Olsen to Cripe, June 23, 1955, Montana Attorney-General Subject Files, MSS, Box 52, Montana Historical Society.

69. Winifred Galloway, "The History of Uranium in Wyoming," B.A. honors thesis (University of Wyoming, 1961), Hebard Library, Laramie, p. 17.

70. Erickson to Woodahl, April 1, 1970, Montana Attorney-General's Official Records, MSS, Box 19, Montana Historical Society.

71. Woodahl to Dorsey, March 19, 1970, ibid.

72. Jared Diamond, *Collapse: How Societies Choose to Fail or Succeed* (New York: Viking Penguin, Inc., 2005), p. 428.

73. Ibid.

CHAPTER 6

1. Statement of Americus Vespucius Lancaster, MSS, Bancroft Library, p. 3.

2. Aulbach to Hawley, July 27, 1897, James H. Hawley Collection, MSS, Correspondence 1897, Folder A-Au, Idaho State Historical Society.

3. Jones to Blackburn, September 17, 1902, William A. Blackburn Papers, MSS, Box 3H60, Eugene C. Barker Texas History Center, University of Texas at Austin. Townsend was married to Blackburn's cousin and had been advised in 1895 that "his mines are undoubtedly valuable but I am afraid they are too inaccessible to be successfully worked without the expenditure first of a large amount to capital, and that he has not got" (Palmer Townsend to William A. Blackburn, October 19, 1895, Box 3H59, ibid.).

4. Brown to McLure, September 16, 1903, and November 9, 1903, Paul A. Fusz Papers, MSS, Box 1, Montana Historical Society.

5. Fowler to Holter, November 27, 1903, Anton M. Holter Papers, MSS, Box 92, Montana Historical Society.

6. Corette to Knapp, December 6, 1915, Corette and Corette Records, MSS, Box 1, Letterpress Book, Montana Historical Society.

7. Smith to Young, October 17, 1911, George U. Young Papers, MSS, Box 2, Arizona Collection, Hayden Library, Arizona State University.

8. Turner to Wood, June 18, 1899, and Turner to Mr. Brown, January 3, 1900, Robert Chester Turner Collection, MSS, Box 2, Huntington Library.

9. Kipp to Folks at Home, May 24, 1927, Ewald Kipp Papers, MSS, Manuscript Division, Special Collections, Accession #777, Box 3, University of Utah Marriott Library.

10. Cooke to White, October 19, 1940, Nevada Porphyry Gold Mining Company Papers, MSS, Box 3, Huntington Library.

11. Davis to Emerson, August 15, 1938, Alonzo E. Emerson Papers, MSS, Box 1, Montana Historical Society.

12. Corette to Carrigan, May 15, 1943, Corette and Corette Records, MSS, Box 11, Montana Historical Society.

13. See Lee Metcalf Papers, May 1958 to May 1959 correspondence, particularly with John A. Kelly of Helena, MSS, Box 371, Montana Historical Society.

14. Jared Diamond, *Collapse: How Societies Choose to Fail or Succeed* (New York: Viking Penguin, Inc., 2005), p. 38.

CHAPTER 7

1. Curtis H. Lindley, *A Treatise on the American Law Relating to Mines and Mineral Lands*, 3 vols. (San Francisco: Bancroft-Whitney, 1914), vol. 2, p. 1294. For an excellent treatment of the subject in the Utah mines, see William T. Parry, *All Veins, Lodes, and Ledges throughout Their Entire Depth: Geology and the Apex Law in Utah Mines* (Salt Lake City: University of Utah Press, 2004). Also see Grant Smith with Joseph V. Tingley, *The History of the Comstock Lode: 1850–1997* (Reno: Nevada Bureau of Mines and the University of Nevada Press, 1998).

2. Smith to Young, September 28, 1911, George U. Young Papers, MSS, Box 2, Arizona Collection, Hayden Library, Arizona State University.

3. McKee to Keating, October 31, 1879, Nevada Mining Companies Collection, MSS, Box 2, Huntington Library. Also see Donald R. Abbe, *Austin and the Rees River Mining District: Nevada's Forgotten Frontier* (Reno: University of Nevada Press, 1985); James W. Hulse, *Lincoln County, Nevada, 1864–1909: A History of a Mining Region* (Reno: University of Nevada Press, 1971).

4. Ringeling to Cuno, April 11, 1891, Hope Mining Company of St. Louis Papers, MSS, Box 4, Montana Historical Society.

5. Ringeling to John C. Porter, December 29, 1897, Box 5, ibid.

6. "Report on Round Mountain Mine by C. S. Thomas, Jr.," July 6, 1908, Nevada Porphyry Gold Mining Company Collection, MSS, Box 5, Huntington Library.

7. The problem with geology in the nineteenth century was the uncertainty of the science. See Rhoda Rappaport, *When Geologists Were Historians, 1665–1750* (Ithaca, N.Y.: Cornell University Press, 1997); Rachel Laudan, *From Mineralogy to Geology: The Foundations of a Science, 1650–1830* (Chicago: University of Chicago Press, 1987).

8. Stanford to Baur, May 27, 1907, Frank L. Sizer Papers, MSS, Box 9, Montana Historical Society.

9. Burton to Scallon, March 23, 1915, William Scallon Papers, MSS, Box 1, Montana Historical Society.

10. Janin to Hague and Brown, June 20, 1908, Louis Janin Collection, MSS, Box 1, Huntington Library.

11. What mining engineers saw on the ground was also a fact of life in the academy. Eliot Backwelder of the Geology Department of the University of Wisconsin wrote to Bailey Willis, a geology professor at Stanford University on March 10, 1906, that "if Lorenz would only let us into the secret of how he manages to

determine these obscure questions without being within 300 miles of them, it would be a great boon to many of us in our future explorations" (Bailey Willis Collection, MSS, Box 9, Huntington Library). On January 23, 1908, William Morris Davis of the Harvard University Geology Department wrote to Willis and observed, "Have you ever attempted to study out the methods of geographers, in their treatment of land forms? And have you noticed that most of them have no special method at all?" (Box 10, ibid.). James F. Kemp of Columbia University confessed to Willis on September 12, 1901, "The importance of a geologic and physiographic foundation for a topographer is a subject that no doubt you feel even more deeply than I, alth' I long for the silver trumpet tones with which to make it sink into the hearts of the engineers to whom I preach this doctrine of salvation" (Box 16, ibid.). Bailey Willis made a even more telling confession to Leason H. Adams in Washington, D.C., on December 7, 1937, writing, "At any rate I agree that our ignorance is both vast and dense" (Box 24, ibid.).

12. Clark C. Spence, *Mining Engineers and the American West: The Lace-Boot Brigade, 1849–1933* (New Haven: Yale University Press, 1970), pp. 199–201, 222–25.

13. Power to Atkinson, June 12, 1925, Thomas C. Power Papers, MSS, Box 416, Montana Historical Society.

14. Eilers to Power, March 2, 1925, and Power to Eilers, March 7, 1925, ibid.

15. Power to Victor Hills, September 15, 1925, ibid.

16. Walsh and Nagle to Power, September 4, 1925, ibid.

17. Turner to Countiss, September 1, 1914, Robert Chester Turner Papers, MSS, Box 1, Huntington Library.

18. Guess to O'Connor, November 10, 1938, Combined Metals Reduction Company, MSS, MS493, Box 51, Manuscript Division, Special Collections, Utah Marriott Library.

19. Corette and Corette to Edward Sampson, June 8, 1943, Corette and Corette Records, MSS, Box 11, Montana Historical Society. The letter describes an extralateral pursuit issue, an agreement, the failure of the parties to perform, and the abrogation of the contract.

20. Scallon to Donahoe, August 18, 1944, William Scallon Papers, MSS, Box 2, Montana Historical Society.

21. Ibid.

22. Donahoe to Scallon, September 9, 1944, ibid.

23. Scallon to Donahoe, September 16, 1944, ibid.

24. Rossiter Worthington Raymond, "Lawyers and Experts," in *Brave Hearts* (1873), quoted in Spence, *Mining Engineers and the American West*, pp. 226–27.

Chapter 8

1. John Phillip Reid, *Law for the Elephant: Property and Social Behavior on the Overland Trail* (San Marino, Calif.: Huntington Library Press, 1980).

2. Malcolm J. Rohrbough, *Aspen: The History of a Silver Mining Town, 1879–1893* (New York: Oxford University Press, 1986), p. 92.

3. C. L. Sonnichsen, *Colonel Greene and the Copper Skyrocket: The Spectacular Rise and Fall of William Cornell Greene: Copper King, Cattle Baron, and Promoter Extraordinary in Mexico, the American Southwest, and the New York Financial District* (Tucson: University of Arizona Press, 1974), p. 65.

4. Ibid., p. 80. Also see Robert L. Spude and Stanley W. Paher, *Tombstone: Arizona Silver Camp* (Las Vegas: Nevada Publications, 1979); Stanley W. Paher and Robert L. Spude, *Colorado River Ghost Towns* (Las Vegas: Nevada Publications, 1976).

5. Kenneth Baxter Ragsdale, *Quicksilver: Terlingua and the Chisos Mining Company* (College Station: Texas A&M University Press, 1976), p. 266.

6. *Proceedings of the Sixth Annual Convention of the California Miners' Association Held at Odd Fellows Hall, San Francisco, California, October 18, 19, and 20, 1897* (San Francisco: Mysell-Rollins Co., 1897), p. 39.

7. Rohrbough, *Aspen*, p. 107.

8. Christian G. Fritz, Michael Griffith, and Janet M. Hunter, eds., *A Judicial Odyssey: Federal Court in Santa Clara, San Benito, Santa Cruz, and Monterey Counties* (San Jose, Calif.: Advisory Committee of the San Jose Federal Court, 1985), pp. 55–58.

9. Louis Janin, "Notebook: California, 1866–," Louis Janin Collection, MSS, Box 2, Huntington Library.

10. The examples abound, but it was clear that an owner needed a paying mine to pay lawyers. See C. B. Glasscock, *The War of the Copper Kings* (New York: Grosset and Dunlap, 1935); Reno H. Sales, *Underground Warfare in Butte* (Caldwell, Idaho: Caxton Printers, 1964); Jerry W. Calvert, *The Gibraltar: Socialism and Labor in Butte, Montana, 1895–1920* (Helena: Montana Historical Society Press, 1988); Joseph E. King, *A Mine to Make a Mine: Financing the Colorado Mining Industry, 1859–1902* (College Station: Texas A&M University Press, 1977); Dan de Quille, *A History of the Comstock Silver Lode and Mines* (New York: Promontory Press, 1974); Grant H. Smith, *The History of the Comstock Lode* (Reno: Nevada Bureau of Mines, 1998); Powell Greenland, *Hydraulic Mining in California: A Tarnished Legacy* (Spokane: Arthur H. Clark Co., 2001); Lee Scamehorn, *Albert Eugene Reynolds: Colorado's Mining King* (Norman: University of Oklahoma Press, 1995), p. 133.

11. Helen Ellsberg, *Mines of Julian* (Glendale, Calif.: La Siesta Press, 1972), p. 22.

12. S. D. Myers, ed., *Pioneer Surveyor, Frontier Lawyer: The Personal Narrative of O. W. Williams, 1877–1902* (El Paso: Texas Western College Press, 1966), p. 195.

13. Scamehorn, *Albert Eugene Reynolds*, p. 91.

14. Sally Zanjani, *Goldfield: The Last Gold Rush on the Western Frontier* (Athens: Swallow Press/Ohio University Press, 1992), p. 38.

15. Turner to Seeley W. Mudd, April 4, 1912, Robert Chester Turner Collection, MSS, Box 1, Huntington Library.

16. Gordon Morris Bakken, *Practicing Law in Frontier California* (Lincoln: University of Nebraska Press, 1991).

17. See the Fred Jason Babcock Collection, MSS, Idaho State Historical Society, containing twenty boxes of business documents regarding nonmining clients as well as mining cases. See also Frank Martin Sr. Collection, MSS, Idaho State Historical Society; Boyd Guthrie Papers, MSS, Box 1, Manuscript Division, Special Collections, University of Utah Marriott Library; William Allen Harris Statement, MSS, Bancroft Library. Harris was a Tennessee attorney who came to California in 1875, practiced law in San Bernardino, combined law and mining in Colorado in 1879 and 1880, and returned to San Bernardino, maintaining connections with several mining companies. See William A. Blackburn Papers, MSS, Eugene C. Barker Texas History Center, University of Texas; John H. Shoper Papers, MSS, Box 1, Montana Historical Society. The John T. Murphy Papers, MSS, Montana Historical Society, contain some litigation information as well as the diverse nature of business in nineteenth-century Montana. See also the E. M. Niles Papers, MSS, Box 1, Montana Historical Society; Harry L. Burns Interview, MSS, Box 1, Montana Historical Society; Hallowell Fernando Clement Sr. Diary, MSS, Montana Historical Society. Clement is an excellent example of the diversity of practice as well as Colorado and Montana experiences. See, finally, the Frank P. Sterling Letterpress Book, 1891–99, MSS, Montana Historical Society. On Lewis O. Evans, a company attorney, see the *Helena Independent*, May 31, 1931; *Montana Standard*, May 31, June 1, June 2, and June 4, 1931.

18. Hedges to Dennis and Alvina Hedges, November 16, 1865, Cornelius Hedges Family Papers, MSS, Box 1, Montana Historical Society.

19. Hedges to Parents, December 31, 1865, ibid.

20. Hedges to Dennis Hedges, September 9, 1967, ibid.

21. Hedges to Mother, December 7, 1867, ibid.

22. *Anaconda Standard*, April 23, 1916.

23. Chumasero and Chadwick to Trumball, November 3, 1871, Chumasero and Chadwick Papers, MSS, Box 1, Montana Historical Society.

24. Bakken, *Practicing Law in Frontier California*, pp. 114–23.

25. Martin, Harvey Hill Mines, to Oliver, Quebec, July 9, 1879, Oliver-Gowen Collection, MSS, Box 3, Huntington Library.

26. Rumsey to Hauser, December 9, 1886, Samuel T. Hauser Papers, MSS, Box 13, Montana Historical Society.

27. Rohrbough, *Aspen*, p. 96.

28. Ibid., p. 98.

29. Kleinschmidt to James C. Aiken, December 13, 1899, James H. Hawley Collection, MSS, 1899 Correspondence, Box 1, Idaho Historical Society. The letter references Idaho courts, but the neutrality of federal courts was noted for the West in general.

30. Rohrbough, *Aspen*, pp. 101–7. The case discussed was not, of course, the only case brewing in Aspen or the Leadville diggings. Fred G. Buckley's nineteen volumes of diaries recorded numerous cases in Colorado in the period and his role as an expert witness. See Fred Buckley Diaries, MSS, 19 vols., Huntington Library. The concerns about juries were noted in his 1884 diary, with "five members of the Eureka jury under arrest for bribery" (entry of April 7, 1884, Fred Buckley Diaries, MSS, 19 vols., Huntington Library). By 1889, Buckley was a millionaire and general manager of the Aspen Mining and Smelting Company.

31. Buckley 1887 Diary, entry of October 20, 1887, Fred G. Buckley Diaries, MSS, Huntington Library.

32. Nolan to Peck, November 7, 1889, Cornelius B. Nolan Family Papers, MSS, Box 1, Montana Historical Society.

33. Nolan to C. S. Fell, February 27, 1889, 1888–91 Letterpress Book, ibid.

34. See generally Bakken, *Practicing Law in Frontier California*. The problem of finding the law (discussed in Bakken, *Practicing Law in Frontier California*, pp. 33–50) was not just a California problem. In 1937 Walter H. Anderson, a Pocatello, Idaho, attorney, wrote to his fellow barrister Fred J. Babcock in Boise that "the worst feature of this shoddy [Idaho] digest is that the old code sections are cited without any parallel citation of the same sections that have been unamended in the new codes." Anderson also complained that Idaho Supreme Court cases were infrequently cited, making research even more difficult. See Anderson to Babcock, December 24, 1937, Fred Babcock Collection, MSS, Idaho State Historical Society.

35. Russell A. Bankson and Lester S. Harrison, *Beneath These Mountains* (New York: Vantage Press, 1966), p. 190.

36. John F. and James W. Forbin to Henley, June 20, 1893, Granite-Bimetallic Consolidated Mining Company Records, MSS, Box 8, Montana Historical Society.

37. Nolan to Teall, September 5, 1895, Cornelius B. Nolan Family Papers, MSS, Box 1, Montana Historical Society.

38. Graham to Street, December 27, 1904, Joseph Alexander Papers, MSS, Box 26, Hayden Library, Arizona State University.

39. Notebook entry, New Almaden Mine Collection, MSS, Box 1, Huntington Library, p. 71.

40. Johnson and Johnson (Boise) to Captain James Hutchinson, Silver City, Idaho, April 9, 1896, Trade Dollar Consolidated Mining Company Collection, MSS, Box 4, Idaho State Historical Society.

41. Scallon to Michael Donahoe, May 15, 1897, Anaconda Copper Mining Company Records, MSS, Box 10, Montana Historical Society.

42. Conglomerate Mining Company, Corporate Minute Book, May 11, 1898, Lavagnino Collection, MSS, Box 1, Huntington Library.

43. *Proceedings of the Sixth Annual Convention of the California Miners' Association Held at Odd Fellows Hall, San Francisco, October 18, 19, and 20, 1897* (San Francisco: Mysell-Rollins Co., 1897), pp. 8–9.

44. Ibid., pp. 14–15.

45. Ibid., p. 56.

46. Bullard to Borah, September 4, 1903, William Wallace Papers, MSS, Box 1, Montana Historical Society.

47. Bullard to Borah, February 22, 1904, ibid.

48. *The Reveille*, August 8, 1904, quoting a Bozeman *Avant Courier* story.

49. Jean Davis, *Shallow Diggin's: Tales from Montana's Ghost Towns* (Caldwell, Idaho: Caxton Printers, 1962), p. 114.

50. Turner to Chester, May 24, 1897, Robert Chester Turner Collection, MSS, Box 2, Huntington Library.

51. Mallen to Turner, July 26, 1914, Box 1, ibid.

CHAPTER 9

1. Jared Diamond, *Collapse: How Societies Choose to Fail or Succeed* (New York: Viking Penguin, Inc., 2005), p. 38.

2. Randall E. Rohe, "Gold Mining Landscapes of the West," *California Geology* 37 (October 1984): 224.

3. Ibid., p. 227.

4. Dennis M. Daley and Jim Mohler, *Historical Resources Identification and Location Study for National Resources Lands: Garnet Mining District* (Boulder: Western Interstate Commission for Higher Education, 1973), p. 12.

5. Publication Committee of the Arvada Historical Society, *More than Gold: A History of Arvada, Colorado, during the Period 1870–1904* (Boulder: Johnson Publishing Co., 1976), p. 12.

6. George W. Morris remembered that "the claims [near Reynolds City, Montana,] were only two hundred feet long and every man had to take care of his tailings" in 1865 (George W. Morris Reminiscence, MSS, Montana Historical Society). The local mining district rules for the Cheyenne Mining District near Custer, Black Hills, Dakota Territory, of June 11, 1875, provided that "no tailings shall be dumped on another miner's claim without his consent" (Watson Parker, *Gold in the Black Hills* [Norman: University of Oklahoma Press, 1966], p. 205). Yet

"the tailings were emptied into any convenient stream" in the same region according to another researcher (Rosalee Ammons, "The Influence of Gold on the Settlement of the Black Hills," M.S. thesis [Black Hills Teachers College, 1962], p. 93).

7. *Lincoln v. Rogers* (1870), Montana Territorial Supreme Court Case Files, MSS, Montana Historical Society, p. 13.

8. Ibid., p. 69.

9. *Lincoln v. Rogers*, 1 Montana 217, 223 (1870).

10. Plummer to Hauser, January 24, 1887, Samuel T. Hauser Papers, MSS, Box 15, Montana Historical Society.

11. Rumley to James K. Pardee, February 24, 1887, ibid.

12. N. B. Ringeling wrote to the home office of the Hope Mining Company in 1898 suggesting the "repair of our old Reservoir or build a new one, as the Ranchers complain of our turning our tailings into Flint Creek." They had the material to do so and just needed more labor. See Ringeling to John C. Porter, July 5, 1898, Hope Mining Company of St. Louis Company Papers, MSS, Box 5, Montana Historical Society.

13. Cavanaugh to Beattie, November 10, 1913, E. W. and G. D. Beattie Records, MSS, Box 4, Montana Historical Society.

14. Nolan to Lee Montgomery, September 13, 1895, Cornelius B. Nolan Family Papers, MSS, Box 1, Montana Historical Society.

15. Richard Z. Johnson and Richard H. Johnson to Hutchinson, March 4, 1896, the Trade Dollar Consolidated Mining Company Collection, MSS, Box 4, Idaho State Historical Society.

16. *Efficiency* was a nineteenth-century watchword for mining. Drain boxes and tailings sluices were highly recommended. B. Preston, ed., *California Gold Milling Practices*, California State Mining Bureau, Bulletin No. 6 (Sacramento: Superintendent of State Printing, 1895), p. 85.

17. Lee Scamehorn, *Albert Eugene Reynolds: Colorado's Mining King* (Norman: University of Oklahoma Press, 1995), p. 154.

18. Diamond, *Collapse*, p. 37.

19. Lucas to Parker, January 27, 1913, John R. Lucas Papers, MSS, Box 7, Montana Historical Society.

20. Turner to Wilson, August 1, 1896, Bailey Willis Collection, MSS, Box 1, Huntington Library.

21. Turner to Wilson, August 8, 1896, Robert Chester Turner Collection, MSS, Box 2, Huntington Library.

22. Burchan to Paymal, September 13, 1918, Yellow Aster Mining and Milling Company Papers, MSS, Box 1, Huntington Library.

23. Rossberg to Gillie, March 15, 1920, Anaconda Copper Mining Company Records, MSS, Box 63, Montana Historical Society. Folder 63-13 contains extensive reports and correspondence on the working of tailings.

24. Templeton to Ford, February 6, 1920, Montana Attorney-General Subject Files, MSS, Box 96, Montana Historical Society.

25. Templeton to Dr. W. J. Butler, August 6, 1920, ibid.

26. Nicholas A. Casner, "Toxic River: Politics and Coeur D'Alene Mining Pollution in the 1930's," *Idaho Yesterdays* 35 (Fall 1991): 2–19.

27. *Humboldt Standard*, June 15, 1939, clipping in Mines and Mineral Resources Clippings File, Humboldt County Collection, Library Special Collections, Humboldt State University.

28. Water Quality Study of Clark Fork River (1970), Montana Attorney-General's Office Records, MSS, Box 10, Montana Historical Society, p. 1.

29. In addition to tailings, smelters dumped slag, a solid product of molten metal extraction, into watercourses. In Arizona, molten slag dropped "into a running stream of water . . . granulated and [was] carried away to the river, where it obtained free river transportation to the Gulf of California. This method was followed for thirty years, reducing operating expenses very materially" (James Colquhoun, *The History of the Clifton-Morenci Mining District* [London: John Murray, 1924], p. 39). So too, the Boston and Montana Smelter in Great Falls, Montana, dumped slag directly into the Missouri River. See Gordon Morris Bakken and J. Elwood Bakken, "The Goldfish Died: Great Falls, Fort Benton, and the Great Flood of 1908," *Montana: The Magazine of Western History* 51 (Winter 2001): 38–51.

30. Diamond, *Collapse*, pp. 461–62.

CHAPTER 10

1. Powell Greenland, *Hydraulic Mining in California: A Tarnished Legacy* (Spokane: Arthur H. Clark Company, 2001), p. 34.

2. Samuel Spooner to Walter R. Spooner, June 4, 1850, Walter R. Spooner Letters, MSS, HM56919, Huntington Library.

3. Downey to Erastus Burr, January 14, 1857, HM56917, ibid.

4. Mark Fiester, *Blasted Beloved Breckenridge* (Boulder: Pruett Publishing, 1973), pp. 30–31.

5. S. Goodale Price, *Ghosts of Golconda* (Deadwood, S.Dak.: Western Publishers, Inc., 1952), p. 23.

6. Charles A. Averill, *Mineral Resources of Humboldt County* (Sacramento: Department of Natural Resources, Division of Mines, 1942), p. 513.

7. Greenland, *Hydraulic Mining in California*, p. 102.

8. Ibid., p. 136.

9. Louis Janin, "Mining Debris Case, July 16–22, 1878, Notebook," July 16, 1878, entry, Louis Janin Collection, MSS, Item #31, Box 3, Huntington Library.

10. Ibid., July 19, 1878, entry.

11. Ibid., July 21, 1878, entry.

12. Greenland, *Hydraulic Mining in California*, p. 222. The best book on the subject is Robert Kelley, *Gold vs. Grain, the Hydraulic Mining Controversy in California's Sacramento Valley* (Glendale, Calif.: Arthur H. Clark Co., 1959).

13. Cox to Morgan, December 19, 1881, William Rollin Morgan Collection, MSS, Box 2, Huntington Library.

14. Cox to Morgan, September 9, 1885, ibid.

15. Cox to Morgan, August 7, 1886, ibid.

16. Fred C. Turner to R. C. Turner, September 20, 1904, Robert Chester Turner Collection, MSS, Box 2, Huntington Library.

17. Turner to Mallen, September 20, 1917, Box 1, ibid.. Mallen wrote to Turner on October 24, 26, and 29, 1917, detailing the progress.

18. Turner to Mallen, November 15, 1917, ibid.

19. Chapman to Morgan, June 5, 1886, William R. Morgan Collection, MSS, Box 1, Huntington Library.

20. Ibid.

21. Julian Dana, *The Sacramento: River of Gold* (New York: Rinehart and Co., 1939), p. 175.

22. Chapman to Morgan, March 19, 1887, Morgan Collection, Box 1, Huntington Library.

23. Chapman to Morgan, June 4, 1887, ibid.

24. Cox to William R. Morgan, January 8, 1888, ibid.

25. Cox to Morgan, March 2, 1890, ibid.

26. Cox to Morgan, February 22, 1891, ibid.

27. Donahue to Morgan, December 27, 1890, ibid.

28. Donahue to Morgan, March 23, 1895, ibid.

29. Cox to Morgan, February 22, 1894, ibid.

30. Donahue to Morgan, April 23, 1896, ibid.

31. Turner to Seeley W. Mudd, May 30, 1912, Robert Chester Turner Collection, MSS, Box 1, Huntington Library.

32. Turner to Countiss, September 17, 1917, ibid.

33. Turner to Mallen, September 8, 1917, ibid.

34. Ibid.

35. Turner to Mallen, November 15, 1917, ibid.

36. David Stiller, *Wounding the West: Montana, Mining, and the Environment* (Lincoln: University of Nebraska Press, 2000), pp. 74–80.

37. Jared Diamond, *Collapse: How Societies Choose to Fail or Succeed* (New York: Viking Penguin, Inc., 2005), p. 36.

38. A. Scheidel, *The Cyanide Process and Its Practical Application and Economic Results* (Sacramento: California State Mining Bureau, 1894), pp. 45–46.

39. Ibid., p. 10.

40. Emil W. Billeb, *Mining Camp Days* (Berkeley: Nowell-North Books, 1968), p. 79.

41. Turner to Fred Chester, June 4, 1897, Robert Chester Turner Collection, MSS, Box 2, Vol. 1 Private Correspondence Letterbook, Huntington Library.

42. Augustus Reeves's Reminiscences, 1888–1942, "A Giant's Dreams," MSS, Utah State Historical Society, pp. 8–9.

43. Otis E. Young Jr., *Western Mining* (Norman: University of Oklahoma Press, 1970), p. 285.

44. Robert L. Spude, "Elusive Gold: George P. Harrington and the Bradshaw Miners, 1887–1925," *Journal of the West* 33 (Summer 1992): 162.

45. William Sampson to Edna Dahl Sampson, September 6, 1903, William Sampson Collection, MSS, Box 2, Huntington Library.

46. William Sampson to Edna Sampson, October 25, 1903, ibid.

47. William Sampson to Edna Sampson, February 4, 1904, Box 3, ibid.

48. William Sampson to Edna Sampson, February 16, 1904, ibid.

49. William Sampson to Edna Sampson, April 3, 1904, ibid.

50. William Sampson to Edna Sampson, April 21, 1904, ibid.

51. Turner to Fred Chester, June 4, 1897, Robert Chester Turner Collection, Box 2, Vol. 1 Private Correspondence Letterbook, Huntington Library.

52. Shotwell to Worthington, August 12, 1933, Little Ben Mining Company Records, MSS, Box 1, Montana Historical Society.

53. W. to Worthington, August 16, 1933, ibid.

54. Worthington to Commissioner of Indian Affairs, Washington, D.C., August 15, 1933, ibid.

55. Hale and Last Chance leases, Joseph A. McDonough Records, MSS, Box 1, Montana Historical Society, p. 2.

56. William Z. Walker Diary, 1849, MSS, Harold B. Lee Library, Brigham Young University, pp. 151–52.

57. Young, *Western Mining*, pp. 118–21.

58. Mineral Resources Analysis Project Staff, California Division of Mines and Geology, "The Mineral Industry of California in 1990," *California Geology* 44 (October 1991): 221.

CHAPTER 11

1. Comptroller General of the United States, General Accounting Office, "Modernization of 1872 Mining Law Needed to Encourage Domestic Mineral Production, Protect the Environment, and Improve Public Land Management," B-118678.

2. Edward H. Peplow Jr., "Land Lessons from the Past," reprinted in *Pay Dirt: A Publication Devoted to the Interests of the Arizona Small Mine Operators* 337 (April 21, 1967): 1.

3. Ibid.

4. Ibid., pp. 2–3.

5. Ibid., p. 3.

6. Dwyer to Metcalf, October 10, 1969, Lee Metcalf Papers, MSS, Box 64, Montana Historical Society.

7. Metcalf to Lindren, November 30, 1970, Lee Metcalf Papers, MSS, Box 32, Montana Historical Society.

8. *Billings Gazette*, September 24, 1970.

9. Aldrich to Montana Congressional Delegation, March 3, 1970, Lee Metcalf Papers, MSS, Box 65, Montana Historical Society.

10. Whirry to Lee Metcalf, April 10, 1970, ibid.

11. Shotliff to Lee Metcalf, October 21, 1970, ibid.

12. Hageman to Lee Metcalf, February 25, 1970, ibid.

13. Mansfield to Cliff, November 5, 1970, Lee Metcalf Papers, MSS, Box 32, Montana Historical Society.

14. Stanley Dempsey to Edward P. Cliff, April 27, 1971, Lee Metcalf Papers, MSS, Box 31, Montana Historical Society.

15. Ibid.

16. "Address Delivered to North American Wildlife Conference," Lee Metcalf Papers, MSS, Box 656, Montana Historical Society, p. 1.

17. Ibid.

18. Ibid, p. 5.

19. Ken Walcheck, "The Long Pines: Armed with the Archaic Mining Law of 1872, Mobil Oil and Other Energy Companies Are Busy in the Long Pines," *Montana Outdoors* 6 (March/April 1975): 16–17.

20. U.S. Congress, Senate, *Legislative History of FLPMA*, Publication #95-99 (Washington, D.C.: U.S. Government Printing Office, 1978).

21. Charles Wallace Miller Jr., *Stake Your Claim! The Tale of America's Enduring Mining Laws* (Tucson: Westernlore Press, 1991), pp. 239–41.

22. Homer E. Milford, "The Threats to Our Mining Heritage: A Provincial Point of View," *Cultural Resource Management: Information for Parks, Federal Agencies, Indian Tribes, States, Local Governments, and the Private Sector* 21, no. 7 (1998): 62.

23. Metcalf to Knoyle, March 7, 1977, Lee Metcalf Papers, MSS, Box 309, Montana Historical Society.

24. Metcalf to Farrey, April 13, 1977, ibid.

25. Lee Metcalf to Willis M. Johns, October 12, 1977, Box 306, ibid.

26. Olson to Morris K. Udall, March 10, 1977, Box 309, ibid.

27. Cannon to Metcalf, February 25, 1877, and Metcalf to Cannon, March 17, 1977, ibid.

28. Metcalf to Charles M. Hauptman, December 22, 1977, Box 306, ibid.

29. Metcalf to Varner, December 12, 1977, ibid.

CHAPTER 12

1. Duane A. Smith, *Mining America: The Industry and the Environment, 1800–1980* (Lawrence: University Press of Kansas, 1987), pp. 123–35.

2. Ibid., pp. 136–48. Richard H. K. Vietor, *Environmental Politics and the Coal Coalition* (College Station: Texas A&M University Press, 1980), pp. 125–93.

3. Frank Wheat, *California Desert Miracle* (San Diego: Sunbelt Publications, 1999), p. 12.

4. "Pettis Pushes Desert Bill," *Hi-Desert Star*, January 11, 1973.

5. K. Ross Toole, "Environmental Degradation in Montana," *Montana Business Quarterly*, Winter 1970: 7.

6. Ibid.

7. Ibid., p. 8.

8. Ibid., p. 9.

9. William L. Lang, "Bad Air, Environmental Politics, and History," in Donald MacMillan, *Smoke Wars: Anaconda Copper, Montana Air Pollution, and the Courts, 1890–1924* (Helena: Montana Historical Society Press, 2000), pp. 4–5.

10. Ibid., pp. 6–7.

11. Ibid., p. 6.

12. James M. McElfish Jr., Tobie Bernstein, Susan P. Bass, and Elizabeth Sheldon, *Hard Rock Mining: State Approaches to Environmental Protection* (Washington, D.C.: Environmental Law Institute, 1996), p. 213.

13. Jared Diamond, *Collapse: How Societies Choose to Fail or Succeed* (New York: Viking Penguin, Inc., 2005), p. 428.

14. Ibid., p. 103.

15. Ibid., p. 159.

16. Owen H. Seiver, *Inventory of Major California Environmental Legislation and Accomplishments since 1970* (Sacramento: Center for California Studies, 1995); Nico Calavita, *Legislative History of the Environmental Goals and Policy Report* (Sacramento: Center for California Studies, 1995).

17. Seiver, *Inventory of Major California Environmental Legislation and Accomplishments since 1970*, pp. 57–58.

18. Norris Hundley Jr., *The Great Thirst*, rev. ed. (Berkeley: University of California Press, 2001), p. 310.

19. William L. Graf, "Mining and Channel Response," *Annals of the Association of American Geographers* 69 (June 1979): 263.

20. Ibid., pp. 265–66.

21. Richard V. Francaviglia, "Hardrock Mining's Effects on the Visual Environment of the West," *Journal of the West* 43 (Winter 2004): 39–51.

22. Smith, *Mining America*, p. 147.

23. Peter Keppler, "An Overview of the Mineral Permitting Process," in *Institute on Mineral Resources Permitting* (Boulder: Rocky Mountain Mineral Law Foundation, 1981), paper 1, p. 1.

24. Ibid., p. 2.

25. Ibid., p. 3.

26. Ibid., p. 19.

27. Stephen M. Voynick, *Climax: The History of Colorado's Climax Molybdenum Mine* (Missoula: Mountain Press Publishing Company, 1996), pp. 315–24.

28. Smith, *Mining America*, pp. 159–60.

29. Ibid., p. 160.

30. Harold Linder, "Hart Mining District, San Bernardino County, California," *California Geology*, 1898: 134–43; Lynn A. Pirozzoli and James S. Poppy, "Implementing an Award Winning Reclamation Plan at Castle Mountain Mine," *California Geology*, 1992: 182–86; Environmental Solutions, Inc., *Castle Mountain Project, San Bernardino County, Draft Environmental Impact Statement/ Environmental Impact Report* (Irvine, Calif.: Environmental Solutions, 1989).

31. "Environmentalists, Mine Firm Call Truce, Common Ground Found in Desert," *Chicago Tribune*, June 7, 1992 (Business Section); "Unusual Accord Opens the Way for a Gold Mine," *New York Times*, November 25, 1990; "Tortoise and Viceroy: Mutual Benefit," *Mining Journal*, February 23, 1992: 148; "New Mojave Gold Mine to Set 'New Standard' for Conservation," *Los Angeles Times*, November 11, 1990.

32. Mel Levine, Member of Congress, to Dear Colleague, "California Desert Protection: Clearing Up the Confusion," November 13, 1991: "An attempt was made to address every site-specific conflict . . . satisfying at least three mining companies. The wilderness designation in the Mojave was reduced for Viceroy Gold" (Frank Wheat Collection, MSS, Box 82, Huntington Library).

33. "Mine Law Is Pure Gold to Speculators," *Los Angeles Times*, May 22, 1989.

34. David L. Callies, "Takings Clause—Take Three," *American Bar Association Journal*, November 1, 1987: 48–56.

35. Louise A. Halper, "*California Coastal Commission v. Granite Rock Co.*, 480 U.S. 572 (1987): Environmental Regulation of Land-Use Control," in *Law in the Western United States*, ed. Gordon Morris Bakken (Norman: University of Oklahoma Press, 2000), pp. 545–50.

36. Ibid., p. 548.

CHAPTER 13

1. "The Mining Law of 1872 Needs Revision: A Report to the Chairman, Subcommittee on Mining and Natural Resources, Committee on Interior and Insular Affairs, House of Representatives" (Washington, D.C.: U.S. General Accounting Office, March 10, 1989), p. 2.

2. Ibid., pp. 2–3.

3. Ibid., p. 3.

4. Ibid., p. 4.

5. Ibid., p. 14.

6. Ibid., p. 18.

7. Ibid., p. 19.

8. Ibid., pp. 19–20.

9. Ibid., p. 20.

10. "Mine Law Is Pure Gold to Speculators," *Los Angeles Times*, May 22, 1989.

11. "Hardscrabble Miners Make Their Last Stand," *San Francisco Chronicle*, May 18, 1990.

12. Frank Wheat Collection, MSS, Box 75, Huntington Library. Other newspapers saw desert preservation as an economic necessity as well as an environmental gain. "Desert Park Foes Square Off," *Bakersfield Californian*, April 19, 1988; "We Need to Save the Desert," *Lansing State Journal* (Inyokern, Calif.), April 23, 1988. Also see David Darling, "Last Standing in the Desert: Will the Sun Soon Set on California's Land of Anarchy? Should It?" *Outside*, August 1988. In an earlier sentiment the *Fresno Bee* in its March 16, 1986, edition opined that "a portion of it, close to its original state, must be preserved for future generations" ("National Parks in the Desert," *Fresno Bee*, March 16, 1986). Also see "Time for Serious Look at Desert Protection," *Sun* (San Bernardino), March 9, 1986; "The Desert Springs Eternal," *Telegram-Tribune* (San Luis Obispo), March 4, 1986; "Decision Year for the California Desert?" *Sunset*, March 1988.

13. "Miners to Sharpen Environmental Skills at Joint Conference in May," *Mining Record*, February 21, 1990.

14. "Gold Fields Mesquite Develops Method to Cover the Mine's Solution Ponds," *Mining Record*, February 21, 1990.

15. "Report Indicates Strong Year for U.S. Mineral Industries," *Mining Record*, February 21, 1990. There was more good news in 1990. The Round Mountain, Nevada, was the largest heap leach gold mine in the world ("Round Mountain Is World's Largest Heap Leach Gold Mine," *Mining Record*, June 6, 1990). And the Hecla Mining Company won an environmental award for its work in Baker County, Oregon ("Hecla Receives Environmental Award," *Mining Record*, June 27, 1990).

16. The best book on this topic is Frank Wheat, *California Desert Miracle: The Fight for Desert Parks and Wilderness* (San Diego: Sunbelt Publications, 1999).

17. "CMA Says Desert Bill Opponents Win the Day in Los Angeles," *Mining Record*, March 21, 1990.

18. Jared Diamond, *Collapse: How Societies Choose to Fail or Succeed* (New York: Viking Penguin, Inc., 2005), p. 465.

19. Michael Searles, "Desert Hearing Draws Thousands," *Southern Sierran*, March 1990. Also see "New Age Meets Old West in Mining Showdown," *New Mexican* (Santa Fe), October 29, 1990; "Scientists Join Arizonans in Opposing Gold Exploration," *New York Times*, December 4, 1990; "*Save Bodie! News*," published by the California State Park Rangers Association, 1, no. 1 (Summer 1990), in Frank Wheat Papers, MSS, Box 85, Huntington Library.

20. Teague to Frank Wheat, February 17, 1993, Frank Wheat Collection, MSS, Box 80, Huntington Library.

21. "U.S. Mining Industry Leads in Pollution Abatement; Still Target," *Mining Record*, April 4, 1990.

22. "Bureau of Mines Planning Activities for Earth Day," *Mining Record*, April 18, 1990.

23. "Mining—Endangered in the Nineties!" *Mining Record*, April 25, 1990.

24. Ibid.

25. "Nevada Governor Opposes Claim Rental Fee," *Mining Record*, June 20, 1990.

26. "Nevada Congress Supports 1872 Law," *Mining Record*, June 20, 1990.

27. "Mountain States Challenges Constitutionality of Superfund," *Mining Record*, July 25, 1990.

28. "Mountain States Legal Foundation Hails Victory in Public Lands Case," *Mining Record*, July 11, 1990.

29. "NMMA Members Critique Proposal to Change the 1872 Mining Law," *Mining Record*, August 1, 1990.

30. "AMC Opposes Moratorium," *Mining Record*, August 15, 1990.

31. "Two Federal Agencies Muzzle U.S. Government Mineral Experts," *Mining Record*, August 29, 1990.

32. "AMC Chides Newspaper on 1872 Mining Law Story," *Mining Record*, August 29, 1990.

33. "Too Many Considerations Unanswered in New Bill," *California Mining* 15, no. 9 (September 1990): 1.

34. Ibid., p. 3.

35. "The Environmental Protection Act of 1990: A Big Green Monster?" *California Mining* 15, no. 9 (September 1990): 2.

36. Ibid.

37. "First California Teacher Manuals Training Set for 1991," *California Mining* 15, no. 9 (September 1990): 5.

38. "The Lead Exposure Reduction Act Poses Adverse Consequences," *Mining Record*, September 5, 1990.

39. "AMC Says Proposed Changes to Mining Law Will Create Problems," *Mining Record*, September 12, 1990. Also see expanded coverage of the testimony in "Delcour Says Mining Law Objectives Not Met by Proposed Legislation," *Mining Record*, September 19, 1990.

40. "GAO Says Some Hardrock Claim Holders Misuse Law," *Mining Record*, September 12, 1990.

41. "The Future Is Up in the Air for Mineral Area in Idaho: Silver Valley Prospects for Tourists to Even Out Economy. The Centerpiece of Its Campaign Is the World's Longest Aerial Gondola," *Los Angeles Times*, September 18, 1990.

42. "IMA Opposes Changes," *Mining Record*, September 19, 1990.

43. "American Mining Congress Disputes Senate Bill's Royalty Provisions," *Mining Record*, September 26, 1990.

44. "Mining Law Controversy Explored at Hearing," *California Mining* 15, no. 10 (October 1990): 4.

45. "New BLM Policy Sets New Bond Standards," *California Mining* 15, no. 10 (October 1990): 6.

46. "Toward a National Minerals Policy," *Mining Record*, October 10, 1990.

47. "Miners and Environmentalists Open Lines of Communication in Oregon," *Mining Record*, October 10, 1990.

48. "Mining Convention '90 Faces Challenges in a Changing World," *Mining Record*, October 17, 1990.

49. "Colorado Mining Association Opposes Federal Mandatory Holding Fee," *Mining Record*, October 24, 1990.

50. "Clean-Air Accord Is Reached in Congress That May Cost Industry $25 Billion a Year," *Wall Street Journal*, October 23, 1990.

51. "Sen. Cranston Withdraws S. 11 in Face of Heated Opposition," *California Mining* 15, no. 11 (November 1990): 5.

52. "South Dakota Rejects Proposed Anti-mining Initiative," *Mining Record*, November 14, 1990.

53. "Major Environmental Problem Is Solved at McCoy/Cove Mine," *Mining Record*, November 14, 1990.

54. "Operations at So. Dakota's Largest Heap Leach Gold Mine," *Mining Record*, November 14, 1990.

55. "Seine River Complete Acquisition of Meridian/Lincoln Property," *Mining Record*, November 14, 1990.

56. "Strawman II Cast as Dangerous 'Weird Witch of the East,'" *Mining Record*, November 28, 1990.

57. "Bill Could Force Small Mining Companies Out of Business," *Mining Record*, December 5, 1990.

58. "Gold Mining Execs Discuss Challenges at Convention," *Mining Record*, December 19, 1990.

59. "Environmental Issues Dominate Convention," *Mining Record*, December 26, 1990.

60. "You'll Find Welfare in Them Thar Hills," *Los Angeles Times*, December 18, 1990. This was not front-page news. The story was on the first page of the Business Section.

CHAPTER 14

1. "Miners Urge Interior Secretary to Support Existing Mining Law," *Mining Record*, February 20, 1991.

2. "EPA Will Develop Mine Water Regulations under a Nonhazardous Title," *Mining Record*, February 13, 1991.

3. "Cost of Land Withdrawal under the Wilderness Act," *Mining Record*, February 20, 1991.

4. "Denver, Reno Field Hearings Scheduled on 1872 Mining Law," *California Mining* 16, no. 3 (March/April 1991): 1. Also see Larry Vredenburg, Russell L. Harttill, and Gary L. Shumway, *Desert Fever: An Overview of Mining in the California Desert* (Canoga Park, Calif.: Living West Press, 1981).

5. "Reclamation Excellence Recognized at Annual Meeting," *California Mining* 16, no. 3 (March/April 1991): 1, 5.

6. Ibid., p. 5.

7. "People for the West Rally Attracts 800 from Six States," *California Mining* 16, no. 4 (May 1991): 1, 4.

8. "Conference Designed to Address Mineral and Mining Education," *California Mining* 16, no. 4 (May 1991): 1.

9. "Open House Celebrates Mesquite's Millionth Ounce," *California Mining* 16, no. 4 (May 1991): 4.

10. "BLM Reports Gold Production Up; Wildlife, Environmental Changes," *California Mining* 16, no. 5 (June 1991): 2.

11. "Colvin Testifies in Congress on 1872 Mining Law," *California Mining* 16, no. 6 (July/August 1991): 1, 3.

12. "Mineral Education Conference Marked with Bright Success," *California Mining* 16, no. 7 (September 1991): 1, 4–5.

13. "BLM Draft Plan Addresses Mining Use of Cyanide on Public Lands," *California Mining* 16, no. 7 (September 1991): 3.

14. "Industry, Environment Groups Join in Testifying against HR 2929," *California Mining* 16, no. 8 (October 1991): 1, 5.

15. "'Old Nevada' Mines Different Lode, but Taxes to Test Its Mettle," *Wall Street Journal*, July 11, 1991.

16. "Few Small Miners Left Now Face the Prospect of a Hostile New Law," *Wall Street Journal*, September 18, 1991.

17. Frank Wheat, *California Desert Miracle* (San Diego: Sunbelt Publications, 1999), pp. 242-62.

18. "Members Host Congressional Staff Tour of Desert Mining Operations," *California Mining* 17, no. 3 (May 1992): 1, 5; "Miners Keep Up the Fight against Desert Wilderness Legislation," *California Mining* 17, no. 3 (May 1992): 4.

19. "Desert Protection Act Remains Unresolved after Hearings," *California Mining* 17, no. 4 (June 1992): 1, 5.

20. "Miners Protest Challenges to 1872 Mining Law," *California Mining* 17, no. 5 (July/August 1992): 3.

21. "Senate Approves Mining Law Amendments to HR 5503," *California Mining* 17, no. 6 (September 1992): 1, 3.

22. "Teachers Give A-Plus to Second Mineral Education Conference," *California Mining* 17, no. 6 (September 1992): 4-5.

23. "Seymour Blocks Cranston's 'Hardball Politics' Attempt to Voce Desert Wilderness Bill," *California Mining* 17, no. 6 (September 1992): 6.

24. "Cranston's Desert Protection Act Dies in Senate Committee," *California Mining* 17, no. 7 (October/November 1992): 1.

25. "BLM Proposed Stricter Rules on Unpatented Mining Claims," *California Mining* 17, no. 7 (October/November 1992): 5.

26. "How to Break the Impasse over Mining Reform," *High Country News*, October 4, 1993.

27. "Gold Company Stymied in Montana's Sweet Grass Hills," *High Country News*, August 9, 1993.

28. "Indians Ask Congress for a First Amendment," *High Country News*, August 9, 1993.

29. "California Desert Protection Act Reintroduced in Congress," *California Mining* 17, no. 11 (February 1993): 1, 6.

30. "$54 Million Sacramento River Clean Up Plan Selected for Iron Mountain Mine," *California Mining* 17, no. 11 (February 1993): 7.

31. "Mine Is Endless Threat to Waters at Iron Mountain," *Los Angeles Times*, April 10, 1993.

32. "Industry Urges Balance in Desert Legislation," *California Mining* 17, no. 3 (April 1993): 3.

33. "Dear Mr. President: A Balanced Approach to Land Management," *California Mining* 17, no. 3 (April 1993): 3.

34. "Women Take Mining Message to Congress," *California Mining* 17, no. 3 (April 1993): 6-7.

35. "A Big Gold Mine Wants to Get Bigger," *High Country News*, May 3, 1993.

36. "California Mining Executives Go to Washington, D.C.," *California Mining* 17, no. 4 (May/June 1993): 6.

37. "U.S. Mining Firms, Unwelcome at Home, Flock to Latin America: Citing Environmental Woes, They Step Up Spending in Newly Friendly Lands," *Wall Street Journal*, June 18, 1993.

38. "Mineral Resource Alliance Makes Fast Track Response on Mining Law," *California Mining* 17, no. 5 (July/August 1993): 3.

39. "Indians and Environmentalists Protest a Montana Gold Mine," *High Country News*, August 23, 1993. Also see "Outrageous Fortune: Mining on Public Lands," *National Wildlife Enviro Action*, March 1993: 6–7. In this column by Phil Pittman, he called the Mining Law of 1872 "archaic, environmentally destructive, and fiscally irresponsible" based in "19th century" principles. This newsletter was a publication of the National Wildlife Federation.

40. "New Mine Disaster Looms over Colorado," *High Country News*, September 6, 1993.

41. "Town Fights Its Designation as the Nation's Worst Superfund Site," *High Country News*, September 20, 1993.

42. "Disappointment Expressed by Institute of S21 'Compromise,'" *California Mining* 17, no. 6 (September/October 1993): 1.

43. "Miners Drop 480,000 Claims to Avoid Fees," *High Country News*, November 15, 1993.

44. Ibid. Also see "Mandatory Rental Fees on Unpatented Mining Claims Due," *California Mining* 17, no. 1 (December/January 1993): 3.

45. Hughes to Strickland, November 22, 1992, "Desert Tidbits 7," Frank Wheat Papers, MSS, Box 82, Huntington Library.

46. "Mining Reform Moves Closer," *High Country News*, December 13, 1993. Also see "How to Break the Impasse over Mining Reform."

47. "Governor Urges 'Reasonable and Fair' Mining Law Reform," *California Mining* 18, no. 1 (February/March 1994): 3.

48. "Senator Reid Speaks Out in Defense of Miners and 1872 Mining Law," *California Miner* 18, no. 2 (April 1994): 5.

49. "Coal Firm May Pull Its Straw out of Aquifer," *High Country News*, April 18, 1994.

50. "Can a Copper Firm Restore a Blasted Ecosystem?" *High Country News*, May 30, 1994.

51. "Gold Mines Are Sucking Aquifers Dry," *High Country News*, June 13, 1994.

52. "Mega Coal Mine Proposed Again in Utah," *High Country News*, July 25, 1994.

53. "Golden Sunlight Spill Cited," *Independent Record*, July 16, 1994.

54. "How Love of Gold Moves Mountains," *High Country News*, July 25, 1994.

55. "Millions Spent at Warm Springs," *Independent Record*, September 28, 1994.

56. "Poisoning Montana's Precious Water: Porkbarrel Senator Burns Will Inflict 1872 Mining Disaster on Montana Taxpayers!" *Independent Record*, September 29, 1994.

57. "Controversies Have Mining Back on Center Stage," *Independent Record*, October 9, 1994.

58. "Gold Near Park Fires Controversy," *Independent Record*, October 10, 1994.

59. "Project Near Lincoln Stirs Fears of Pollution," *Independent Record*, October 11, 1994.

60. "Asarco Is Told to Pay $28 Million in Lawsuit over Denver Cleanup," *Wall Street Journal*, April 27, 1993.

61. "Butte: Out of the Pits. City Reaping a Bonanza as Old Mine Oozes Poisons," *Los Angeles Times*, March 27, 1994.

62. "Mining the Sagebrush," *Wall Street Journal*, June 22, 1994.

63. "Mining Reform Is Dead," *Independent Record*, September 30, 1994.

64. "Mining Reform: Dead or Alive?" *High Country News*, October 3, 1994.

65. "Superfund Vote Upsets Yellowtail," *Independent Record*, October 7, 1994.

66. "Conservationists Fete Desert Act's Passage; Miners Call It Major Blow," *Los Angeles Daily News*, October 10, 1994.

67. Ibid.

68. "California Desert Protection Act Passes," *Sierra Club: The Planet*, December 1994/January 1995, at http://www.sierraclub.org/planet/199412/ftr-cadesert.asp.

CHAPTER 15

1. One sacred places, see Peter Nabokov, *Where the Lightning Strikes: The Lives of American Indian Sacred Places* (New York: Viking, 2006). For a more popular approach, see Brad Olsen, *Sacred Places North America: 108 Destinations* (Santa Cruz, Calif.: Consortium of Collective Consciousness, 2003).

2. Final Environmental Impact Statement: Flambeau Mining Co.–Copper Mine Ladysmith, Wisconsin, March 1990, State of Wisconsin, Department of Natural Resources, Madison.

3. Wisconsin made its mining history part of tourism. See "Book Brings Wisconsin's Mining Days Back to Life," *Wisconsin State Journal*, November 17, 2002. Minnesota had an elaborate program for visiting the Hibbing mines in the Iron Range of northern Minnesota. See "Mining History: Museums Mix with Working Mines on Minnesota's Iron Range," *Wisconsin State Journal*, April 27, 1997.

4. "Mining Protesters Removed," *Wisconsin State Journal*, July 8, 1991. The *Journal* noted that Flambeau Mining had launched a $10,000 television and radio campaign to get its message out in northern counties.

5. "Fence Work Starts at Mine," *Wisconsin State Journal*, July 10, 1991.

6. "Environment Study at Mine Site Urged," *Wisconsin State Journal*, July 11, 1991.

7. "State Denies Tribe's Bid to Suspend Mine Permits," *Wisconsin State Journal*, July 12, 1991.

8. "Park Mining Bill Vetoed," *Wisconsin State Journal*, July 13, 1991.

9. "Mine Protest Leads to 7 Arrests," *Wisconsin State Journal*, July 13, 1991; "Protesters Urge Survey at Mine Site," *Wisconsin State Journal*, July 16, 1991.

10. "Mining Firms Dig for Support," *Wisconsin State Journal*, August 1, 1991.

11. "DNR Wants New Study for Mine, Work to Continue," *Wisconsin State Journal*, August 3, 1991; "Mining Firm Gets OK to Join Suit," *Wisconsin State Journal*, August 6, 1991.

12. "Judge Halts Mine Project," *Wisconsin State Journal*, August 30, 1991. This was the front-page headline.

13. "Mining Halt Faces Appeal," *Wisconsin State Journal*, August 31, 1991.

14. "Mining Company Warns of Job Loss," *Wisconsin State Journal*, September 1, 1991.

15. "Dem Blasts Study That Boosts Mining," *Wisconsin State Journal*, October 24, 1991; "Mining, Pollution Bills Pass," *Wisconsin State Journal*, November 7, 1991.

16. "Doubts Remain as Mine Opens," *Wisconsin State Journal*, May 16, 1993.

17. "Mine Disclosure Sought," *Wisconsin State Journal*, September 8, 1993. Also see "Mining Limits Advance," *Wisconsin State Journal*, September 30, 1993.

18. "New Life for Mine Project," *Wisconsin State Journal*, September 15, 1993.

19. "Mining Opponents: Sierra Club and Tribes Oppose Exxon's Project," *Wisconsin State Journal*, September 18, 1993. See for a comparative analysis of American Indian opposition to mining Saleem H. Ali, *Mining, the Environment, and Indigenous Development Conflicts* (Tucson: University Press of Arizona, 2003). Ali argues that the root of the opposition is in tribal sovereignty.

20. "Old Foes Now Allies," *Wisconsin State Journal*, February 11, 1994.

21. "Mining Notice Is Filed: Crandon Co. Seeks Permits to Operate in Forest County," *Wisconsin State Journal*, February 16, 1994.

22. "Forest County Mine Opposed," *Wisconsin State Journal*, March 15, 1994.

23. "Mining Concern Changes Agenda," *Wisconsin State Journal*, April 10, 1994.

24. "Vote Pleases Mine Opposition," *Wisconsin State Journal*, April 14, 1994.

25. "Tribes Firm in Opposition to Mine," *Wisconsin State Journal*, April 20, 1994.

26. "Crandon Mine Battle Begins," *Wisconsin State Journal*, April 23, 1994; "DNR Hears Mine Concerns," *Wisconsin State Journal*, April 24, 1994; "Exxon's PR Man: J. Wiley Bragg," *Wisconsin State Journal*, April 25, 1994.

27. "Mining Permit Not a Given. . . ," *Wisconsin State Journal*, May 14, 1994; "Company Lobbying for Disputed Mine: Tribes, Sierra Club Oppose, Zinc, Copper Mine," *Wisconsin State Journal*, August 17, 1994.

28. "92 Candidates against Mining, Environmental Groups Say," *Wisconsin State Journal*, July 30, 1996.

29. "Anti-mining Crowd Digs for Trouble," *Wisconsin State Journal*, July 22, 1996; "Today's Mail," *Wisconsin State Journal*, August 3, 1996.

30. "Crandon Mine Fate May Rest on Computer Measurements," *Wisconsin State Journal*, August 11, 1996; "Crandon Weighs Plan for Mine," *Wisconsin State Journal*, August 11, 1996; "Mining Firm Protests Environmental Report," *Wisconsin State Journal*, August 16, 1996; "EPA Jardens: Its Stance on Mine," *Wisconsin State Journal*, August 18, 1996; "New Ways Make It Safer to Mine, DNR Report Says," *Wisconsin State Journal*, August 20, 1996; "Mining Charges Raise Questions," *Wisconsin State Journal*, September 14, 1996; "DNR Says No Merit in Report on Mining 'Bias,'" *Wisconsin State Journal*, November 24, 1996.

31. "Local Governments Say No Thanks to Mine Plan" and "Village Boards Oppose Crandon Mine," *Wisconsin State Journal*, November 3, 1996.

32. "Town Board Says Resolution Illegal," *Wisconsin State Journal*, December 9, 1996; "Copper Mine Gets Town's Blessing" and "Judge Won't Block Mining Vote," *Wisconsin State Journal*, December 13, 1996.

33. "A Taste of the Mine: Is Open Pit Mining Really As Bas as Its Critics Claim?" *Wisconsin State Journal*, September 9, 1996; "Flambeau Mine Being Refilled," *Wisconsin State Journal*, September 29, 1996; "Official Wants Panel to Help with Search for Minerals," *Wisconsin State Journal*, November 12, 1996.

34. "Politicians Turn 'Green' on Issues," *Wisconsin State Journal*, October 21, 1996.

35. "Mining Wastes Trouble Board," *Wisconsin State Journal*, January 10, 1997; "DNR Concerned about Mine's Water Claims," *Wisconsin State Journal*, January 14, 1997.

36. "Mining Moratorium Vote Slated for Today," *Wisconsin State Journal*, January 21, 1997; "Thompson's Plan for Environment Called 'Just Nickel and Dime Stuff,'" *Wisconsin State Journal*, February 10, 1997.

37. "Spectators with a Cause? Environmental Group Borrows Super Bowl Hoopla," *Wisconsin State Journal*, January 18, 1997; "Crandon Mining Begins TV Ads," *Wisconsin State Journal*, January 30, 1997; "Mining Proponents Outspend

Foes 3-to-1," *Wisconsin State Journal*, February 6, 1997; "Mining Company Defends TV Ads," *Wisconsin State Journal*, February 14, 1997.

38. "Crandon Mining Protests Moratorium Extension," *Wisconsin State Journal*, February 7, 1997; "Governor Criticized for Silence on Mining," *Wisconsin State Journal*, February 10, 1997; "Thompson Back Mining-Community Cushion," *Wisconsin State Journal*, February 12, 1997; "Environment: Plan to Change Mining Law Called 'Sideshow,'" *Wisconsin State Journal*, February 13, 1997; "Mining Bill among Those Set for Hearings," *Wisconsin State Journal*, February 17, 1997.

39. "Advocates Fight Back with 'Mining Success' Examples," *Wisconsin State Journal*, February 18, 1997.

40. "Critics Say Crandon Mining Report Has Flaws," *Wisconsin State Journal*, March 4, 1997; "Group Warns of Danger from Mine," *Wisconsin State Journal*, April 22, 1997; "More Mail: Don't Be Fooled by Crandon Mine Ads," *Wisconsin State Journal*, March 9, 1997.

41. "Senate Panel Passes Anti-mining Bill," *Wisconsin State Journal*, March 6, 1997.

42. "Anti-mining Bill Should Be Rejected," *Wisconsin State Journal*, March 9, 1997.

43. "Moratorium Won't Close Mining Company," *Wisconsin State Journal*, March 11, 1997.

44. "Bill Retains Specific Permit Requirements," *Wisconsin State Journal*, March 12, 1997.

45. "Thompson, Mine Foes Cross Swords," *Wisconsin State Journal*, March 14, 1997.

46. "A Referendum on Crandon Mine: Forest County Town Candidates Are Pro or Con," *Wisconsin State Journal*, March 28, 1997; "Recount Secures Seats for Anti-mining Candidates," *Wisconsin State Journal*, April 8, 1997.

47. "Whether to Mine Should Be a Decision Made Locally," *Wisconsin State Journal*, April 26, 1997.

48. "Outsiders Enter Crandon Struggle: Environmentalists vs. Supporters of Property Rights," *Wisconsin State Journal*, July 6, 1997; "Environmentalists Prepare for Crandon Mine Protest," *Wisconsin State Journal*, July 7, 1997; "Crandon Mine Protest Results in 29 Arrests," *Wisconsin State Journal*, July 8, 1997; "Many Mine Protesters Remaining in Jails," *Wisconsin State Journal*, July 10, 1997.

49. "To Mining Outsiders: It's Our Debate," *Wisconsin State Journal*, July 9, 1997; "Editorial Missed Mark on Mining, 'Outsiders,'" *Wisconsin State Journal*, July 19, 1997; "More Mail: Earth First!, Mining's Long-Term Effects," *Wisconsin State Journal*, July 26, 1997.

50. "Crandon Mining Wins Approval of Water Plan for Proposed Mine," *Wisconsin State Journal*, August 13, 1997.

51. "Mining Company's Promise of Prosperity a Flat-Out Lie," "More Mail: Toxic Tailings Would Produce Sulfuric Acid," and "No Reason to Trust Mining Company's Claims," *Wisconsin State Journal*, August 24, 1997; "Underground Mine Could Harm 'Precious' Rice Beds," *Wisconsin State Journal*, September 16, 1997; "Black: Mining Moratorium Necessary," *Wisconsin State Journal*, September 27, 1997; "Mining Bill Advocates Push Case at Capitol," *Wisconsin State Journal*, October 9, 1997; "DNR Secretary Urges Lawmakers to Abandon Mine Bill," *Wisconsin State Journal*, October 12, 1997; "Speaking Out on Mining Bill," *Wisconsin State Journal*, October 14, 1997; "1,000 Gather to Be Heard on Mining Issue," *Wisconsin State Journal*, October 15, 1997; "GOP Proposing Changes in Mining Bill," *Wisconsin State Journal*, November 9, 1997; "Mining Sides Dig in for Assembly Debate," *Wisconsin State Journal*, November 12, 1997; "Scientific Evidence Counters Claims of Mining Company," *Wisconsin State Journal*, November 14, 1997; "Crandon Foes Unite Online: Mining Activists Stress Value of Communication," *Wisconsin State Journal*, November 21, 1997.

52. "Tighter Pollution Rules Eyed for Mines," *Wisconsin State Journal*, December 2, 1997; "Black, Meyer Spar over Mine Rule," *Wisconsin State Journal*, December 4, 1997; "DNR's Mining Decision May Be Years Away," *Wisconsin State Journal*, December 20, 1997.

53. "40,000 Sign Petition to Back Mining Bill," *Wisconsin State Journal*, January 9, 1998.

54. "Today's Mail: Don't Let Wisconsin River Be Crandon Mining Sewer" and "Exxon Should Prove Mine Technology's Safe," *Wisconsin State Journal*, January 11, 1998; "Poll: Crandon Mine Unpopular," *Wisconsin State Journal*, January 12, 1998; "Poll Indicates Many Oppose Crandon Mine," *Wisconsin State Journal*, January 13, 1998; "Today's Mail: Politicians Will Try to Cripple Mining Bill" and "Seniors Wise Enough to Value Environment," *Wisconsin State Journal*, January 17, 1998; "Our Opinion: Scrutinize Mining, Don't Abandon It," *Wisconsin State Journal*, January 21, 1998; "Our Opinion: Dig for Middle Ground on Mining," "More Mail: Facts Don't Support Case for More Mining," and "Where's Harm in Keeping Ore in Ground?" *Wisconsin State Journal*, February 1, 1998.

55. "UW Sociologist a Doubter on Mine," *Wisconsin State Journal*, January 14, 1998.

56. "Moratorium on Mines Gains Momentum," *Wisconsin State Journal*, January 18, 1998.

57. "DNR Says It's Seeking Best Science on Mining," *Wisconsin State Journal*, January 18, 1998.

58. "Mining Bill Locked Up for the Night," *Wisconsin State Journal*, January 22, 1998; "Mining Bill at a Glance" and "GOP Alters Moratorium Mining Bill," *Wisconsin State Journal*, January 23, 1998.

59. "Exxon Abandons Crandon Mining," *Wisconsin State Journal*, January 24, 1998.

60. "No Light at End of Tunnel in Mine Fight," *Wisconsin State Journal*, January 25, 1998.

61. "Rio Algom Trying a 'New Approach,'" *Wisconsin State Journal*, January 30, 1998; "Exxon's Ex-Partner Cites Different Ideas," *Wisconsin State Journal*, February 1, 1998; "Crandon Mining Co. Outspends Its Opponents by 4–1 in Lobbying," *Wisconsin State Journal*, February 3, 1998.

62. "Mine Foes Look to Senate," *Wisconsin State Journal*, February 3, 1998; "Mining Moratorium Bill Approved," *Wisconsin State Journal*, February 5, 1998.

63. "A Mining Step in the Right Direction," *Wisconsin State Journal*, February 8, 1998; "Thompson Urged to Sign Mining Moratorium," *Wisconsin State Journal*, March 3, 1998; "Thompson Questions Mining Plan," *Wisconsin State Journal*, February 19, 1998; "Thompson Says He'll Sign Moratorium Bill," *Wisconsin State Journal*, March 20, 1998; "Governor Signs Mining Moratorium Bill," *Wisconsin State Journal*, April 23, 1998.

64. "Crandon Mine Has New Idea on Water," *Wisconsin State Journal*, March 20, 1998; "Nicolet Minerals Explains New Waste-Water Proposal," *Wisconsin State Journal*, June 16, 1998.

65. "Here's How to Lobby if Other Side Has $1 Million" and "Pipeline Issue Got Democracy Rolling up North," *Wisconsin State Journal*, March 21, 1998.

66. "DNR Criticized for Its Work on Mining Law," *Wisconsin State Journal*, June 4, 1998; "Coalition Asks DNR to Enforce Mining Law," *Wisconsin State Journal*, July 16, 1998.

67. "Environmentalists Sue over Proposed Mine," *Wisconsin State Journal*, June 5, 1998; "Now Is Time to Stop Pollution of Mining," *Wisconsin State Journal*, July 20, 1998.

68. "Rules Mocked to Make a Point on Mining Law," *Wisconsin State Journal*, September 25, 1999.

69. "Flambeau Mining Co. Says Ladysmith Mine Didn't Pollute," *Wisconsin State Journal*, May 26, 1997; "What You Should Know about the Flambeau Mine," *Real Mining News* (Rusk County Citizens Action Group), March 1999.

70. "Former Copper Mine Leaking Acid, Metals, but Levels Are Too Low to Hurt Flambeau River, Say State, Company Officials," *Milwaukee Journal Sentinel*, July 8, 1999.

71. See Flambeau Mine at http://www.miningmatters.org/Flambeau_Mine.htm, accessed June 23, 2004.

72. "The Truth behind the Rusk County 'Economic Miracle,'" at http://www.nocrandonmine.com/wsn/mining/Ladysmithecon.html, accessed June 23, 2004.

73. "Mining Added to Toxic Emissions," *Wisconsin State Journal*, May 12, 2000. The report lumped hard rock with electrical utilities emissions and effluents.

74. "Water Contamination Concerns Delay Crandon Mine," *Wisconsin State Journal*, June 18, 2000; "Validity of Crandon Mine Deal to Be Tested," *Wisconsin State Journal*, July 3, 2000; "Mine Company Plans Wetlands," *Wisconsin State Journal*, October 4, 2000; "Judge Delays Mine Rulings," *Wisconsin State Journal*, October 20, 2000.

75. "Town Calls Off Mine Mediation," *Wisconsin State Journal*, January 6, 2001; "Crandon Mine Mediation Never Happened," *Green Bay News-Chronicle*, February 6, 2001; "Mining Opponents Seek Cyanide Legislation to Block Mine," *Green Bay News-Chronicle*, May 11, 2001; "Cyanide Ban at Mines Sought," *Wisconsin State Journal*, May 1, 2001; "Ruling Victory for Mine Supporters," *Wisconsin State Journal*, March 9, 2001; "Review Sought for Mine Ruling," *Wisconsin State Journal*, March 17, 2001; "Company Wins Dispute in Crandon Mine Case," *Wisconsin State Journal*, August 14, 2001.

76. "State Senate Approves Ban on Cyanide in Mining," *Green Bay News-Chronicle*, November 7, 2001; "Banning Cyanide Use in Mining," at http://www.serconline.org/mining/background.html, accessed June 23, 2004; "Mine Opponents Rally to Support Passage of Cyanide Ban," *Wisconsin State Journal*, October 14, 2001.

77. "Mine Action Challenged," *Wisconsin State Journal*, January 27, 2001; "Study of Planned Crandon Mine Nearly Finished," *Wisconsin State Journal*, October 1, 2001.

78. "State Might Buy Mine Site," *Wisconsin State Journal*, June 21, 2002; "State May Buy Crandon Mine," *Green Bay News-Chronicle*, June 21, 2002.

79. "State Can't Afford to Buy Mine Lands," *Wisconsin State Journal*, June 23, 2002.

80. "Plan to Buy Mine Site Would Protect a Jewel—the Wolf River," *Wisconsin State Journal*, July 6, 2002.

81. "Plan Can Protect Crandon Mine Site," *Wisconsin State Journal*, August 1, 2002; "Tribe Takes Its Anti-mine Appeal Global," *Wisconsin State Journal*, August 23, 2002; "Chippewa Optimistic after Talks about Mine," *Wisconsin State Journal*, September 3, 2002.

82. "First Appraisal of Crandon Mine Property Completed," *Green Bay News-Chronicle*, September 6, 2002.

83. "State Won't Try to Buy Mine Site," *Wisconsin State Journal*, September 14, 2002.

84. "Mine Site May Be Tough Sell," *Wisconsin State Journal*, September 18, 2002; "Company Pulls Out of Crandon Mine," *Wisconsin State Journal*, September 17, 2002; "Industry Official: Selling Crandon Mine Won't Be Easy," *Green Bay News-Sentinel*, September, 18, 2002. Another reason for folding was the fact that the DNR had rejected one of the three model mines proposed by Nicolet Minerals. See "New Concern Raised on Pollution," *Wisconsin State Journal*, August 31, 2002.

85. "Crandon Mine Site Ownership Moves," *Wisconsin State Journal*, April

12, 2003; "New Owners of Proposed Mine Looking for Mining Company for Partnership," *Green Bay News-Chronicle*, April 19, 2003.

86. "Crandon Council Scrapped," *Wisconsin State Journal*, April 21, 2003.

87. "Environmentalists Worry about New Mine Ownership," *Wisconsin State Journal*, April 17, 2003; "Final Crandon Mine Report Nears End," *Wisconsin State Journal*, April 24, 2003; "Crandon Mine Firm Seeks Delay," *Wisconsin State Journal*, June 3, 2003; "Groups Signal Intent to Sue DNR over Crandon Mine," *Wisconsin State Journal*, June 20, 2003; "Owners of Crandon Mine Rip DNR Pace," *Wisconsin State Journal*, July 8, 2003; "Mine Company Wants Money Back," *Wisconsin State Journal*, July 19, 2003; "Crandon Mine Panel Defunct, but Will Report," *Wisconsin State Journal*, July 26, 2003; "Good Riddance to Mining Group," *Wisconsin State Journal*, September 12, 2003.

88. "Crandon Mine's New Owners Offer to Sell Parcel of Land to Tribes," *Green Bay News-Chronicle*, July 30, 2003.

89. "Tribe to Buy Mineral Rights to Proposed Mine," *Wisconsin State Journal*, October 28, 2003; "Tribes Will Pay $16.5 Million for Mine Site," *Wisconsin State Journal*, October 29, 2003; "Crandon Mine's New Owners Offer to Sell Parcel of Land to Tribes"; "Tribes Buy Crandon Mine," *Green Bay News-Chronicle*, August 29, 2003.

90. "Mine Promoter Disappointed: He Calls Crandon Sale 'End of Mining in the State," *Wisconsin State Journal*, October 30, 2003.

91. "Tribes Make It Official: There Won't Be Mining," *Wisconsin State Journal*, October 31, 2003; "State Tribes' Influence Has Broadened over Years," *Wisconsin State Journal*, November 2, 2003; Peter Rebhahn and John Dipko, "Tribes Buy Crandon Mine Site," *Green Bay Press-Gazette*, October 29, 2003. Sokagon Chairwoman Sandra Rachal said that "this purchase protects lands of great cultural, religious and historic importance to our people" (Rebhahn and Dipko, "Tribes Buy Crandon Mine Site").

92. "Crandon Mine Victory Won by Historic Alliance," at http://www.wsn.org/mining/crandon_mine-victory.html, accessed June 23, 2004. Here Debra McNutt and Zolfan Grossman observed that the movement "was inspired by the historic perseverance of Native American nations to protect their treaty rights and sovereignty."

93. "Tribes Honored for Buying Mine Site," *Wisconsin State Journal*, February 7, 2004.

CONCLUSION

1. Jon Christensen, "After the Gold Rush," *High Country News*, April 3, 1995.

2. Ibid.

3. "How Montana Fouled a Family's Water," *High Country News*, March 6, 1995.

4. Gordon Morris Bakken, "Property Rights," in *By and For the People: Constitutional Rights in American History*, ed. Kermit L. Hall (Arlington Heights, Ill.: Harlan Davidson, Inc., 1991), pp. 102–12.

5. "Pay Me to Be Good—or I'll Sue," *Los Angeles Times*, March 10, 1995.

6. "Timbisha Shoshone Tribe Challenges Plan for Inyo County Gold Mine," *Los Angeles Times*, July 29, 1995.

7. "Sacred Claims: American Indian Tribes Win Some, Lose Some, on Federal Land," *High Country News*, November 14, 2005.

8. "Judge Sets Back Bid by Noranda for Mine Near Yellowstone," *Wall Street Journal*, October 16, 1995.

9. "Proposed Gold Mine Stirs Up a Rural Washington County," *High Country News*, December 11, 1995.

10. "Did Toxic Stew Cook the Geese?" *High Country News*, December 11, 1995.

11. Ibid. Edwin Dobb, "Pennies from Hell: In Montana, the Bill for America's Copper Comes Due," *Harper's Magazine*, October 1996: 39–54.

12. "Yellowstone: A Park Boss Goes to Bat for the Land," *High Country News*, April 29, 1996.

13. "Bill to 'Protect' Park from Mine Upcoming," *Bozeman Daily Chronicle*, May 8, 1996.

14. "Critics Pan Pit-Mine Plan on Yellowstone," *Bozeman Daily Chronicle*, May 8, 1996.

15. "Mine Study Gets 'Unprecedented' Review," *Bozeman Daily Chronicle*, May 9, 1996.

16. "Burns, Baucus Say Bill to Stop Mine Has No Chance," *Bozeman Daily Chronicle*, May 9, 1996.

17. "Report Says Mine No Threat to Park," *Bozeman Daily Chronicle*, May 17, 1996.

18. "Feds Near Land-Swap Deal to Stop Controversial Mine," *Wisconsin State Journal*, August 10, 1996; "Yellowstone Mine a Goner," *High Country News*, August 19, 1996.

19. Ray Ring, "The Bigger the Mine, the Better the Deal," *High Country News*, September 30, 1996.

20. "Mining Act of 1872 Needs Major Changes," *Orange County Register*, December 22, 1996.

21. "Yellowstone Mine Swap Is in a Very Deep Pit," *High Country News*, April 28, 1997.

22. "Federal Negligence Turns Ordinary Montanans Hostile," *High Country News*, February 19, 1996; "Montana on the Edge: A Fight over Gold Forces the

Treasure State to Confront Its Future," *High Country News*, December 22, 1997; "Mine Wastes Haunt a Mythic River," *High Country News*, December 22, 1997.

23. "Plan Bans Mining in Sweet Grass Hills," *Bozeman Daily Chronicle*, May 19, 1996.

24. Mineral Policy Center, *1996 Annual Report* (Washington, D.C.: Mineral Policy Center, 1996), pp. 2–3.

25. "On the Trail of Mining's Corporate Nomads," *High Country News*, June 23, 1997; "While the New West Booms, Wyoming Mines, Drills . . . and Languishes," *High Country News*, July 7, 1997.

26. "Toxics Pour into Our Air, Water, Land," *High Country News*, September 16, 1996.

27. "Asarco Will Pay $6.4 Million in Fines, Spend $61.5 Million to Clean Two Sites," *Wall Street Journal*, January 26, 1998.

28. "Homestake Shows How Good a Mine Can Be," *High Country News*, January 19, 1998.

29. "Voters to Decide Mining's Future," *High Country News*, September 28, 1998; "Re-vote Proposal on Cyanide Issue Sees Fiery Debate," *Billings Gazette*, February 25, 2003. In 2004 the ban withstood I-147, an initiative to reintroduce cyanide heap leaching and a political means to returning to cyanide processing, and a court challenge. See "Montana's Ban on Cyanide Heap Leach Mining Doesn't Constitute a Property Taking," *High Country News*, June 27, 2005.

30. "Mining Industry Gets More than Enough Chances," *High Country News*, February 2, 1998.

31. "Proposed Mine Threatens Ecosystem," *High Country News*, October 12, 1998; "Activists Join Forces against Mining Law," *High Country News*, June 22, 1998; "Mined-Over Region Resents EPA Scrutiny," *High Country News*, March 30, 1998; "Excavating Ecotopia: A Proposed Gold Mine Tests Washington's Green Credentials," *High Country News*, August 31, 1998.

32. "Tribes Strike Back at Mining," *High Country News*, August 31, 1998.

33. "After the Gold Rush," "Superfund Strives for Accountability," "Turning the Old West into the New West," "A Few Plants Love Mine Waste," "A Radical Approach to Mine Reclamation," and "The Reclamation Plan Uses Waste to Bury Waste," *High Country News*, January 19, 1998.

34. "Mining May Need Some Brakes," *High Country News*, November 8, 1999.

35. "Mining on the Run," *High Country News*, July 5, 1999.

36. "The Last Mine Closes in Leadville," *High Country News*, February 15, 1999.

37. "Gold Mine Capsizes in Westwater Canyon," *High Country News*, April 12, 1999.

38. "The Feds Poke a Hole in the 1872 Mining Law" and "New Twist in an Old Law Has Everyone Screaming," *High Country News*, May 24, 1999; "It's Time to Enforce Waste Dump Limits, and Reform the Mining Law," *Mineral Policy Center Newsletter*, Winter 1999: 4.

39. "Blasting the Past: Farewell to Stacks," *Salt Lake Tribune*, August 5, 2000.

40. "Mining the Past," *High Country News*, June 7, 1999. San Diego, California, also was using its mining past to lure tourists. See "San Diego Gold Rush Country," *California Chronicle* 12, no. 2 (Spring 2001): 5. Leadville, Colorado, found the same fame a tourist attraction. "In Search of the Glory Days," *High Country News*, December 23, 2002.

41. "Is a Gold Mine's Discharge Illegal?" *High Country News*, December 18, 2000.

42. "Reclaiming a Golden Landscape," *High Country News*, April 10, 2000.

43. "Colorado Considers a Mining Ban," *High Country News*, June 19, 2000.

44. Jared Diamond, *Collapse: How Societies Choose to Fail or Succeed* (New York: Viking Penguin, Inc., 2005), p. 428.

45. "Mining Legacy: Mile Tailings Leave Yellowstone at Risk Say Park Service, Environmentalists," *Bozeman Daily Chronicle*, August 6, 2000.

46. "The Mine That Turned the Red River Blue," *High Country News*, August 28, 2000.

47. "Libby's Dark Secret: For Decades, Mine Dust Has Been Killing People in Libby, Montana. Why Didn't Anyone Do Anything about It?" *High Country News*, March 13, 2000; "Company Leaves Victims in Its Dust," *High Country News*, April 23, 2001.

48. "Small Mines Stay under the Radar: Environmental Laws, Designed to Regulate the Big Boys, Overlook Some Big Messes," *High Country News*, August 14, 2000.

49. "Coalition Ushers a Mine Off Sacred Ground," *High Country News*, September 11, 2000; "Navajos Issue Call to Save the Peaks," *Mineral Policy Center Newsletter*, Spring 2000: 14.

50. Walter Swain, "The Environmental Effects of Mining in California," *California Studies Newsletter* 9, no. 3 (Spring 2000): 4. In 2005 the Navajo Tribal Council closed 17 million acres of tribal land to uranium mining. See "Navajos Put More than 17 Million Acres Off Limits," *High Country News*, June 13, 2005.

51. "Mining Out the Middleman: In Montana, Locals and Industry Bypass Agencies and Forge a New Road," *High Country News*, July 31, 2000. Over a thousand people are employed at the mine, and buses bring them in from miles around. There is so much traffic in the area that on a 2003 elk hunt in the Absaroka-Beartooth Wilderness Area I had to wait for buses and trucks to clear intersections.

52. "Mining Tops EPA's Toxics Polluter List," *Mineral Policy Center Newsletter*, Winter 2000: 7.

53. "Mining Regs Slip into the Rulebooks" and "Bush Hits the Brakes," *High Country Register*, February 12, 2001.

54. "Mining Reform Gets the Shaft," *High Country News*, November 19, 2001; "Stop the Rollbacks," *Mineral Policy Center Newsletter*, Summer 2001: 1, 4–5.

55. "Mining Boom! The Impact on Wildlands," *Redrock Wilderness Newsletter* 18, no. 2 (Summer 2001): 11.

56. "Gold May Bury Tribe's Path to Its Past," *High Country News*, December 17, 2001.

57. "Closing the Wounds: A Plucky Group of New Mexico Activists Pushes Mining Reclamation into the 21st Century," *High Country News*, December 3, 2001.

58. "An Orange River Runs Through It," *Chronicle of Higher Education*, March 22, 2002.

59. "EPA Wants to Supersize Idaho Superfund Site," *High Country News*, March 4, 2002.

60. "Life in the Wasteland," *High Country News*, December 9, 2002.

61. "Superfund . . . On the Hill . . . On the Ground," *High Country News*, December 9, 2002.

62. "Gold-Plated Cleanup: State Spends $700,000 to Reclaim Pony Mill Site," *Bozeman Daily Chronicle*, August 2, 2002.

63. "Battle Brews over a Wilderness Mother Lode," *High Country News*, February 18, 2002; "Forest Service Gives Green Light to Rock Creek Mine," *Mineral Policy Center Newsletter*, Winter 2002: 4; "Forest Service Forced to Yank Rock Creek Mine Permit," *Mineral Policy Center Newsletter*, Summer 2002: 4.

64. "Bears and Bull Trout May Block Mine," *High Country News*, May 2, 2005.

65. "Protecting Sacred Lands," *Mineral Policy Center Newsletter*, December 2002: 1, 3. There should be little surprise in this relationship between earth and the American Indian. For example, the Navajo believe that their "Holy People" were the spirit forces present at creation, and following the creation and exodus of the Navajo people to their present living place, these Holy People went into the rocks and earth where they still reside to help the Navajo in their daily lives. See Robert Yazzie, "'Life Comes from It': Navajo Justice Concepts," in *Navajo Nation Peacemaking: Living Traditional Justice*, ed. Marianne O. Nielsen and James W. Zion (Tucson: University of Arizona Press, 2005), p. 55.

66. "Black Thunder: What Is It Like to Work at North America's Largest Surface Coal Mine?" *Uwyo*, November 2002: 32–33.

67. "Planning for Positive Growth Patterns," *Greater Yellowstone Report*, Early Winter 2002: 10–12.

68. "Lila Canyon Coal Mine Stopped . . . for Now," *Redrock Wilderness Newsletter* 19, no. 1 (Spring/Summer 2002): 27.

69. "New Legislation Requires Mine Backfill," *Mineral Policy Center Newsletter*, Summer 2003: 5; "Mining Rules Put Industry on Rocky Ground," *High Country News*, May 26, 2003.

70. Reed Karaim, "Losing Sacred Ground," *Preservation*, March/April 2003: 30–35.

71. "Highway Robbery: Make-Believe Roads Threaten Real Wilderness," *Sierra*, July/August 2003: 11; "The 1866 Mining Act: What Is It and What Does It Have to Do with Utah Wilderness?" *Redrock Wilderness Newsletter* 20, no. 1 (Spring 2003): 8; "R.S. 2477: Highway Robbers Plot Unprecedented Heist of Wilderness Jewels," *Redrock Wilderness Newsletter* 20, no. 1 (Spring 2003): 13.

72. "Of Mines and Men," *Wall Street Journal*, October 24, 2003.

73. "As Threat of Old Mines Grows, a Legislative Fix Isn't Working," *Wall Street Journal*, June 4, 2003.

74. Ian Frazier, "At 12:30 in the Morning of October 11, 2000," *OnEarth*, Spring 2003: 14–23.

75. "A Mine Fall, and a Tribe May Get the Shaft," *High Country News*, January 20, 2003.

76. "Wyoming at a Crossroads," *High Country News*, February 17, 2003.

77. "Gold Mining Proposed in Historic South Pass Area," *High Country News*, May 16, 2005.

78. "Rock Jocks Fight a Mining Company for a Popular Climbing Spot: Land Swap Would Undo a Presidential Order for Land Protection," *High Country News*, April 4, 2005.

79. "Who Owns the West?" *Earthworks Journal*, Winter 2004/2005: 4.

80. "A Motherlode of State History: Mineral Point, Shullsburg, Platteville and the Like Offer Rich Stories of Wisconsin's Lead-Mining Past," *Wisconsin State Journal*, August 29, 2004.

81. Noelle Straub, "Enviros Critical as House OKs Mining Change," *Billings Gazette*, November 19, 2005.

82. Mike Stark, "Mining by Yellowstone at Issue," *Billings Gazette*, November 19, 2005.

83. Tania Soussan, "Got $2.50? Get Yourself an Acre: Old Law Makes Fed Land a Steal," *Albuquerque Journal*, October 25, 2005.

84. John Heilprin, "Old Mining Law Paves Way for Cheap-Land Grab: An Obscure Mining Law Allows the Government to Sell Public Lands Containing Minerals to Mining Companies for Only $2.50 to $5 an Acre. Currently, There Are 50 Sales Pending in 11 States in the West," *The New Mexican*, October 17, 2005.

85. "Company Staking Mining Claims to Preserve Land," *Albuquerque Journal*, October 8, 2005.

86. "Asarco to Expand Demolition Work at East Helena Smelter: The Plan Calls for Tearing Down about a Dozen Structures at the East Helena Site by the End of the Year," *Bozeman Daily Chronicle*, July 16, 2006.

87. "Mine Rules: State Board Tables Plan to Toughen Regulations," *Bozeman Daily Chronicle*, June 3, 2006.

88. "Indian Tribe Gets $8 Million Gift: Mining Company Sets Up Trust for Mole Lake Chippewa with the Band's Final Payment for Proposed Mine Site," *Wisconsin State Journal*, May 31, 2006. Meanwhile the Winnemem lands are about to be submerged in California. "Six Hundred Feet and Rising: California's Shasta Dam Soars High above the Sacramento River; Any Higher, and the Winnemem Tribe Is History," *OnEarth*, Summer 2006: 23–27.

89. Alan Septoff, "Let's Make This Dinosaur Extinct," *Earthworks*, August 7, 2007: 1–2.

90. Alan Septoff and Lauren Pagel, "Victory! House Passes 1872 Mining Law Reform 244 to 166," *Earthworks*, November 5, 2007: 1–2.

INDEX